The Perfect DIABETES COMFORT FOOD COLLECTION

9 Essential Recipes You Need to Create
90 Amazing Complete Meals

ROBYN WEBB, MS

American Diabetes Association®

Director, Book Publishing, Abe Ogden; *Managing Editor, Project Manager,* Rebekah Renshaw; *Acquisitions Editor,* Victor Van Beuren; *Production Manager,* Melissa Sprott; *Composition,* pixiedesign, llc; *Cover Design,* Vis-à-vis Creative; *Photography,* Renee Comet; *Printer,* R.R. Donnelly.

Printed in the United States of America
1 3 5 7 9 10 8 6 4 2

♾ The paper in this publication meets the requirements of the ANSI Standard Z39.48-1992 (permanence of paper).

ADA titles may be purchased for business or promotional use or for special sales. To purchase more than 50 copies of this book at a discount, or for custom editions of this book with your logo, contact the American Diabetes Association at the address below or at booksales@diabetes.org.

American Diabetes Association
1701 North Beauregard Street
Alexandria, Virginia 22311

DOI: 10.2337/9781580406024

Library of Congress Cataloging-in-Publication Data

Names: Webb, Robyn.
Title: The perfect diabetes comfort food collection : the 9 essential recipes
you need to create 90 amazing complete meals / Robyn Webb.
Identifiers: LCCN 2016014828 | ISBN 9781580406024 (paperback)
Subjects: LCSH: Diabetes--Diet therapy--Recipes. | Diabetes--Nutritional
aspects. | Cooking. | BISAC: COOKING / Health & Healing / Diabetic &
Sugar-Free. | COOKING / Health & Healing / Weight Control. | COOKING /
Health & Healing / Heart. | HEALTH & FITNESS / Nutrition.
Classification: LCC RC662 .W34 2016 | DDC 641.5/6314--dc23
LC record available at https://lccn.loc.gov/2016014828

DEDICATION

This book is dedicated to my late mother, Ruth:
for me, it was and always will be, about her.

ACKNOWLEDGMENTS

I'm often asked what it is like to write a cookbook. After penning quite a few, I always say it is usually solitary work that takes every ounce of concentration, a strong vision, and a healthy sense of humor. It also takes enrolling others in your project, for even though I work alone most of the time, without the following people, this book would not have been possible.

To my long-time agent Beth Shepard, who is probably at this point more like my sister than agent, as she truly knows how I think and can center me when I'm off in different directions. Her wise words always help to make each project shine with my signature.

To my two long-time testers Ramzi Faris and Cecilia Stoute, and new tester chef Kara Hunt, your feedback and meticulous testing is what inspires me to make each book better than the one before. Your enthusiasm for this book is appreciated more than you know and your honesty is something that keeps me on my toes.

To food photographer Renee Comet and food stylist Lisa Cherkasky, I'm not sure where I'd be without you both. Your talents far exceed any words I can express here and I hope you both know how much I love working with you. May we continue to have many years and projects together!

To Abe Ogden, Rebekah Renshaw, and Lyn Wheeler, thank you once again for the opportunity to serve the diabetes population, their caregivers, relatives, colleagues and friends. Thank you for all the support you've bestowed upon me for so many years.

To Kelly Rawlings for your creativity and your collaboration to produce my column "The Plate" in *Diabetes Forecast* magazine, which was the inspiration for this book. Thank you for always listening and allowing me to spread my wings and try new things under your masterful direction.

And finally, thank you to the loyal readers of my books. It is my hope and wish that I can support the diabetes community with healthy, delicious, and easy-to-prepare foods, and ease the burden of diabetes in some small way. I wish all of you the strength to face the challenges along the way and enjoy my creations with every bite.

Robyn Webb

TABLE OF CONTENTS

CHAPTER 4 *Meatloaf* • 79

• • • • • • •

CHAPTER 5 *Pasta and Sauce* • 101

• • • • • • •

CHAPTER 6 *Salads* • 127

• • • • • • •

CHAPTER 7 *Soup* • 155

CHAPTER 8 *Stir Fry* • 181

• • • • • • •

CHAPTER 9 *Tacos* • 205

Lasagna Cupcakes page 68, and Master Chicken Sear page 37

INTRODUCTION

As I began to write *The Perfect Diabetes Comfort Food Collection*, a neighbor of mine who is always supportive of my cookbooks, said to me: "This is the one I've been waiting for, Robyn." She explained that despite having hundreds of cookbook, she was relieved when I shared that the theme revolves around only needing to know 9 solid techniques to create infinite wonderful meals. Despite her huge collection of books and insatiable thirst for more recipes, she admitted that she only prepared a handful of the same recipes over and over again. She is also a person with diabetes, so she really needed a cookbook that was streamlined for her needs.

My friend is not alone in her sentiments. It's more than okay to rely on a few foods and recipes that you know you can prepare well. But if you long to have a small but great repertoire, you really should strive to make your short list the best it can be. For example, if you know how to create the perfect stir fry, then you can also create hundreds of variations once you have the technique mastered.

First, let me explain that the title of this book is not implying "you" need to be perfect to prepare these meals. It means that I've devised a system of meal planning that will make your life much easier. By learning the techniques, preparing a meal will become so easy that you'll have more time for the other things in life that are important to you. And if that's not the perfect arrangement, I don't know what is.

When designing the concept for this book, I researched several sources. First, I remembered the cooking I grew up with. My mother was a person with diabetes, so we always ate healthy meals. As a full-time working mom, she also made simple meals and relied on a few simple techniques to get dinner on the table quickly. Second, I asked many of my clients and readers what dishes they prepare over and over again. I also looked at dishes that have stood the test of time through every culinary trend. In this book, you will learn the master techniques to prepare stir fry, lasagna, meatloaf, burgers, tacos, chicken, soups, main dish salads, and pasta.

Each chapter begins with a blueprint: a step-by-step plan to master the technique of each dish. These directions were honed through many years of trial and error—I made all the mistakes and missteps, so you don't have to. Once you learn these techniques, you can create many more recipes of your own. The first recipe in each chapter will start you off with the technique, and each subsequent recipe will be very similar in preparation, but with different ingredients. In order to build your confidence and skill level, your pantry and kitchen equipment need to be stocked as well. Fortunately, *The Perfect Diabetes Comfort Food Collection* calls for the simplest ingredients and minimal equipment. Let's look at these a bit more closely.

THE PERFECT PANTRY

Creating a well-stocked pantry is important in every kitchen. You want to make sure you have what you need when you are ready to cook, but you also want to keep tabs on how long it's been stored. Expired ingredients do you no good, so it's a little bit of an art to stock the pantry so that everything gets used in proper time. The best way to keep an eye on everything is to attach a label to the bottom of the jar, can, or bag that indicates the day you purchased it. Most dry, unopened products will last for a year and still retain their freshness. I'd advise that you work through your pantry goods often; fortunately, they will get a lot of use with the recipes in this book since I reuse many of the same ingredients over and over again.

Plan your pantry in the following categories and you'll never run out of ingredients:

Olive oil: Keep two kinds on hand. One that's inexpensive for cooking (it can even be a virgin olive oil) and one that's a bit more flavorful for the main dish salads. A good, slightly more costly olive oil is worth the investment for cold food preparation. Store the oil no more than a year. If the oil comes in a clear bottle, transfer it to a dark container. Light is one of the enemies of oil, and can cause the oil to spoil faster. I like olive oil from many different countries, it doesn't need to be from Italy.

Vinegar: Stock both red and white vinegars. You really don't need to go beyond that, as those two choices can serve most of your cooking needs. While you'll need them to prepare salads, think about splashing a small amount at the end of making a soup or stew. The acidity will liven up any soup. If you want to go beyond red and white, consider storing balsamic, champagne, and herb vinegars. Despite popular belief, vinegar does not last forever. Check the bottom of the bottle; if there is a lot of sediment swirling around, it's time to put them in the trash. Vinegar also gets cloudy as it ages. It is still useable at this point, but should be replaced relatively soon. Once opened, it's best to store vinegar in the refrigerator.

Mustard: Many of the recipes in this book use mustard, so it pays to always have it on hand. I actually prefer smaller bottles of mustard as large jars tend to lose their flavor potency over time. One bottle of

Dijon mustard should be sufficient. I like the coarse ground variety, but it's entirely up to you. Watch out for some of the "fancier" mustards—they can be loaded with sugar, honey, or other ingredients that really aren't necessary, or particularly healthful.

Canned tomatoes: While I prefer mostly fresh ingredients, there are a few canned items that are staples for me and canned tomatoes are one of them. Fortunately, canned products are now being sealed in BPA-free containers, and glass jars are always an option instead of metal. When I say canned, it could be something you do yourself. DIY canning projects have risen dramatically in popularity. Having canned tomatoes always available is a real plus to make many of these recipes. In the pasta chapter (page 101), I teach you how to prepare your own marinara sauce. Canned tomatoes are the main ingredient. Fresh tomatoes are lovely, but with their short peak time, it makes sense to defer to the canned.

Fresh tomatoes (in season): I give instructions for crushing your own, so there is no need to buy already crushed or diced tomatoes. It's less expensive and much more flavorful to buy them whole.

Soy Sauce: Soy sauce falls into a category called the "fifth taste," after salt, bitter, sweet, and sour. Asian foods are popular for that reason. Although soy sauce is typically a high-sodium condiment, a little goes a very long way, and when used right, it can add much appeal to normally bland-tasting foods. But you have to buy the right soy sauce. First, I'll tell you what to avoid. Chemical soy sauces should stay right on the grocer's shelf and not yours. These distasteful sauces are made over the course of two days by hydrolyzing soy protein and combining it with other flavors. The taste is far removed from traditional soy sauces that are made with fermented soybeans.

I prefer Japanese-style soy sauces over Chinese ones. Japanese-style are clearer, thinner, and less harsh tasting than Chinese sauces. Japanese sauces use an even ratio of soybeans and wheat, whereas the Chinese soy sauces are traditionally all soy. I typically use reduced-sodium soy sauce. It's made the same way regular soy sauce is made but about 40% of the salt is taken out post-brewing. I also use tamari, which actually is more akin to traditional Chinese soy sauce. Tamari is made with soybeans and has an assertive flavor, so a little goes a long way. Also for people who need to avoid wheat, tamari is available wheat free.

There is a little more finesse needed when storing soy sauce. Its main enemies are light and heat. Soy sauce can actually develop fishy flavors if not stored properly. Store an unopened bottle far away from any heat source in your kitchen. Once opened, keep it in the refrigerator.

Panko breadcrumbs: While I only call for these breadcrumbs in the meatloaf chapter (page 79), they are vastly different from typical commercially prepared breadcrumbs. Panko crumbs, also known as Japanese breadcrumbs, may sound fancy, but they are now easy to find in major supermarkets throughout the country. The crumbs are cut thicker than the standard breadcrumbs and may look more like flakes then crumbs. They are offered in a whole-wheat version, which is the version used throughout this book.

Beans: Rich in fiber, beans are an excellent source of meatless protein. They are also inexpensive. While you are welcome to soak and cook dry beans, I typically just use canned. Look for BPA-free cans. Beans will last a year on your shelf, so stock up. Feel free to substitute one bean for another depending on what's in your pantry.

Grains/pasta: You'll notice that a majority of the recipes center on lean protein and non-starchy vegetables; however, I also include high-fiber whole-grain starches in the recipes as well as in the suggested side dishes. Depending on your eating plan, you will need to decide how much grain and pasta you wish to include in a meal. Keep all grains and pasta well sealed in airtight containers. They should last up to 1–1/2 years.

Dried spices, herbs, and salt: While I recommend fresh herbs, do keep a small supply of dried herbs on hand. They are convenient and will be potent for up to a year. Keep them tightly sealed and away from heat and light. You will need to discuss with a registered dietitian your personal sodium restrictions, but all of my recipes call for a very small amount of salt. I don't eliminate it entirely, however, just a touch can really boost the flavor of the recipe. Use kosher or sea salt for best results (these are not lower in sodium than iodized salt). Black pepper should be freshly ground, so a pepper mill is necessary.

And that's about it! Except for buying fresh produce and lean proteins, your stock need not be extensive. In fact, I'd rather you be well stocked, but not overstocked, as so many home pantries are.

THE PERFECT EQUIPMENT LIST

My chef friends and I always get a kick out of catalogs filled with expensive, shiny new pots and pans. We know all too well those pieces of equipment will never look the same after one use. Truly, there is no need to have a lot of kitchen equipment; it will only clog up your shelf space and cause you to feel overwhelmed. Fortunately, the recipes in this book only require a few pieces of equipment.

Wok: To make the perfect stir fry, I highly suggest a wok. I explain in the stir fry chapter (page 181) why a wok helps to produce a really great stir fry. No need to invest in anything expensive, just make sure it's deep enough.

Heavy skillet, preferably cast iron: To make the perfect chicken, perfect pasta sauces, and perfect burgers, a cast iron skillet is

essential. Cast iron skillets are inexpensive, indestructible, and indispensable. Cooking in cast iron ensures even cooking. An 8- or 10-inch skillet is all you need. You can purchase pre-seasoned cast iron pans with easy instructions for care.

Casserole dishes: To make the perfect lasagnas, a casserole dish is all you need. A good 9 × 13-inch pan made of porcelain or glass is just fine. I'm usually not a big fan of nonstick cookware, but something like lasagna, which tends to be a little messy, can benefit from a nonstick coating, so that can be an option if you desire.

Dutch oven and/or 6-quart saucepot: To make the perfect soups, a sturdy Dutch oven or saucepot with a lid will be needed. My favorite brand of all time to prepare my soups is called Staub. Similar to Le Creuset, the interior surface of this brand of pots does not scratch and I love the gorgeous colors that are available. Just make sure you use a heavy pot; onions and garlic shouldn't burn as you slowly sauté them. A thin pot made of aluminum will cause your base vegetables to scorch. Also, certain vegetables will turn unappealing colors (cauliflower turns a dull purple when cooked in aluminum). If you want to purchase a stainless steel pot, be sure it has several layers of construction including copper for even heating.

Salad spinner: An extremely useful tool for drying greens. To make perfect main dish salads, the spinner will reduce any excess water. The dressing will better adhere to dry leaves, earning the spinner a place in your kitchen drawer. You can even use the insert as a colander!

That's all! Just make sure you have a good sharp 8–10-inch chef's knife and a large cutting board and you'll be all set.

PERFECT MEAL PLANNING

All of the recipes are paired with other accompanying foods to round out a meal. Unlike many meal planners you may have seen or used, mine is incredibly easy to implement. While it's ambitious to create completely different meals for every day of the week, I know that people just want to make their everyday meals simple. So you will see the same accompanying foods over and over again. Why waste that bag of apples you bought on sale? The same goes for a bunch of broccoli. Maybe you are a small family and couldn't possibly finish a large head of broccoli in one sitting. Serve it again the following night, but choose a different recipe to pair it with.

The recipes are paired with 1–3 suggestions. I want you to spend your effort on main recipes I've featured; however, you will see several times that two of the recipes are paired because they go so well with each other. I always want to save time, so the easiest ideas are presented. Feel free to add or delete the suggestions or swap the sides for a similar food. Many of the ideas are for non-starchy vegetables, such as 1 cup salad or 1/2 cup cooked vegetables. Don't like asparagus? No problem! You can easily choose another vegetable you prefer, as most non-starchy vegetables have the same nutritional profile. I'm not much of a baker and I'm not really fond of the taste of many sugar-free commercially prepared desserts, so my dessert suggestions are mostly fruit. Dessert was always fruit in my house growing up. Remember, your own unique nutritional needs should be the first consideration when altering whatever I may suggest. Consulting a registered dietitian can help guide you toward the right decisions for your needs.

Enjoy, share, and eat well.

Healthfully yours,
Robyn

THE QUESTION OF CARBOHYDRATES

Mention the word carbohydrates and people with diabetes are often confused. Should I eat pasta or should I avoid it? Is fruit okay to eat? How much? No two people with diabetes will have the same response to any food, so choosing the right amount of carbohydrates will be different from one person to the next.

This book has built-in flexibility with respect to controlling your blood glucose levels. For example, you can leave out the bun in any of the burger recipes, or, instead of a corn or flour tortilla, wrap fillings in a crunchy and crisp romaine lettuce leaf. Go ahead and enjoy any of the stir frys without rice or noodles. You can always pile the savory mixtures on a bed of shredded cabbage or diced cauliflower for an interesting and flavorful variation

Remember that vegetables are carbohydrates, but not all of them contain starch, so be careful calculating the amount of starchy and nonstarchy vegetables in your eating program. Have that bun or taco shell if you can, enjoy some rice or pasta, and remember many people with diabetes manage their blood sugar just fine while including these foods in their meal plans.

For a complete understanding of your carbohydrate needs and the science of carbohydrates, I recommend consulting with your physician or a registered dietitian.

MASTER PROTEINS

Many of the recipes in this book include what I call "Master Protein" recipes along with the featured recipe. Often the featured recipe, by virtue of its nutritional profile, can be considered more of a side dish. In order to balance your meal, I've included master protein recipes for tofu, chicken, fish, shrimp, and pork that you can mix and match with the featured recipes, depending upon your nutritional needs and taste preferences. By learning these master recipes, you'll be able to create lots of variations and never tire of any one meal. Each of these proteins can also be added to salads, soups, stews, turned into lettuce wraps, or added to a vegetable stir fry.

• • • • • • •

TOFU

Serves: 4 | Serving size: 3 1/2 ounces

14 ounces extra-firm tofu, cut into 3/4-inch slices, then cut into 2-inch triangles
1 tablespoon vegetable or peanut oil
1/2 teaspoon salt
1/2 teaspoon freshly ground black pepper

1. Freeze the tofu triangles, uncovered, on a cookie sheet overnight. In the morning, set the frozen tofu in the refrigerator to thaw. Before cooking, dry the tofu with paper towels to remove any excess surface moisture.
2. Heat the oil in a large heavy skillet. Add the tofu in batches, if necessary, seasoning both sides with salt and pepper. Turn the tofu every 3 minutes for a total cooking time of 10 minutes.

SEASONED BROILED FISH

Serves: 4 | Serving size: 4 ounces

2 teaspoons chipotle chili powder
1/2 teaspoon dried oregano leaves
1/2 teaspoon sweet paprika
1/4 teaspoon ground cumin
1/4 teaspoon freshly ground black pepper
1/4 teaspoon salt
1 pound fish filets, about 1 inch thick
1 tablespoon olive oil

1. Preheat the oven to broil. Line a broiler pan with nonstick foil. In a small ramekin, combine the chili powder, oregano, paprika, cumin, pepper, and salt.
2. Coat both sides of the fish lightly with the seasoning. Drizzle the fish with the olive oil.
3. Broil the fish about 5 minutes per side or until cooked through.

SEASONED SAUTÉED SHRIMP

Serves: 4 | Serving size: 4 ounces

2 teaspoons chipotle chili powder
1/2 teaspoon dried oregano leaves
1/2 teaspoon sweet paprika
1/4 teaspoon ground cumin
1/4 teaspoon freshly ground black pepper
1/4 teaspoon salt
1 pound peeled and deveined large shrimp
1 tablespoon olive oil

1. In a large bowl, combine the chili powder, oregano, paprika, cumin, black pepper, and salt. Add in the shrimp and toss well.
2. Heat the olive oil on medium heat in a large skillet. Add the shrimp and sauté for 5–7 minutes or until shrimp is cooked through.

PAN-GRILLED PORK CHOPS

Serves: 4 | Serving size: 3 ounces

Cooking spray
1 pound boneless pork loin chops, trimmed of fat, brought to room temperature
1/2 teaspoon kosher salt
1/4 teaspoon freshly ground black pepper

1. Coat a nonstick ridged grill pan with cooking spray. Set the pan on high heat until hot, about 2 minutes. Sprinkle the chops with salt and pepper. Add the chops and cook on each side for about 2 minutes per side.
2. Lower the temperature to medium and cook for an additional 3–4 minutes per side or until an internal temperature of 135°F is reached. Remove from the pan and set aside. The internal temperature will reach 145°F as the pork rests.

SEARED CHICKEN BREASTS

Serves: 4 | Serving size: 3 ounces

1 pound boneless, skinless chicken breasts, remove any tenderloins so chicken lays flat
1/2 teaspoon kosher salt
1/4 teaspoon freshly ground black pepper
1 1/2 tablespoons olive or vegetable oil

1. Pound the chicken breasts if necessary so they are even in thickness. Season the chicken with salt and pepper.
2. Heat the oil in a heavy cast iron skillet over medium-high heat. Add the chicken breasts and sear on both sides for about 5 minutes per side. Be sure to let one side of the chicken thoroughly sear before turning over to the other side. This will ensure even cooking and will prevent sticking.
3. Cover the skillet, lower the heat to low, and cook for about 5–6 minutes until the chicken is cooked through.

CHAPTER 1
Burgers

THE PRINCIPLES OF BURGER MAKING

For as long as Americans have had indoor and outdoor grills and broilers, the quest for making the perfect burger has been one that every home cook strives for. The burger pairs well with so many side dishes. I learned how to make the best burger from the chefs at the hotel where I grew up. They taught me the "blueprint for burgers" that I could easily change by just substituting different meats. I grew so confident in the burger-making business, that making seafood and vegetarian versions produced the same great results. And the truth is, even though creating the perfect burger looks straightforward, it's the little nuances you need to perfect. The first lesson? Don't overcomplicate making burgers; proper cooking technique is key. Just follow these simple instructions:

1. Cook your burgers in a cast iron skillet, not the grill. I know that sounds counterintuitive, but the cast iron skillet or griddle is the perfect piece of equipment to get that crusty burger. With a skillet, all the juices remain in the pan, and you want to capture and retain that flavor.
2. Don't form large burgers. In keeping with your dietary plan, make burgers relatively small, approximately 4 ounces each. In addition, you must get the heat to the center of the burger and too much meat will produce a giant undercooked meat loaf.
3. Don't over-handle the meat. When you rough-handle the meat, you'll cause the meat to compact and it will end up tough and dry after cooking.
4. Have the butcher grind the meat for you. This might sound like a luxury, but in fact most butchers are happy to do this for you and often the quality is much better. Pre-ground meat can be too fine, causing it to feel mushy. Ask your butcher to coarse-grind the meat.
5. Keep the meat in the refrigerator until you are ready to use.
6. Use medium heat for cooking burgers. No need to set the heat up so high to show off, just a steady medium heat will do.
7. All the burgers in this chapter are cooked in a small amount of fat. This is to keep the burgers juicy and to help form a crust. I wouldn't skip this step, but do check about your daily fat allotment.

Once you can create the Basic Burger, the Spiced Turkey Burger, Juicy Lamb Burger,

Asian Style Pork Burgers, Meatloaf Burgers, and Italian Meatball Burgers are created in the same format, with just a few additional ingredients. Resist the temptation to throw the contents of the refrigerator and pantry into a burger. The best burgers taste clean and pure with the great flavor of lean meat shining through.

The Zesty Salmon and Fresh Tuna Burgers are handled a little differently. You will form compact burgers so they don't fall apart in the skillet. I recommend always using fresh fish for these instead of canned. There's nothing wrong with canned fish products, but fresh seafood is easier to work with and the texture will be silky, almost buttery, as compared with the drier texture of the canned product. The Chickpea Patties with Mango Chutney are a great jumping-off point for experimenting with any kind of beans. Remember that beans are like blank canvases, and unlike beef, turkey, and pork, they need additional ingredients to make them taste delicious.

All the toppings for these burgers primarily consist of lettuce and tomato. I believe that burgers should be simple and underdressed—after all, the burger is the star here. A little good-quality ketchup or mustard works nicely. In the case of the Meatloaf Burgers (which use a typical meatloaf sauce), simple sauces keep your burgers nicely unadorned. Depending on your dietary plan, choose to add a bun, or not. If so, choose a whole-wheat or multi-grain whole-wheat bun or roll. Or try a whole-wheat pita bread or tortilla wrap. But honestly, these burgers are so good all by themselves—I recommend just grabbing your fork and knife and digging in!

THE BASIC BURGER

Serves: 6 | Serving size: 1 burger | Prep time: 5 minutes | Cook time: 8 minutes

For this basic burger, I'd buy grass-fed, organic meat if you can. It may or may not be a bit pricier than what you'd usually pay; however, I think the taste is worth it. The chuck beef will produce a slightly juicier burger than the ground sirloin, but by following this recipe exactly, you can't go wrong with either choice of beef.

- 1 pound lean 95% fat-free ground chuck or sirloin, preferably coarse grind
- 1/4 cup finely minced onion, shallot, or scallion
- 1 teaspoon coarse kosher salt
- 4 slices fresh tomato
- 4 lettuce leaves
- Mustard or low-sugar ketchup (optional)
- 4 whole-grain buns, toasted (optional)

1. Combine the beef with the onion and form into six patties (handling the meat as little as possible) and sprinkle with salt.
2. Spray a large cast iron skillet with nonstick cooking spray and heat over medium-high heat. Add the patties and cook for 4 minutes per side.
3. Serve with a slice of tomato, a leaf of lettuce, and mustard or ketchup. Serve with or without whole-grain buns.

CALORIES	CALORIES FROM FAT	TOTAL FAT	SATURATED FAT	TRANS FAT	CHOLESTEROL	SODIUM	POTASSIUM
100	30	3.5 g	1.6 g	0.1 g	45 mg	350 mg	270 mg

TOTAL CARBOHYDRATE	DIETARY FIBER	SUGARS	PROTEIN	PHOSPHORUS	EXCHANGES/CHOICES:
1 g	0 g	1 g	15 g	135 mg	2 Protein, lean

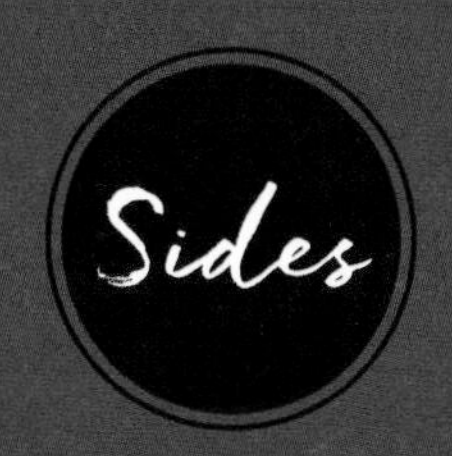

ROASTED PEPPER SALAD

Serves: 6 | Serving size: 1 cup
Prep time: 30 minutes | Cook time: 35 minutes

2 large red peppers
2 large yellow or orange peppers
2 large green peppers
2 tablespoons extra virgin olive oil, divided use
2 teaspoons balsamic vinegar
1 small garlic clove, very finely chopped or crushed

GARNISH
12 black olives, pitted
A handful of small fresh basil leaves

1. Preheat the oven to 400°F. Brush the peppers with 1 tablespoon of the olive oil and arrange them in a shallow roasting pan. Roast for about 35 minutes or until the pepper skins are evenly darkened, turning them 3 or 4 times. Place the peppers in a bowl, cover with plastic wrap, and leave until they are cool enough to handle.
2. Working over a bowl to catch the juice, peel the peppers. Cut them in half and discard the cores and seeds (strain out any seeds that fall into the juice), then cut into thick slices.
3. Measure 1 1/2 tablespoons of the pepper juice into a small bowl (discard the remainder). Add the vinegar and garlic and whisk in the remaining 1 tablespoon of olive oil.
4. Arrange the peppers on a serving platter or on individual salad plates. Drizzle over the dressing and garnish with the olives and basil.

EXCHANGES / CHOICES
2 Nonstarchy Vegetable; 1 Fat

Calories 100; Calories from Fat 50; Total Fat 6.0 g; Saturated Fat 0.8 g; Trans Fat 0.0 g; Cholesterol 0 mg; Sodium 85 mg; Potassium 380 mg; Total Carbohydrate 12 g; Dietary Fiber 3 g; Sugars 6 g; Protein 2 g; Phosphorus 45 mg

This recipe also in Salads page 148

APPLE WITH CINNAMON

Serves: 1 | Serving size: 1 apple

1 small (4-ounce) sliced apple
Pinch cinnamon

1. Top apple slices with a pinch of cinnamon

EXCHANGES / CHOICES
1 Fruit

Calories 50; Calories from Fat 0; Total Fat 0.0 g; Saturated Fat 0.0 g; Trans Fat 0.0 g; Cholesterol 0 mg; Sodium 0 mg; Potassium 110 mg; Total Carbohydrate 14 g; Dietary Fiber 3 g; Sugars 11 g; Protein 0 g; Phosphorus 10 mg

ZESTY SALMON BURGERS

Serves: 4 | Serving size: 1 burger | Prep time: 10 minutes | Cook time: 13 minutes

While frozen salmon burgers are certainly available, freshly made salmon burgers are far superior. Avoid the temptation to purchase canned salmon for this recipe. I prefer wild salmon as its rich taste is more scrumptious than farm-raised salmon. These burgers freeze well. Just place cooked burgers in a freezer container with waxed paper between each one and freeze up to 3 months.

2 teaspoons olive oil
1/2 cup finely chopped red onion
1/4 cup finely chopped celery
1 garlic clove, minced
1 pound skinned salmon filet, cut into 1-inch pieces
1 tablespoon Dijon mustard
1/4 cup panko breadcrumbs
1/16 teaspoon Old Bay seasoning
1 tablespoon olive oil

SAUCE
1/4 cup nonfat mayonnaise
1 teaspoon small capers
1 teaspoon fresh lemon juice
1/4 teaspoon lemon zest

4 thin slices tomato
4 lettuce leaves

1. Heat the olive oil in a cast iron skillet over medium heat. Add the red onion, celery, and garlic and sauté for 3 minutes. Add the mixture to a bowl and let cool.
2. Add the salmon to a food processor and pulse just until coarsely chopped. Add to the sautéed vegetables.
3. Add the mustard, breadcrumbs, and Old Bay seasoning and mix well. Shape into 4 (3–4 inch) patties.
4. Heat the oil in the cast iron skillet over medium heat. Add the salmon burgers and cook 4–5 minutes per side.
5. Combine sauce ingredients.
6. Serve the salmon burgers on whole-grain buns with some of the sauce drizzled on top with a slice of tomato and lettuce. Or serve the salmon bunless with the sauce, tomato, and lettuce.

CALORIES	CALORIES FROM FAT	TOTAL FAT	SATURATED FAT	TRANS FAT	CHOLESTEROL	SODIUM	POTASSIUM
270	130	14.0 g	2.6 g	0.0 g	65 mg	330 mg	560 mg
TOTAL CARBOHYDRATE	**DIETARY FIBER**	**SUGARS**	**PROTEIN**	**PHOSPHORUS**	**EXCHANGES/CHOICES:**		
10 g	2 g	3 g	24 g	345 mg	1/2 Carbohydrate; 1 Nonstarchy Vegetable; 3 Protein, lean; 1 1/2 Fat		

STEAMED SPINACH

Serves: 1 | Serving size: 1/2 cup

1/2 cup spinach

1. Steam spinach for 2 minutes or until wilted.

EXCHANGES / CHOICES
1 Nonstarchy Vegetable

Calories 20; Calories from Fat 0; Total Fat 0.0 g; Saturated Fat 0.0 g; Trans Fat 0.0 g; Cholesterol 0 mg; Sodium 65 mg; Potassium 420 mg; Total Carbohydrate 3 g; Dietary Fiber 2 g; Sugars 0 g; Protein 3 g; Phosphorus 50 mg

. . . .

TANGERINES

Serves: 1 | Serving size: 2 tangerines

2 small tangerines

1. Serve alongside salmon burgers and spinach.

EXCHANGES / CHOICES
1 1/2 Fruit

Calories 80; Calories from Fat 5; Total Fat 0.5 g; Saturated Fat 0.1 g; Trans Fat 0.0 g; Cholesterol 0 mg; Sodium 0 mg; Potassium 250 mg; Total Carbohydrate 20 g; Dietary Fiber 3 g; Sugars 16 g; Protein 1 g; Phosphorus 30 mg

CHICKPEA PATTIES WITH MANGO CHUTNEY

Serves: 4 | Serving size: 1 patty | Prep time: 12 minutes | Cook time: 14 minutes

My chickpea patties first made their appearance in the pages of *Diabetes Forecast* magazine. We received so many compliments about this recipe that I want to share it again. Similar in flavor to falafel, but with an Indian flair, these can be prepared, placed on a plate, covered, and refrigerated hours before you plan to cook them.

2 teaspoons olive oil
1 small onion, diced
3 tablespoons minced celery
2 tablespoons minced red bell pepper
2 tablespoons minced parsley
2 garlic cloves, minced
2 teaspoons curry powder
1/4 teaspoon ground cumin
pinch cayenne
pinch sea salt and pepper
2 cups chickpeas, drained and rinsed
1 egg, beaten
1 1/3 cups whole-wheat panko breadcrumbs
1 tablespoon olive oil
4 whole-grain buns, toasted (optional)
4 slices tomato
4 lettuce leaves

1. Heat the oil in a cast iron skillet over medium heat. Add the onion and sauté for 3 minutes. Add in the celery, red pepper, parsley, and garlic, and sauté for 2 minutes. Add in the curry powder, cumin, cayenne, and a pinch of sea salt and pepper, if desired, and remove from the heat.
2. Puree the chickpeas in a food processor or blender, adding a little water, if necessary. Pulse until you have a coarse puree. Add the chickpeas to a bowl. Add in the vegetable mixture, egg, and breadcrumbs and mix well. Adjust the seasonings with additional salt and pepper, if necessary.
3. Form the mixture into four patties. Heat the cast iron skillet over medium-high heat. Add the olive oil. Add the patties and brown on both sides for about 5–6 minutes per side. Add the patties to toasted whole-grain buns and top with tomato, lettuce leaves, and mango chutney, if desired.

CALORIES	CALORIES FROM FAT	TOTAL FAT	SATURATED FAT	TRANS FAT	CHOLESTEROL	SODIUM	POTASSIUM
310	90	10.0 g	1.6 g	0.0 g	45 mg	200 mg	460 mg
TOTAL CARBOHYDRATE	**DIETARY FIBER**	**SUGARS**	**PROTEIN**	**PHOSPHORUS**	**EXCHANGES/CHOICES:**		
45 g	10 g	7 g	13 g	225 mg	2 1/2 Starch; 1 Nonstarchy Vegetable; 1 Protein, lean; 1 Fat		

CUCUMBER AND VINEGAR SALAD

Serves: 1 | Serving size: 1 cup

1 cup diced cucumber
1 teaspoon balsamic vinegar

1. Toss cucumber with balsamic vinegar and serve.

EXCHANGES / CHOICES
1 Nonstarchy Vegetable

Calories 20; Calories from Fat 0; Total Fat 0.0 g; Saturated Fat 0.0 g; Trans Fat 0.0 g; Cholesterol 0 mg; Sodium 0 mg; Potassium 160 mg; Total Carbohydrate 5 g; Dietary Fiber 1 g; Sugars 2 g; Protein 1 g; Phosphorus 25 mg

SPICED TURKEY BURGERS

Serves: 4 | Serving size: 1 burger | Prep time: 8 minutes | Cook time: 14 minutes

My testers couldn't believe a turkey burger could be this juicy, they tested it several times just to be sure the first test wasn't some kind of fluke. Cooking the burger in the skillet is the key to keeping the burger moist. The yogurt sauce gives this burger a Moroccan feel. Use the yogurt sauce on chicken and fish as well.

1 1/4 pounds ground turkey
1/4 cup seasoned breadcrumbs
1 egg, beaten
1/4 cup minced parsley
1/4 cup finely minced onion
2 teaspoons reduced-sodium soy sauce
1 teaspoon Worcestershire sauce
1/2 teaspoon ground cumin
1/2 teaspoon paprika
1/4 teaspoon freshly ground black pepper

2 teaspoons olive oil

YOGURT SAUCE

1/2 cup plain nonfat Greek yogurt
2 teaspoons finely minced dill
1 teaspoon apple cider vinegar
1/2 teaspoon grated lemon zest

4 whole-grain hamburger buns, toasted (optional)

1. Combine all burger ingredients, except the oil, and form into patties, being careful to handle the meat lightly.
2. Heat a medium-sized skillet over medium heat. Add the olive oil and turkey burgers. Cook for about 5–7 minutes per side until turkey is cooked through (an internal temperature reading should be 180°F).
3. Combine the ingredients for the Yogurt Sauce. Add the turkey burgers to a whole-grain bun and top with the yogurt sauce. Or serve the turkey burgers with the sauce and without the bun.

CALORIES	CALORIES FROM FAT	TOTAL FAT	SATURATED FAT	TRANS FAT	CHOLESTEROL	SODIUM	POTASSIUM
300	140	15.0 g	3.6 g	0.1 g	140 mg	350 mg	450 mg

TOTAL CARBOHYDRATE	DIETARY FIBER	SUGARS	PROTEIN	PHOSPHORUS	EXCHANGES/CHOICES:
9 g	1 g	2 g	34 g	350 mg	1/2 Carbohydrate; 5 Protein, lean; 1 Fat

STEAMED CARROTS

Serves: 1 | Serving size: 1/2 cup

1/2 cup steamed carrots
1/4 teaspoon lemon zest

1. Top steamed carrots with lemon zest and serve.

EXCHANGES / CHOICES
1 Nonstarchy Vegetable

Calories 25; Calories from Fat 0; Total Fat 0.0 g; Saturated Fat 0.0 g; Trans Fat 0.0 g; Cholesterol 0 mg; Sodium 45 mg; Potassium 180 mg; Total Carbohydrate 6 g; Dietary Fiber 2 g; Sugars 3 g; Protein 1 g; Phosphorus 25 mg

. . . .

PLUMS

Serves: 1 | Serving size: 2 plums

2 small plums, halved and pitted

1. Serve plums alongside turkey burger and carrots.

EXCHANGES / CHOICES
1 Fruit

Calories 60; Calories from Fat 5; Total Fat 0.5 g; Saturated Fat 0.0 g; Trans Fat 0.0 g; Cholesterol 0 mg; Sodium 0 mg; Potassium 210 mg; Total Carbohydrate 15 g; Dietary Fiber 2 g; Sugars 13 g; Protein 1 g; Phosphorus 20 mg

JUICY LAMB BURGERS

Serves: 4 | Serving size: 1 burger | Prep time: 8 minutes | Cook time: 8 minutes

Make everyone feel special when you serve them this treat. It's not every day that you'd serve lamb, but it's a nice change from beef and turkey. The lamb provides all the juices you need, so there's no need for cooking oil.

- 1 pound lean ground lamb (ask butcher to bone lamb, trim off visible fat, and grind)
- 1/2 cup dry whole-wheat breadcrumbs
- 1/4 cup diced rehydrated sun-dried tomatoes
- 1/4 cup minced fresh parsley
- 1/4 cup finely minced shallot
- 2 tablespoons freshly grated Pecorino Romano cheese
- 1/4 teaspoon kosher salt
- 1/4 teaspoon freshly ground black pepper

- 4 tomato slices
- 4 lettuce leaves

1. Combine all the ingredients for the burger, handling the meat as little as possible. Form into four patties.
2. Heat a cast iron skillet over medium-high heat. Add the patties and cook for 3–4 minutes per side. Serve with tomato and lettuce on a whole-grain bun or serve bunless.

CALORIES	CALORIES FROM FAT	TOTAL FAT	SATURATED FAT	TRANS FAT	CHOLESTEROL	SODIUM	POTASSIUM
190	45	5.0 g	2.1 g	0.1 g	60 mg	240 mg	620 mg

TOTAL CARBOHYDRATE	DIETARY FIBER	SUGARS	PROTEIN	PHOSPHORUS	EXCHANGES/CHOICES:
15 g	3 g	3 g	22 g	235 mg	1/2 Starch; 1 Nonstarchy Vegetable; 3 Protein, lean

ASPARAGUS SPEARS

Serves: 1 | Serving size: 6 spears

6 spears asparagus
Pinch lemon zest

1. Steam asparagus spears for 6-8 minutes and top with lemon zest.

EXCHANGES / CHOICES
1 Nonstarchy Vegetable

Calories 20; Calories from Fat 0; Total Fat 0.0 g; Saturated Fat 0.0 g; Trans Fat 0.0 g; Cholesterol 0 mg; Sodium 15 mg; Potassium 200 mg; Total Carbohydrate 4 g; Dietary Fiber 2 g; Sugars 1 g; Protein 2 g; Phosphorus 50 mg

PLUMS

Serves: 1 | Serving size: 2 plums

2 small plums, halved and pitted

1. Serve plums alongside lamb burger and asparagus.

EXCHANGES / CHOICES
1 Fruit

Calories 60; Calories from Fat 5; Total Fat 0.5 g; Saturated Fat 0.0 g; Trans Fat 0.0 g; Cholesterol 0 mg; Sodium 0 mg; Potassium 210 mg; Total Carbohydrate 15 g; Dietary Fiber 2 g; Sugars 13 g; Protein 1 g; Phosphorus 20 mg

ASIAN STYLE PORK BURGERS

Serves: 4 | Serving size: 1 burger | Prep time: 5 minutes | Cook time: 10 minutes

Pork can be terribly dry, but with juices from the finely minced garlic and moisture from the soy sauce, these remain succulent. Using hoisin sauce as a substitute for the ketchup is a fun change. Dark sesame oil imparts rich flavor and a teaspoon goes a long way.

1 pound 96% lean ground pork
1 tablespoon finely minced garlic
1 tablespoon lite soy sauce
2 scallions, finely minced
1 teaspoon dark sesame oil

1 tablespoon vegetable oil
2 tablespoons hoisin sauce
4 slices tomato
4 lettuce leaves

1. Combine the first five ingredients for the burgers, handling the meat as little as possible. Form into four patties.
2. Heat the vegetable oil in a cast iron skillet over medium-high heat. Add the burgers and cook for 4–5 minutes per side.
3. Spread each burger with hoisin sauce. Serve with tomato, lettuce, and a toasted whole-grain bun, if desired.

CALORIES	CALORIES FROM FAT	TOTAL FAT	SATURATED FAT	TRANS FAT	CHOLESTEROL	SODIUM	POTASSIUM
220	90	10.0 g	2.1 g	0.0 g	65 mg	350 mg	440 mg

TOTAL CARBOHYDRATE	DIETARY FIBER	SUGARS	PROTEIN	PHOSPHORUS	EXCHANGES/CHOICES:
7 g	1 g	3 g	26 g	225 mg	1/2 Carbohydrate; 3 Protein, lean; 1 Fat

GARDEN SALAD WITH BALSAMIC VINAIGRETTE

Serves: 8 | Serving size: 1 cup
Prep time: 7 minutes | Cook time: 4 minutes

3/4 cup walnuts
2 tablespoons sugar

DRESSING
1/4 cup balsamic vinegar
1 garlic clove, minced
1 teaspoon coarse Dijon mustard
1 teaspoon honey or sugar
3 tablespoons olive oil
1/4 teaspoon sea salt
1/4 teaspoon freshly ground black pepper

SALAD
5 cups mixed greens
1 cup halved cherry tomatoes
2 large carrots, peeled and grated
1/2 medium red onion, thinly sliced

1. In a small sauté pan or skillet over medium-high heat, toss the walnuts with the sugar for 3 to 4 minutes or until the sugar melts and caramelizes. Watch that the nuts do not burn. Remove the nuts from the pan and let cool.
2. In a large bowl, combine dressing ingredients and whisk well.
3. Add the salad ingredients to the dressing and quickly toss together. Serve on individual plates, top with the nuts.

EXCHANGES / CHOICES
1/2 Carbohydrate; 1 Nonstarchy Vegetable; 2 1/2 Fat

Calories 160; Calories from Fat 120; Total Fat 13.0 g; Saturated Fat 1.4 g; Trans Fat 0.0 g; Cholesterol 0 mg; Sodium 105 mg; Potassium 250 mg; Total Carbohydrate 11 g; Dietary Fiber 2 g; Sugars 7 g; Protein 3 g; Phosphorus 65 mg

This recipe also in Salads page 150

ORANGE

Serves: 1 | Serving size: 1 orange

1 small orange

1. Serve orange alongside pork burgers and salad.

EXCHANGES / CHOICES
1 Fruit

Calories 45; Calories from Fat 0; Total Fat 0.0 g; Saturated Fat 0.0 g; Trans Fat 0.0 g; Cholesterol 0 mg; Sodium 0 mg; Potassium 170 mg; Total Carbohydrate 11 g; Dietary Fiber 2 g; Sugars 9 g; Protein 1 g; Phosphorus 15 mg

FRESH TUNA BURGERS

Serves: 4 | Serving size: 1 burger | Prep time: 38 minutes | Cook time: 8 minutes

This burger is prepared and cooked in almost the same fashion as the Salmon Burgers. When buying fresh tuna, look for a beautiful rich red, almost crimson color. There should be no dry edges or brown spots. Ask for a whiff of the tuna before you buy it. Fresh tuna should be odorless.

1 pound fresh tuna steaks, finely chopped
1/2 cup whole-wheat panko breadcrumbs
2 tablespoons Dijon mustard
1 tablespoon vegetable oil
2 scallions, finely minced
1/4 teaspoon coarse kosher salt
1/4 teaspoon freshly ground black pepper

1 tablespoon olive oil
4 lettuce leaves
4 slices tomato
2 tablespoons coarse Dijon mustard (optional)

1. Combine all burger ingredients and form into patties. Place on a plate and refrigerate for 30 minutes.
2. Heat the olive oil in a large cast iron skillet over medium heat. Add the patties and cook for 4 minutes per side.
3. Serve the burgers with lettuce, tomato, mustard, and a whole-grain bun, if desired.

CALORIES	CALORIES FROM FAT	TOTAL FAT	SATURATED FAT	TRANS FAT	CHOLESTEROL	SODIUM	POTASSIUM
280	120	13.0 g	2.3 g	0.0 g	45 mg	360 mg	420 mg
TOTAL CARBOHYDRATE	**DIETARY FIBER**	**SUGARS**	**PROTEIN**	**PHOSPHORUS**	**EXCHANGES/CHOICES:**		
10 g	2 g	2 g	30 g	335 mg	1/2 Starch; 4 Protein, lean; 1 Fat		

LEMON ASPARAGUS SOUP

Serves: 12 | Serving size: 1 cup | Prep time: 20 minutes | Cook time: 30 minutes

1 tablespoon olive oil
1 small leek, bottom portion only, washed and chopped
1 medium onion, chopped
2 garlic cloves, minced
2 pounds asparagus, stems trimmed, sliced into 2-inch pieces
2 large russet potatoes, peeled and cubed
6 cups fat-free, low-sodium chicken broth
1 tablespoon lemon pepper seasoning
1/2 cup half and half

GARNISHES
1 fresh lemon, zested
1/4 cup toasted chopped pistachio nuts

1. Heat the olive oil in a large saucepan over medium heat. Add the leek, onion, and garlic and sauté for about 7–9 minutes until vegetables are soft. Add in the asparagus, potatoes, and broth. Bring to a boil, lower the heat to medium, and cook, covered, until potatoes are tender, about 15–17 minutes.
2. Ladle the soup into a food processor or blender and process until the soup is smooth, working in batches if necessary. Return the soup to the saucepan and add in the lemon pepper seasoning and half and half. Heat through for 1 minute.
3. Garnish each bowl with lemon zest and pistachio nuts.

EXCHANGES / CHOICES
1 Starch; 1 Nonstarchy Vegetable; 1/2 Fat

Calories 110; Calories from Fat 30; Total Fat 3.5 g; Saturated Fat 1.1 g; Trans Fat 0.0 g; Cholesterol 5 mg; Sodium 170 mg; Potassium 510 mg; Total Carbohydrate 17 g; Dietary Fiber 2 g; Sugars 3 g; Protein 5 g; Phosphorus 120 mg;

This recipe also in Soups page 176

MEATLOAF BURGERS

Serves: 4 | Serving size: 1 burger | Prep time: 8 minutes | Cook time: 10 minutes

Everything you love about meatloaf, the ultimate comfort food, is packed into this burger. The three types of meat work together in harmony to provide an excellent range of flavors. Have your butcher grind all the meats for you. I avoid the prepackaged meatloaf mixture found in the meat department. Freshly ground meats make these burgers a special treat.

6 ounces 93% lean ground beef
6 ounces 96% lean ground pork
4 ounces lean ground veal
1/2 cup whole-wheat panko breadcrumbs
1/4 cup minced fresh parsley
1/4 cup finely minced shallots
1 egg
1 tablespoon low-sugar, low-sodium ketchup (such as Walden Farms)
1 teaspoon sweet paprika

1 tablespoon olive oil
3 tablespoons commercial barbecue sauce
1 tablespoon Dijon mustard
4 lettuce leaves
4 slices tomato

1. Combine the burger ingredients. Form into patties, handling the meat as little as possible.
2. Heat the oil in a large cast iron skillet over medium-high heat. Add the burgers and cook for 4–5 minutes per side. Combine the barbecue sauce and mustard in a small bowl. Brush the mixture over the burgers and cover and cook for 1 minute.
3. Serve the burgers with tomato, lettuce, and a whole-grain bun, if desired.

CALORIES	CALORIES FROM FAT	TOTAL FAT	SATURATED FAT	TRANS FAT	CHOLESTEROL	SODIUM	POTASSIUM
260	100	11.0 g	2.9 g	0.2 g	110 mg	380 mg	500 mg
TOTAL CARBOHYDRATE	**DIETARY FIBER**	**SUGARS**	**PROTEIN**	**PHOSPHORUS**	**EXCHANGES/CHOICES:**		
16 g	2 g	5 g	25 g	245 mg	1/2 Starch; 1 Nonstarchy Vegetable; 3 Protein, lean; 1 Fat		

FRESH SPINACH SALAD

Serves: 1 | Serving size: 1 1/2 cups

1 cup fresh spinach leaves
5 cherry tomatoes halved
1/4 cup red onion, thinly sliced
1 teaspoon olive oil
1/2 teaspoon lemon juice

1. Combine spinach, tomatoes, and onion, and drizzle with olive oil and lemon juice.

EXCHANGES / CHOICES
1 Nonstarchy Vegetable; 1 Fat

Calories 70; Calories from Fat 45; Total Fat 5.0 g; Saturated Fat 0.7 g; Trans Fat 0.0 g; Cholesterol 0 mg; Sodium 25 mg; Potassium 360 mg; Total Carbohydrate 7 g; Dietary Fiber 2 g; Sugars 3 g; Protein 2 g; Phosphorus 40 mg

• • • • • • •

APPLE

Serves: 1 | Serving size: 1 apple

1 (4-ounce) apple
Pinch cinnamon

1. Slice apple and sprinkle with a pinch of cinnamon.

EXCHANGES / CHOICES
1 Fruit

Calories 50; Calories from Fat 0; Total Fat 0.0 g; Saturated Fat 0.0 g; Trans Fat 0.0 g; Cholesterol 0 mg; Sodium 0 mg; Potassium 110 mg; Total Carbohydrate 14 g; Dietary Fiber 3 g; Sugars 11 g; Protein 0 g; Phosphorus 10 mg

ITALIAN MEATBALL BURGERS

Serves: 4 | Serving size: 1 burger | Prep time: 10 minutes | Cook time: 10 minutes

Growing up in New York, I had my fair share of the best Italian meatballs served "as is" or stuffed into submarine bread. The aroma of sizzling Italian sausage is a permanent food memory seared into my mind. So, I streamlined a previously high-fat recipe into something that's more in line with better nutrition.

- 8 ounces lean turkey sausage, casings removed
- 4 ounces 93% lean ground beef
- 4 ounces 96% lean ground pork
- 1 tablespoon finely minced fresh basil
- 2 teaspoons fresh minced oregano
- 1/8 teaspoon coarse kosher salt
- 1/4 teaspoon freshly ground black pepper

- 1 tablespoon olive oil
- 1/2 cup low-sodium fat-free marinara sauce, heated
- 4 fresh basil leaves
- 1 tablespoon freshly grated Parmesan cheese
- 4 whole-grain buns, toasted

1. Combine the burger ingredients. Form into four patties, handling the meat as little as possible.
2. Heat the oil in a cast iron skillet over medium-high heat. Add the burgers and cook for 4–5 minutes per side.
3. Spoon the heated marinara sauce over the burger, top with a basil leaf, and sprinkle with Parmesan cheese. Serve open-faced on a bun.

CALORIES	CALORIES FROM FAT	TOTAL FAT	SATURATED FAT	TRANS FAT	CHOLESTEROL	SODIUM	POTASSIUM
240	110	12.0 g	2.8 g	0.3 g	65 mg	430 mg	430 mg
TOTAL CARBOHYDRATE	**DIETARY FIBER**	**SUGARS**	**PROTEIN**	**PHOSPHORUS**	**EXCHANGES/CHOICES:**		
12 g	2 g	3 g	23 g	230 mg	1/2 Starch; 1 Nonstarchy Vegetable; 3 Protein, lean; 1 Fat		

FRESH SPINACH SALAD

Serves: 1 | Serving size: 1 cup

1 cup fresh spinach leaves
5 cherry tomatoes, halved
1/4 cup thinly sliced red onion
1 teaspoon olive oil
1/2 teaspoon lemon juice
1/4 teaspoon balsamic vinegar

1. Combine first five ingredients and drizzle with balsamic vinegar.

EXCHANGES / CHOICES
1 Nonstarchy Vegetable; 1 Fat

Calories 70; Calories from Fat 45; Total Fat 5.0 g; Saturated Fat 0.7 g; Trans Fat 0.0 g; Cholesterol 0 mg; Sodium 25 mg; Potassium 360 mg; Total Carbohydrate 7 g; Dietary Fiber 2 g; Sugars 3 g; Protein 2 g; Phosphorus 40 mg

• • • • • • •

STRAWBERRIES

Serves: 1 | Serving size: 3/4 cup

3/4 cup fresh strawberries

1. Serve strawberries with burgers and salad.

EXCHANGES / CHOICES
1/2 Fruit

Calories 40; Calories from Fat 5; Total Fat 0.5 g; Saturated Fat 0.0 g; Trans Fat 0.0 g; Cholesterol 0 mg; Sodium 0 mg; Potassium 190 mg; Total Carbohydrate 10 g; Dietary Fiber 2 g; Sugars 6 g; Protein 1 g; Phosphorus 30 mg

SPICY MUSTARD SAUCE

Serves: 4 | Serving size: 1 tablespoon
Prep time: 5 minutes

Although I believe a burger is best when simply dressed, sometimes you just need to jazz it up a bit! This all-purpose sauce is not only great for any of the burgers in this chapter, it's also perfect to slather on top of the meatloaf recipes as well! Double or triple the recipe if you are feeding a crowd.

2 tablespoons nonfat mayonnaise
2 teaspoons low-sodium ketchup
1 teaspoon drained, chopped capers
1 teaspoon spicy mustard
1 teaspoon minced chopped chives
1/8 teaspoon cayenne pepper

1. Combine all ingredients in a small bowl. Store in an airtight container in the refrigerator for up to 3 days.

EXCHANGES / CHOICES
Free food

Calories 10; Calories from Fat 0; Total Fat 0.0 g; Saturated Fat 0.0 g; Trans Fat 0.0 g; Cholesterol 0 mg; Sodium 95 mg; Potassium 20 mg; Total Carbohydrate 2 g; Dietary Fiber 0 g; Sugars 1 g; Protein 0 g; Phosphorus 5 mg

CHAPTER 2

Chicken

THE PRINCIPLES OF CHICKEN PREPARATION

Chicken is recognizable, comforting, and available everywhere. While we may drool over photographs of elaborately prepared delicacies, it is chicken that has always weathered the storm through the latest culinary trends. Ask someone their favorite food memory and chances are they will mention their mother's succulent, crisp roast chicken. Like basic black, chicken can be dressed up or served simply, but no matter what, it probably appears on the dinner plate more frequently than any other protein.

So the challenge in preparing a great piece of chicken is to cook it just right so it's not boring or overly fussed with. Yes, I'd say chicken is the perfect blank canvas; you have unlimited flavor possibilities and with the right cooking techniques, chicken's neutrality becomes its advantage and allows for some terrific and varied meals.

Your results will be better if you begin with high-quality poultry. It's certainly up to you (and your budget) which type of chicken you prefer, but I always lean toward organic chicken. Although "organic" and "free-range" chicken are loosely defined, I try to buy my chicken at our local farmers market each week. The taste is wonderful and certainly better than some of the off-color and fatty birds I've purchased in the past at the grocery store.

One of the greatest features of keeping poultry on your cooking calendar, is that it freezes beautifully. Go ahead and stock up on chicken when it's on sale. Just remove the chicken from its original packaging, wrap in butcher paper, and seal in a Ziploc bag. Use chicken within 2 months for best freshness. Once chicken has been thawed, it will keep up to 2 days in the refrigerator.

The best way to defrost the chicken is to simply remove it from the freezer and place in the refrigerator for overnight thawing. Be sure to place the chicken within a container to prevent any juices from spilling out onto the refrigerator shelves. If you decide to speed up the process and thaw the chicken in the microwave or in a cold water bath, cook the chicken immediately. By either method, the chicken may have temporarily warmed up to a temperature above 40°F, and harmful bacteria may begin to multiply. Cooking will be required to destroy it.

To wash or not to wash chicken? When you wash chicken prior to it being cooked, you can end up accidentally distributing bacteria on surfaces all over your kitchen, including the sink, kitchen utensils, counters, and cutting boards. The bacteria that is present on raw chicken, if any, will be destroyed when it is cooked. Cleaning and disinfecting cutting utensils, cutting boards, and counters is the best way to guard against bacteria in chicken.

In this chapter, I'll show you three methods for cooking chicken that I think every home cook should master. You'll learn to properly sear, poach, and grill chicken. These three techniques will give you endless menu options. Let's look at each method in depth:

SEARING

The purpose of searing is to create an intense layer of flavor where the proteins brown or caramelize. The result is a very flavorful piece of meat. It's a common myth that searing seals in the juices. It actually doesn't do that at all. The chicken will develop a crusty outside that has tons of flavor, but it's just as easy to dry out a seared piece of chicken as one that is not seared.

To sear chicken properly:

- Make sure the pan is very hot, just under the point of actual smoking. Use a cast iron or stainless steel pan for the best results. Nonstick is a poor choice for these recipes, as the chicken needs to leave residue in the pan to be incorporated into the sauce. You also simply cannot heat a nonstick pan safely to the temperature needed for a proper sear.
- Make sure the chicken is very dry. Pat it with paper towel, if necessary (I leave marinated chicken for grilling).
- Add oil to the pan and then add the chicken. You should hear a loud sizzle. If you don't, remove the chicken and wait until the pan is hot enough. Be patient!
- Do not move or flip the chicken for at least 3 minutes. If you flip or move the chicken around you lessen the amount of heat, which means you have to wait longer for the chicken to develop a good sear, or at worse, you'll never sear it at all.
- After 3–4 minutes, flip the chicken and check to see that you have a golden brown surface.
- After the chicken has been seared properly, it is flavorful to eat it as is; however, I prefer searing to be the first step to making a flavorful sauce to pair with the chicken. The tasty residue chicken leaves behind in the pan is perfect for making a flavorful sauce.

POACHING

Some home cooks go one step beyond the gentle moist heat of proper poaching to rapid boiling to cook chicken. Unless you want dried-out bites of chicken, poaching is the only way to produce a silken-textured chicken that is perfect for chicken salads and casseroles. Poaching prevents the proteins in the chicken from contracting tightly. When the proteins tighten, it squeezes the moisture out of the chicken, and takes all of the flavor with it.

To poach chicken properly:

- Start with a flavorful broth. Use chicken stock or water and then add peppercorns, garlic, and/or celery leaves. You can also add pieces of onion and parsley stems, if desired. Adding a tablespoon of white wine will also round out the flavor of the broth.
- Bring the mixture to a simmer to allow the flavors to infuse.
- Bring the liquid to a boil, turn off the heat, and add the chicken. Cover with a lid and the chicken will gently poach in this hot liquid for 10–12 minutes, with no chance of becoming rubbery, and will remain moist and tender.
- Use this poaching method for making chicken salads, casseroles, or to just eat with a simple sauce.

GRILLING

For grilling chicken, here is the basic rule — choose only bone-in, chicken thighs. Save the chicken breasts for poaching or searing. Grilled chicken thighs work the very best on the grill, just remember to take the skin off before eating it. And bone-in chicken thighs are the most economical part of the chicken. The thigh bones continuously feed flavor to the meat and the darker meat stays moist and juicy at high grilling temperatures.

- Coat your grill rack with cooking spray or oil it well using a brush. This will avoid the chicken sticking to the grill.
- Make sure the grill comes to a medium-high temperature. Too hot a fire causes rubbery, stringy chicken.
- Start with grilling the thighs using direct heat (uncovered) for 8–10 minutes per side and then switch to indirect (covered) heat for 10–12 minutes per side. This combination ensures the outside will brown nicely, but the meat will remain moist.
- Resist the urge to keep flipping the thighs or moving them around. Not only will the non-stick spray prevent stickiness, but also leaving the chicken alone will keep it from sticking to the grill.
- I prefer the use of marinades rather than slathering on a BBQ sauce. If you want to use BBQ sauce, make your own or use a low-sugar variety. And remember to add the BBQ sauce in the last 10 minutes of the cooking process, otherwise the sauce will cause the chicken to burn easily.
- Clean your grill after cooking chicken to remove any grease and excess bits. You don't have to clean it perfectly; a little leftover residue can impart a great flavor to the next batch of food to be grilled, but avoid a massive pile-up of leftover chicken bits.

MASTER CHICKEN SEAR

Serves: 4 | Serving size: 1 breast or thigh
Cook time: 6–8 minutes

FOR BONELESS BREASTS AND THIGHS

1. Season 4 boneless skinless chicken breasts or 4 boneless skinless chicken thighs with 1/8 teaspoon kosher salt and 1/4 teaspoon ground black pepper.
2. In a 12–14-inch heavy skillet, preferably cast iron or stainless (NOT nonstick), heat 1 1/2 tablespoons olive or canola oil over medium-high heat.
3. Add the chicken and sear until well browned on both sides for 3–4 minutes per side for the breasts, 2–3 minutes for the thighs.
4. Transfer the chicken to a plate and tent with foil.
5. Choose and prepare one of the sauce recipes.
6. Return the chicken and accumulated juices to the skillet and simmer gently until cooked through, about 4–5 minutes.

TO TEST: Chicken should feel firm to the touch. Using closed tongs, press on the center of the chicken. It should feel firm. Alternately, you may make a very small incision in the center of the meat and check to be sure the meat is cooked through with no traces of pink.

FOR BONE-IN BREASTS AND THIGHS

Follow step 1, but instead of removing the chicken to a plate, transfer the chicken to a baking sheet. Roast the chicken at 375°F for about 10–15 minutes until chicken is cooked through. Add back to the skillet with the sauce and cook for 3–4 minutes more.

EXCHANGES / CHOICES
3 Protein, lean;
1 Fat

Calories 180; Calories from Fat 90; Total Fat 10.0 g; Saturated Fat 2.0 g; Trans Fat 0.0 g; Cholesterol 85 mg; Sodium 120 mg; Potassium 200 mg; Total Carbohydrate 0 g; Dietary Fiber 0 g; Sugars 0 g; Protein 21 g; Phosphorus 170 mg;

MASTER POACHED CHICKEN

Serves: 4 | Serving size: 1 breast
Prep time: 5 minutes
Cook time: 20–22 minutes

3 cups fat-free, reduced-sodium chicken broth or water
1 bay leaf
Handful celery leaves
1 teaspoon black peppercorns
1 peeled and smashed garlic clove
3 tablespoons dry white wine
1 pound boneless, skinless chicken breasts

1. Add the chicken broth or water, bay leaf, celery leaves, peppercorns, garlic, and wine to a skillet with lid. Bring to simmer, uncovered, and simmer for 10 minutes.
2. Raise the heat to boil, then turn off the heat. Add the chicken to the pot and cover with a lid. Let the chicken sit in the hot liquid for 10–12 minutes until cooked through.
3. With a slotted spoon or skimmer, remove the chicken from the liquid and place on a cutting board.
4. The chicken is now ready to be sliced, cubed, or shredded into various dishes. You may also serve the chicken uncut with a sauce.

EXCHANGES / CHOICES
3 Protein, lean

Calories 130; Calories from Fat 20; Total Fat 2.5 g; Saturated Fat 0.7 g; Trans Fat 0.0 g; Cholesterol 65 mg; Sodium 70 mg; Potassium 160 mg; Total Carbohydrate 0 g; Dietary Fiber 0 g; Sugars 0 g; Protein 24 g; Phosphorus 140 mg

SCALLION AND GINGER SAUCE WITH SEARED CHICKEN

Serves: 4 | Serving size: 1 breast or thigh
Prep time: 15 minutes | Cook time: 8 minutes + time to prepare Master Chicken Sear

Scallion and ginger sauce is so versatile; you can use it over salmon, pork, or stir it into steamed vegetables. When mincing scallions, be sure to use all of the scallion, right up to the root end. Grate the entire amount of ginger called for below; the taste will be deep and rich.

Master Chicken Sear (see page 37)
1 1/2 teaspoons olive oil
1/4 cup minced scallions
3 garlic cloves, minced
1 tablespoon grated fresh ginger
3/4 cup fat-free, reduced-sodium chicken broth
1/4 cup rice wine vinegar
2 tablespoons hoisin sauce
1 teaspoon sugar
Chopped scallions (for garnish)

1. Sear chicken as in Master recipe (page 37), using breasts or thighs, boneless or bone in. Add 1 1/2 teaspoons oil to the pan over medium heat.
2. Add the scallions, garlic, and ginger. Cook for 1 minute. Add the broth, vinegar, hoisin sauce, and sugar and bring to a boil. Cook for 3 minutes.
3. Return the chicken and juices to the pan and reduce the heat to low. Cook for 4 minutes.

CALORIES	CALORIES FROM FAT	TOTAL FAT	SATURATED FAT	TRANS FAT	CHOLESTEROL	SODIUM	POTASSIUM
220	110	12.0 g	2.2 g	0.0 g	85 mg	360 mg	290 mg
TOTAL CARBOHYDRATE	**DIETARY FIBER**	**SUGARS**	**PROTEIN**	**PHOSPHORUS**	**EXCHANGES/CHOICES:**		
7 g	1 g	4 g	22 g	190 mg	1/2 Carbohydrate; 3 Protein, lean; 1 Fat		

BROWN RICE

Serves: 1 | Serving size: 1/2 cup

1/2 cup cooked brown rice

1. Cook brown rice according to package directions.

EXCHANGES / CHOICES
1 1/2 Starch

Calories 110; Calories from Fat 10; Total Fat 1.0 g; Saturated Fat 0.2 g; Trans Fat 0.0 g; Cholesterol 0 mg; Sodium 0 mg; Potassium 40 mg; Total Carbohydrate 22 g; Dietary Fiber 2 g; Sugars 0 g; Protein 3 g; Phosphorus 80 mg

. . . .

ASPARAGUS SPEARS

Serves: 1 | Serving size: 6 spears

6 spears steamed asparagus

1. Steam asparagus spears for 6–8 minutes and serve alongside chicken and brown rice.

EXCHANGES / CHOICES
1 Nonstarchy Vegetable

Calories 20; Calories from Fat 0; Total Fat 0.0 g; Saturated Fat 0.0 g; Trans Fat 0.0 g; Cholesterol 0 mg; Sodium 15 mg; Potassium 200 mg; Total Carbohydrate 4 g; Dietary Fiber 2 g; Sugars 1 g; Protein 2 g; Phosphorus 50 mg

APPLE CIDER CHICKEN

Serves: 4 | Serving size: 1 breast or thigh
Prep time: 15 minutes | Cook time: 10–12 minutes + time to prepare Master Chicken Sear

This is a great dish to prepare in the fall and around the holidays. When you tire of turkey, change to this chicken recipe chock full of tart Granny Smith apples. If you can't find fresh cider, substitute unsweetened, unfiltered apple juice.

- Master Chicken Sear (see page 37)
- 1 1/2 teaspoon olive oil
- 1 Granny Smith apple, peeled and diced
- 1/4 cup minced shallots
- 2 teaspoons fresh minced thyme
- 1/2 cup apple cider
- 1/2 cup fat-free, low-sodium chicken broth
- 2 tablespoons reduced-fat sour cream
- 1 tablespoon minced fresh parsley

1. Sear chicken as in Master Recipe (page 37) using chicken breasts or thighs, boneless or bone-in.
2. Add the oil to the pan on medium heat. Add the apples, shallots, and thyme to the pan and cook for 2 minutes. Add the apple cider and broth and bring to a simmer. Cook for 3 minutes.
3. Return the chicken and juices to the skillet and reduce to low. Simmer for 4 minutes. Add in the sour cream and parsley and serve.

CALORIES	CALORIES FROM FAT	TOTAL FAT	SATURATED FAT	TRANS FAT	CHOLESTEROL	SODIUM	POTASSIUM
240	110	12.0 g	2.7 g	0.0 g	85 mg	150 mg	340 mg

TOTAL CARBOHYDRATE	DIETARY FIBER	SUGARS	PROTEIN	PHOSPHORUS	EXCHANGES/CHOICES:
10 g	1 g	7 g	22 g	200 mg	1/2 Fruit; 3 Protein, lean; 1 1/2 Fat

GARDEN SALAD WITH BALSAMIC VINAIGRETTE

Serves: 8 | Serving size: 1 cup
Prep time: 7 minutes | Cook time: 4 minutes

3/4 cup walnuts
2 tablespoons sugar

DRESSING
1/4 cup balsamic vinegar
1 garlic clove, minced
1 teaspoon coarse Dijon mustard
1 teaspoon honey or sugar
3 tablespoons olive oil
1/4 teaspoon sea salt
1/4 teaspoon freshly ground black pepper

SALAD
5 cups mixed greens
1 cup halved cherry tomatoes
2 large carrots, peeled and grated
1/2 medium red onion, thinly sliced

1. In a small sauté pan or skillet over medium-high heat, toss the walnuts with the sugar for 3 to 4 minutes or until the sugar melts and caramelizes. Make sure the nuts do not burn. Remove the nuts from the pan and let cool.
2. In a large bowl, combine dressing ingredients and whisk well.
3. Add the salad ingredients to the dressing and quickly toss together. Serve on individual plates. Top with the nuts.

EXCHANGES / CHOICES
1/2 Carbohydrate; 1 Nonstarchy Vegetable; 2 1/2 Fat

Calories 160; Calories from Fat 120; Total Fat 13.0 g; Saturated Fat 1.4 g; Trans Fat 0.0 g; Cholesterol 0 mg; Sodium 105 mg; Potassium 250 mg; Total Carbohydrate 11 g; Dietary Fiber 2 g; Sugars 7 g; Protein 3 g; Phosphorus 65 mg

This recipe also in Salads page 150

BROCCOLI

Serves: 1 | Serving size: 1/2 cup

1/2 cup steamed broccoli or broccolini

1. Steam broccoli or broccolini for 4–5 minutes until crisp and tender, and serve alongside Apple Cider Chicken and the salad.

EXCHANGES / CHOICES
1 Nonstarchy Vegetable

Calories 25; Calories from Fat 5; Total Fat 0.5 g; Saturated Fat 0.1 g; Trans Fat 0.0 g; Cholesterol 0 mg; Sodium 30 mg; Potassium 230 mg; Total Carbohydrate 6 g; Dietary Fiber 3 g; Sugars 1 g; Protein 2 g; Phosphorus 50 mg

PROVENÇAL CHICKEN

Serves: 4 | Serving size: 1 breast or thigh
Prep time: 15 minutes | Cook time: 10–12 minutes + time to prepare Master Chicken Sear

Much more flavorful than chicken with tomato sauce, this is a great balance of sweet and savory, just perfect to dress up chicken's blank canvas.

- Master Chicken Sear (see page 37)
- 1 1/2 teaspoons olive oil
- 3 garlic cloves, minced
- 1 small onion, chopped
- 1/2 teaspoon anchovy paste
- 1/2 cup fat-free, low-sodium chicken broth
- 1/2 cup dry white wine
- 1 (14-ounce) can diced tomatoes
- 1/4 cup fresh chopped basil
- 2 tablespoons black olives, chopped

1. Sear the chicken as in Master Recipe (page 37) using breasts or thighs, boneless or bone-in.
2. Add the oil to the skillet over medium heat. Add the garlic, onion, and anchovy paste and cook for 2 minutes. Add the broth, wine, and tomatoes and bring to a simmer. Cook for 4–6 minutes.
3. Return the chicken to the skillet and juices. Simmer for 4 minutes. Add in the basil and olives and serve.

CALORIES	CALORIES FROM FAT	TOTAL FAT	SATURATED FAT	TRANS FAT	CHOLESTEROL	SODIUM	POTASSIUM
240	110	12.0 g	2.3 g	0.0 g	85 mg	360 mg	490 mg

TOTAL CARBOHYDRATE	DIETARY FIBER	SUGARS	PROTEIN	PHOSPHORUS	EXCHANGES/CHOICES:
8 g	2 g	4 g	23 g	215 mg	2 Nonstarchy Vegetable; 3 Protein, lean; 1 1/2 Fat

BROCCOLI

Serves: 1 | Serving size: 1/2 cup

1/2 cup steamed broccoli
or broccolini

1. Steam broccoli or broccolini for 4–5 minutes until crisp and tender, and serve alongside Provençal Chicken and orzo.

EXCHANGES / CHOICES
1 Nonstarchy Vegetable

Calories 25; Calories from Fat 5; Total Fat 0.5 g; Saturated Fat 0.1 g; Trans Fat 0.0 g; Cholesterol 0 mg; Sodium 30 mg; Potassium 230 mg; Total Carbohydrate 6 g; Dietary Fiber 3 g; Sugars 1 g; Protein 2 g; Phosphorus 50 mg

ORZO

Serves: 1 | Serving size: 1/2 cup

1/2 cup whole-wheat orzo

1. Cook according to package directions.

EXCHANGES / CHOICES
1 Starch

Calories 90; Calories from Fat 5; Total Fat 0.5 g; Saturated Fat 0.1 g; Trans Fat 0.0 g; Cholesterol 0 mg; Sodium 0 mg; Potassium 30 mg; Total Carbohydrate 18 g; Dietary Fiber 2 g; Sugars 1 g; Protein 4 g; Phosphorus 60 mg

CLASSIC CHICKEN SALAD

Serves: 5 | Serving size: 1 cup
Prep time: 15 minutes | Cook time: time to prepare Master Poached Chicken

Simple can be a good thing. Although I'll branch out and add more ingredients in the next two chicken salads, you can never go wrong with this simple salad. The perfect chicken salad has only enough dressing to lightly coat it, so there's no need for this to swim in heavy mayonnaise.

1 recipe Master Poached Chicken, cooled (page 37)
1/4 cup minced red onion
1/4 cup minced celery
2 tablespoons minced parsley
2 tablespoons low-fat mayonnaise
1 tablespoon plain nonfat yogurt
2 teaspoons fresh lemon juice
2 teaspoons Dijon mustard

Lettuce leaves
Wedges of lemon or lime

1. Slice, cube, or shred the poached chicken and add to a serving bowl.
2. Add in the remaining ingredients, except lettuce leaves and lemon, and toss gently. Serve on lettuce leaves with lemon or lime wedges.

CALORIES	CALORIES FROM FAT	TOTAL FAT	SATURATED FAT	TRANS FAT	CHOLESTEROL	SODIUM	POTASSIUM
120	20	2.5 g	0.6 g	0.0 g	50 mg	160 mg	180 mg

TOTAL CARBOHYDRATE	DIETARY FIBER	SUGARS	PROTEIN	PHOSPHORUS	EXCHANGES/CHOICES:
3 g	0 g	1 g	20 g	125 mg	3 Protein, lean

SPINACH SALAD WITH HOT BACON DRESSING

Serves: 11 | Serving size: 1 1/2 cups
Prep time: 15 minutes | Cook time: 6 minutes

7 cups fresh baby spinach leaves
1 small head romaine lettuce, washed, dried, and broken into bite-sized pieces
10 large white mushrooms, cleaned, peeled, if necessary, stemmed, and sliced

DRESSING
4 slices lean bacon (40% or more less fat), chopped
1 small onion, finely chopped
2 cloves garlic, minced
1/2 cup cider vinegar
1 tablespoon sugar
2 tablespoons tomato paste

1. Toss together the spinach, lettuce, and mushrooms.
2. Cook the bacon in a large heavy skillet over medium heat until crisp. Add the onion and sauté for 2 minutes. Add the garlic, vinegar, sugar, and tomato paste. Stir to blend and season with salt and pepper, if desired. Toss salad with dressing and serve.

EXCHANGES / CHOICES
1 Nonstarchy Vegetable

Calories 40; Calories from Fat 10; Total Fat 1.0 g; Saturated Fat 0.3 g; Trans Fat 0.0 g; Cholesterol 0 mg; Sodium 80 mg; Potassium 300 mg; Total Carbohydrate 5 g; Dietary Fiber 1 g; Sugars 3 g; Protein 3 g; Phosphorus 50 mg

This recipe also in Salads page 146

APPLE

Serves: 1 | Serving size: 1 apple

1 (4-ounce) apple, sliced

1. Slice apple and serve alongside Chicken Salad and spinach salad.

EXCHANGES / CHOICES
1 Fruit

Calories 50; Calories from Fat 0; Total Fat 0.0 g; Saturated Fat 0.0 g; Trans Fat 0.0 g; Cholesterol 0 mg; Sodium 0 mg; Potassium 110 mg; Total Carbohydrate 14 g; Dietary Fiber 3 g; Sugars 11 g; Protein 0 g; Phosphorus 10 mg

FRUITED CHICKEN SALAD

Serves: 8 | Serving size: 2/3 cup
Prep time: 15 minutes | Cook time: time to prepare Master Poached Chicken

You'll get your fiber-rich fruit and protein together in this lunch salad—or serve it for a light dinner. Any apple variety will work; however, I think sweet Gala tempers the slightly gamey flavor of the poultry.

1 recipe Master Poached Chicken (see page 37)
2 small gala apples, unpeeled and diced
1/2 cup halved red seedless grapes
1/4 cup sliced dried apricots
1/4 cup dried cherries
2 celery stalks, diced
1/4 cup minced red onion
2 tablespoons low-fat mayonnaise
2 tablespoons plain, nonfat yogurt
1/2 teaspoon sea salt
1/4 teaspoon freshly ground black pepper

1. Cut the chicken into cubes or slices.
2. In a large bowl, combine the chicken with the apples, grapes, apricots, cherries, celery, and onion.
3. Gently fold in the mayonnaise, yogurt, salt, and pepper. Cover and refrigerate for 30 minutes to meld flavors.

CALORIES	CALORIES FROM FAT	TOTAL FAT	SATURATED FAT	TRANS FAT	CHOLESTEROL	SODIUM	POTASSIUM
130	15	1.5 g	0.4 g	0.0 g	30 mg	220 mg	260 mg

TOTAL CARBOHYDRATE	DIETARY FIBER	SUGARS	PROTEIN	PHOSPHORUS	EXCHANGES/CHOICES:
16 g	2 g	12 g	13 g	120 mg	1 Fruit; 2 Protein, lean

WHOLE-WHEAT CRACKERS

Serves: 1 | Serving size: 1 ounce

1 ounce baked whole-wheat crackers, such as Triscuits or Wheat Thins

1. Serve with chicken salad and tomato slices.

EXCHANGES / CHOICES
1 Starch; 1 Fat

Calories 130; Calories from Fat 40; Total Fat 4.5 g; Saturated Fat 0.8 g; Trans Fat 0.1 g; Cholesterol 0 mg; Sodium 180 mg; Potassium 105 mg; Total Carbohydrate 20 g; Dietary Fiber 3 g; Sugars 2 g; Protein 3 g; Phosphorus 95 mg

....

TOMATO SLICES

Serves: 1 | Serving size: 1 tomato

1 small tomato

1. Slice and serve with chicken salad and crackers.

EXCHANGES / CHOICES
1 Nonstarchy Vegetable

Calories 25; Calories from Fat 5; Total Fat 0.5 g; Saturated Fat 0.0 g; Trans Fat 0.0 g; Cholesterol 0 mg; Sodium 5 mg; Potassium 330 mg; Total Carbohydrate 5 g; Dietary Fiber 2 g; Sugars 4 g; Protein 1 g; Phosphorus 35 mg

ASIAN CHICKEN SALAD

Serves: 12 | Serving size: 1 cup
Prep time: 15 minutes | Cook time: time to prepare Master Poached Chicken

Use the dressing in this recipe as another vinaigrette to have in your collection. Asian Chicken Salad is something you see often on restaurant menus, and while it sounds healthy, it's often laden with so much fat and sodium that it quickly becomes a less healthy choice. Choose green cabbage or change to Napa or even red cabbage.

1 recipe Master Poached Chicken (page 37)
1 small head green cabbage, cored and shredded
2 medium carrots, peeled and shredded
1/2 cup sliced scallions
1/2 cup diced red bell pepper

DRESSING
1/4 cup lite soy sauce
3 tablespoons rice vinegar
2 tablespoons canola oil
2 teaspoons dark sesame oil
2 teaspoons fresh grated ginger
1 garlic clove, finely minced
1/2 teaspoon brown sugar

12 lettuce leaves
1 tablespoon toasted sesame seeds

1. Slice, cube, or shred the chicken. Add the chicken to a bowl with green cabbage, carrots, scallions, and red pepper.
2. Whisk together the dressing ingredients and pour over the salad. Mix well. Serve on lettuce leaves and top with toasted sesame seeds.

CALORIES	CALORIES FROM FAT	TOTAL FAT	SATURATED FAT	TRANS FAT	CHOLESTEROL	SODIUM	POTASSIUM
100	40	4.5 g	0.6 g	0.0 g	20 mg	230 mg	250 mg

TOTAL CARBOHYDRATE	DIETARY FIBER	SUGARS	PROTEIN	PHOSPHORUS	EXCHANGES/CHOICES:
7 g	2 g	3 g	10 g	85 mg	1 Nonstarchy Vegetable; 1 Protein, lean; 1/2 Fat

WHOLE-WHEAT CRACKERS

Serves: 1 | Serving size: 1 ounce

1 ounce baked whole-wheat crackers, such as Triscuits or Wheat Thins

1. Serve with chicken salad and strawberries.

EXCHANGES / CHOICES
1 Starch; 1 Fat

Calories 130; Calories from Fat 40; Total Fat 4.5 g; Saturated Fat 0.8 g; Trans Fat 0.1 g; Cholesterol 0 mg; Sodium 180 mg; Potassium 105 mg; Total Carbohydrate 20 g; Dietary Fiber 3 g; Sugars 2 g; Protein 3 g; Phosphorus 95 mg

. . . .

STRAWBERRIES

Serves: 1 | Serving size: 3/4 cup

3/4 cup fresh strawberries, sliced

1. Cut strawberries into slices and serve alongside chicken salad and crackers.

EXCHANGES / CHOICES
1/2 Fruit

Calories 40; Calories from Fat 5; Total Fat 0.5 g; Saturated Fat 0.0 g; Trans Fat 0.0 g; Cholesterol 0 mg; Sodium 0 mg; Potassium 190 mg; Total Carbohydrate 10 g; Dietary Fiber 2 g; Sugars 6 g; Protein 1 g; Phosphorus 30 mg

BASIC GRILLED CHICKEN THIGHS

Serves: 4 | Serving size: 1 thigh | Prep time: 5 minutes | Cook time: 26-30 minutes + marinating time

Use the simple marinade here or try one of the three additional marinades that follow. Although chicken thighs contain more fat than chicken breasts, they hold up on the grill much better than chicken breasts.

4 bone-in skinless chicken thighs
1/4 cup olive oil
3 tablespoons lemon juice
2 garlic cloves, smashed
1 tablespoon chopped fresh herbs (parsley, rosemary, thyme, or basil)

1. Add the thighs to either a shallow baking pan, a deep bowl, or a plastic Ziploc bag. Whisk together the oil, lemon juice, garlic, and herbs. Pour over the chicken, cover or seal, and place in the refrigerator for 2–6 hours.
2. Heat a gas grill to medium-high heat. Set the rack 6 inches from the heat source. Coat the grill rack with cooking spray. Remove the chicken from the marinade.
3. Grill the chicken for 8–10 minutes per side on direct heat and then switch to indirect heat for another 10–12 minutes per side or until the chicken reaches an internal temperature of 165°F, turning once. This may occur before the cooking time is complete, so check the chicken and make sure it doesn't overcook.

CALORIES	CALORIES FROM FAT	TOTAL FAT	SATURATED FAT	TRANS FAT	CHOLESTEROL	SODIUM	POTASSIUM
100	50	6.0 g	1.4 g	0.0 g	65 mg	45 mg	140 mg

TOTAL CARBOHYDRATE	DIETARY FIBER	SUGARS	PROTEIN	PHOSPHORUS	EXCHANGES/CHOICES:
0 g	0 g	0 g	12 g	105 mg	2 Protein, lean

LEMON ASPARAGUS SOUP

Serves: 12 | Serving size: 1 cup
Prep time: 20 minutes | Cook time: 30 minutes

1 tablespoon olive oil
1 small leek, bottom portion only, washed and chopped
1 medium onion, chopped
2 garlic cloves, minced
2 pounds asparagus, stems trimmed, sliced into 2-inch pieces
2 large russet potatoes, peeled and cubed
6 cups fat-free, low-sodium chicken broth
1 tablespoon lemon pepper seasoning
1/2 cup half and half

GARNISHES
1 fresh lemon, zested
1/4 cup toasted chopped pistachio nuts

1. Heat the olive oil in a large saucepan over medium heat. Add the leek, onion, and garlic and sauté for about 7–9 minutes until vegetables are soft. Add in the asparagus, potatoes, and broth. Bring to a boil, lower the heat to medium and cook, covered, until potatoes are tender, about 15–17 minutes.
2. Ladle the soup into a food processor or blender and process until the soup is smooth, working in batches, if necessary. Return the soup to the saucepan and add in the lemon pepper seasoning and half and half. Heat through for 1 minute.
3. Garnish each bowl with lemon zest and pistachio nuts.

EXCHANGES / CHOICES
1 Starch; 1 Nonstarchy Vegetable; 1/2 Fat

Calories 110; Calories from Fat 30; Total Fat 3.5 g; Saturated Fat 1.1 g; Trans Fat 0.0 g; Cholesterol 5 mg; Sodium 170 mg; Potassium 510 mg; Total Carbohydrate 17 g; Dietary Fiber 2 g; Sugars 3 g; Protein 5 g; Phosphorus 120 mg

This recipe also in Soups page 176

CUCUMBER AND TOMATO SALAD

Serves: 1 | Serving size: 1 cup

1/2 cup sliced cucumber
1 small sliced plum tomato
1/2 teaspoon balsamic vinegar

1. Slice the cucumber and tomato and drizzle with balsamic vinegar.

EXCHANGES / CHOICES
1 Nonstarchy Vegetable

Calories 25; Calories from Fat 0; Total Fat 0.0 g; Saturated Fat 0.0 g; Trans Fat 0.0 g; Cholesterol 0 mg; Sodium 5 mg; Potassium 230 mg; Total Carbohydrate 5 g; Dietary Fiber 1 g; Sugars 3 g; Protein 1 g; Phosphorus 30 mg

CHICKEN MARINADES

Follow the directions for Basic Grilled Chicken Thighs (page 50) and use one of these three marinades. Chicken can be marinated for up to 24 hours in a nonreactive bowl or you can use a plastic bag. For the Port Wine Marinade, marinate for only 5–6 hours, as longer marinating time results in a bitter flavor. Turn the chicken pieces on occasion. After marinating, drain the marinade from the chicken and discard or pour the marinade into a small saucepan and bring to a boil. Serve the heated marinade with the cooked chicken. Use a food processor, blender, or just whisk the ingredients for these marinades in a bowl.

• • • • • • •

SOUTHWESTERN MARINADE

Serves: 16
Serving size: 1 tablespoon
Prep time: 5 minutes

1/2 cup olive oil
1/3 cup fresh lime juice
1 tablespoon hot chile powder
2 tablespoons minced scallions
1 garlic clove, minced

EXCHANGES / CHOICES
1 1/2 Fat

Calories 60; Calories from Fat 60; Total Fat 7.0 g; Saturated Fat 0.9 g; Trans Fat 0.0 g; Cholesterol 0 mg; Sodium 5 mg; Potassium 15 mg; Total Carbohydrate 1 g; Dietary Fiber 0 g; Sugars 0 g; Protein 0 g; Phosphorus 5 mg

PORT WINE CHINESE FIVE SPICE

Serves: 12
Serving size: 1 tablespoon
Prep time: 5 minutes

1/2 cup port wine
1/4 cup canola oil
1 tablespoon white wine vinegar
2 teaspoons fresh orange zest
1 teaspoon Chinese five spice

EXCHANGES / CHOICES
1 Fat

Calories 60; Calories from Fat 40; Total Fat 4.5 g; Saturated Fat 0.3 g; Trans Fat 0.0 g; Cholesterol 0 mg; Sodium 0 mg; Potassium 10 mg; Total Carbohydrate 1 g; Dietary Fiber 0 g; Sugars 1 g; Protein 0 g; Phosphorus 0 mg

MINT MARINADE

Serves: 16
Serving size: 1 tablespoon
Prep time: 5 minutes

1/2 cup olive oil
1/2 cup minced mint
1/2 cup fresh lemon juice
2 tablespoons white wine vinegar
2 teaspoons Dijon mustard
Fresh ground black pepper to taste

EXCHANGES / CHOICES
1 1/2 Fat

Calories 60; Calories from Fat 60; Total Fat 7.0 g; Saturated Fat 0.9 g; Trans Fat 0.0 g; Cholesterol 0 mg; Sodium 15 mg; Potassium 20 mg; Total Carbohydrate 1 g; Dietary Fiber 0 g; Sugars 0 g; Protein 0 g; Phosphorus 5 mg

Basic Grilled Chicken Thighs page 50

CHAPTER 3
Lasagna

THE PRINCIPLES OF LASAGNA MAKING

Lasagna for people with diabetes? Oh yes you can! But the classic creation oozing with a ton of cheese and stuffed with fatty meats is not what I am referring to. The first five recipes in this chapter are based on a technique that utilizes vegetables and grains (not traditional noodles) to create luscious layers. Zucchini, eggplant, cauliflower, spinach, and polenta stand in for the more starchy noodles, and are easy to assemble as well. For the remaining five recipes, I use noodles; however, in lesser quantity, so that each serving contains less than a traditional lasagna.

All of these lasagna recipes call for making your own marinara sauce or purchasing low-sodium varieties. I would encourage you to prepare your own sauce. While it cooks, you can prepare the other parts of the dish. The recipe for the marinara sauce is from the Pasta chapter, but I've repeated it here so you don't have to flip pages. Once you've prepared this staple sauce, you can close the book and prepare it all by memory. Now that's what makes a great cook!

Here are some important additional tips to make these vegetable and grain-based lasagnas:

1. For lasagnas that include zucchini and/or eggplant, it is very important to salt both vegetables prior baking. Salt will draw the moisture out of the vegetable so you don't end up with a soggy mess once everything is baked together. Both vegetables are also cooked once prior to being cooked again in the assembled lasagna. This will further dry out the vegetables so they remain sturdy and not water logged. Leave the skins on both vegetables, as that will help to hold them together. I sliced the vegetables with a knife while testing, but if you are adept at using a mandolin, feel free to use one. The mandolin creates perfectly sliced vegetables.
2. For the No Noodle Cauliflower Lasagna, follow each step carefully. While it may appear like a lot of steps, the instructions are easy. When you add the cauliflower to the food processor, the end result should look like small pieces of rice, not a smooth puree. After baking the cauliflower and adding it to the cheesecloth, make sure you squeeze every ounce of water out of the cauliflower. This might take a little muscle, but it's really important, otherwise the cauliflower noodles will not come together.

3. The fillings for all five lasagnas are very similar. This will make it easier for grocery shopping, and any leftover ingredients can be parlayed into the next lasagna you wish to prepare. In the first, the No Noodle Zucchini lasagna, I use tofu as a predominant part of the filling. Once cooked, tofu has a very similar quality to ricotta cheese. I add ricotta cheese as well, as the tofu and ricotta complement each other very well. The filling of the No Noodle Cauliflower Lasagna is a bit simpler. By eliminating the tofu, cottage cheese and ricotta complement the cauliflower nicely. In the No Noodle Polenta lasagna, only mozzarella and Parmesan cheeses are used as a topping. In the No Noodle Spinach Lasagna, cottage cheese is blended to smooth it out and then it's combined with ricotta for an almost sauce-like filling. Always purchase small curd cottage cheese as it will release less water than large curd. Make sure the Parmesan is freshly grated from a wedge and not pre-grated from a can.

4. For the No Noodle Polenta Lasagna: polenta is either labeled as such or it's just labeled as cornmeal. Use a yellow, not white, grain and make sure the grain is coarse, not fine. Imported brands usually taste a bit better so find one if you can. I would avoid using the pre-made polenta or instant polenta; both suffer in quality.
5. Let all the lasagnas sit at room temperature for at least 10 minutes after they come out of the oven. It will be easier to slice into pieces once the ingredients have had a chance to settle. These lasagnas will make fine leftovers, but since they are so vegetable based, it's best to eat them quickly. I'm sure you'll have no trouble sharing these warm, delicious dishes with your friends and family.

The last five recipes are what I term "alternative lasagnas." The usual layering is replaced with creative ways to present the ingredients. As you will probably have leftover ingredients from the No Noodle recipes, you can easily prepare these alternatives without being repetitive in your menu planning.

In Lasagna Cupcakes, thin wonton noodles stand in for heavy noodles. I created this recipe with complete portion control in mind. I don't know about you, but when I used to prepare a traditional lasagna, it was kind of difficult to stick to one portion! These cute muffins with the same great lasagna flavor make portion control a snap.

For the Lasagna Soup you'll need heatproof soup bowls to create a broiled crusty topping with the mozzarella and Parmesan cheeses. This recipe is also designed for perfect portion control. You'll get a few pieces of lasagna noodles in every bite, but nowhere near the amount of noodles you would eat with a traditional lasagna.

For the Corn Tortilla Lasagna, more fiber-rich and lower-calorie corn tortillas are the noodles. I've slipped in a few beans to complement the corn flavor, but left in the traditional lasagna ingredients so you don't have to shop for additional foods you might not have. The bottom layer will get very soft. Be sure not to spread the sauce all the way to the edges. That way, you get a nice balance of crispy edges with a soft middle.

It was my Mom who taught me how to make my recipe for Lasagna Roll Ups! She got tired of all the layering and fuss and one day just rolled a noodle with the cheese filling, and it made her life in the kitchen much easier. Look for lasagna with curly edges to make the spiraled lasagna really elegant.

Use your skillet instead of your casserole dish to make Skillet Lasagna. I love free-formed food, and in this lasagna, all the ingredients come together faster on the stovetop. Personally, I think it tastes richer with all the ingredients melding into each other.

No Noodle Zucchini Lasagna page 60

NO NOODLE ZUCCHINI LASAGNA

Serves: 18 | Serving size: 2 × 3-inch square | Prep time: 45 minutes | Cook time: 1 hour 25 minutes

Zucchini lasagna was the very first lasagna I ever made. Originally, I prepared it with noodles, but now I realize that long strips of zucchini stand in for the noodles beautifully.

MARINARA SAUCE

2 tablespoons olive oil
5 garlic cloves, minced
1 (28-ounce) can good-quality canned tomatoes, preferably packed in its own juice, drained, liquid reserved
5 fresh basil leaves with stems, sliced or whole
1/4 teaspoon kosher salt
1/4 teaspoon freshly ground black pepper
1/4 teaspoon ground red chili flakes (optional)

3 large zucchini

FILLING

16 ounces firm lite tofu
1/2 cup minced parsley
Juice of 1/2 lemon
2 teaspoons lemon zest
1 garlic clove, minced
1 cup low-fat ricotta cheese
1 cup shredded part-skim mozzarella cheese
1 egg, beaten
1/4 teaspoon kosher salt
1/4 teaspoon freshly ground black pepper

TOPPING

1/4 cup grated fresh Parmesano Reggiano or Pecorino Romano cheese

1. Line two baking sheets with parchment paper and set aside.
2. Heat the olive oil and garlic in a large skillet with a lid over low heat (do not use a deep pot, as you want the water to quickly evaporate and the sauce to become thick). Cook the garlic for about 6–7 minutes, stirring occasionally.
3. Meanwhile, add the drained tomatoes to a deep bowl. Crush the tomatoes with your hands, until coarse. Add the tomatoes and basil to the skillet and simmer, uncovered, for 20–25 minutes until thick. Add some of the reserved liquid from the can of tomatoes if the sauce is too thick.
4. Preheat the oven to 400°F. As the sauce simmers, slice the zucchini lengthwise into 1/8-inch thick slices with a knife or mandolin. Arrange the zucchini on the prepared baking sheet. Sprinkle the zucchini lightly with salt. Bake the zucchini for about 10–12 minutes until lightly browned. Remove the zucchini from the oven. Gently roll up the zucchini slices in a towel to get rid of the excess moisture, or just use paper toweling and blot very well. Be careful to keep the slices intact. Add in the salt, pepper, and crushed red pepper (if using) to the tomato sauce.

CALORIES	CALORIES FROM FAT	TOTAL FAT	SATURATED FAT	TRANS FAT	CHOLESTEROL	SODIUM	POTASSIUM
80	35	4.0 g	1.6 g	0.0 g	20 mg	240 mg	260 mg
TOTAL CARBOHYDRATE	**DIETARY FIBER**	**SUGARS**	**PROTEIN**	**PHOSPHORUS**	**EXCHANGES/CHOICES:**		
5 g	1 g	3 g	6 g	115 mg	1 Nonstarchy Vegetable; 1 Protein, medium fat		

5. In a food processor or blender, process the tofu, parsley, lemon juice, lemon zest, and garlic until smooth. Add to a large bowl and mix in the ricotta cheese, mozzarella cheese, egg, salt, and pepper.
6. Pour about 1/3 cup of the marinara sauce over the bottom of a 9 × 12 baking pan. Add a layer of zucchini slices, overlapping them slightly. Add 1/3 of the filling mixture over the zucchini, spreading evenly with a spatula. Add about 1/3 of the remaining marinara sauce over the tofu cheese filling. Repeat the layering process until all ingredients are used up, finishing with marinara sauce. Sprinkle the top of the lasagna with the Parmesan or Romano cheese.
7. Cover loosely with foil and bake for 35 minutes. Remove the cover and bake for 15 minutes more. Remove the lasagna from the oven, let stand at room temperature for 10–15 minutes so lasagna can settle and it will be easier to cut. Cut into squares.

YOUR CHOICE OF ANY MASTER PROTEIN

See page 8.

• • • • • • •

BLUEBERRIES

Serves: 1 | Serving size: 1/3 cup

1/3 cup of blueberries

1. Serve blueberries alongside lasagna and protein.

EXCHANGES / CHOICES
1/2 Fruit

Calories 25; Calories from Fat 0; Total Fat 0.0 g; Saturated Fat 0.0 g; Trans Fat 0.0 g; Cholesterol 0 mg; Sodium 0 mg; Potassium 35 mg; Total Carbohydrate 7 g; Dietary Fiber 1 g; Sugars 5 g; Protein 0 g; Phosphorus 5 mg

NO NOODLE CAULIFLOWER LASAGNA

Serves: 18 | Serving size: 2 × 3-inch square
Prep time: 30 minutes | Cook time: 30 minutes for the cauliflower, 45 minutes for the lasagna

When I first heard that you could make "noodles" from cauliflower, I was quite skeptical. But when I sampled a noodle-less cauliflower lasagna at a local restaurant, it caused me to pause and reconsider. Intrigued, I begged the chef to part with his recipe. Don't shy away from the bit of labor involved; you will have created not only cauliflower lasagna sheets, but you can also form the mixture into a great pizza crust.

CAULIFLOWER NOODLES

- 2 large heads cauliflower, leaves and stems removed, coarsely chopped (about 6 cups)
- 2 eggs, beaten
- 1/2 cup part-skim mozzarella cheese
- 1/4 teaspoon freshly ground black pepper

FILLING

- 1 cup low-fat (1%) cottage cheese
- 1 cup nonfat ricotta cheese
- 1/2 cup shredded part-skim mozzarella cheese
- 1 egg, beaten
- 1/4 teaspoon kosher salt
- 1/4 teaspoon freshly ground black pepper

- 2 cups favorite low-sodium store-bought marinara sauce
- 1/4 cup grated fresh Parmesan cheese

1. Preheat the oven to 375°F. Line a large baking sheet with parchment paper. Add the cauliflower to a food processor and pulse until the cauliflower looks riced (flaky, not puréed). Spread the cauliflower in one thin, even layer onto the baking sheet. Bake the cauliflower for 10–15 minutes.
2. Line a bowl with a double layer of cheesecloth, leaving overhang over the sides of the bowl. Add the baked cauliflower to the cheesecloth and bring up the ends of cheesecloth so you form a ball. Allow to cool a few minutes. Protecting your hands with pot holders, squeeze the excess water from the cauliflower until there is no water left.
3. Rinse the bowl and add the cauliflower, discarding the cheesecloth. Add in the eggs, mozzarella cheese, and black pepper. Mix well. Reline the baking sheet with parchment paper. Increase the oven temperature to 450°F. Spread the cauliflower on the baking sheet into an even layer. Bake the crust for 15 minutes until lightly browned.

CALORIES	CALORIES FROM FAT	TOTAL FAT	SATURATED FAT	TRANS FAT	CHOLESTEROL	SODIUM	POTASSIUM
70	20	2.0 g	1.1 g	0.0 g	40 mg	160 mg	250 mg

TOTAL CARBOHYDRATE	DIETARY FIBER	SUGARS	PROTEIN	PHOSPHORUS	EXCHANGES/CHOICES:
5 g	1 g	3 g	7 g	120 mg	1 Nonstarchy Vegetable; 1 Protein, lean

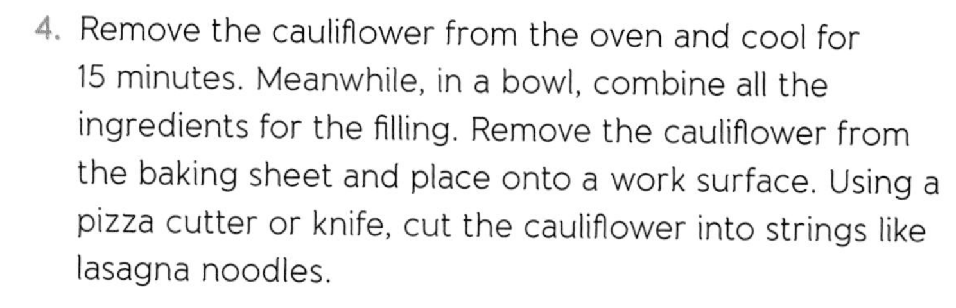

4. Remove the cauliflower from the oven and cool for 15 minutes. Meanwhile, in a bowl, combine all the ingredients for the filling. Remove the cauliflower from the baking sheet and place onto a work surface. Using a pizza cutter or knife, cut the cauliflower into strings like lasagna noodles.
5. In the bottom of a 9 × 12 baking pan, spread about 1/3 cup of sauce. Add a layer of cauliflower noodles. Using a spatula, spread some of the filling over the noodles, then add more sauce. Repeat the layers until all ingredients are used. Top the lasagna with the Parmesan cheese.
6. Lower the oven temperature to 400°F. Cover the lasagna with aluminum foil and bake for 25 minutes. Uncover, and bake an additional 15–20 minutes until lasagna is bubbly and browned. Remove the lasagna from the oven, and let rest 15 minutes before slicing. Cut into squares.

YOUR CHOICE OF ANY MASTER PROTEIN

See page 8.

BLUEBERRIES

Serves: 1 | Serving size: 1/3 cup

1/3 cup of blueberries

1. Serve blueberries alongside lasagna and protein.

EXCHANGES / CHOICES
1/2 Fruit

Calories 25; Calories from Fat 0; Total Fat 0.0 g; Saturated Fat 0.0 g; Trans Fat 0.0 g; Cholesterol 0 mg; Sodium 0 mg; Potassium 35 mg; Total Carbohydrate 7 g; Dietary Fiber 1 g; Sugars 5 g; Protein 0 g; Phosphorus 5 mg

NO NOODLE POLENTA LASAGNA

Serves: 18 | Serving size: 2 × 3-inch square | Prep time: 20 minutes | Cook time: 80 minutes

Polenta was a dish my mom made frequently, especially on cold, wintry upstate New York nights. Mom always made too much and once the polenta was refrigerated, it hardened and we would slice and sauté it into a crispy side dish. When I wanted to create noodle-less lasagnas, I remembered how well polenta went from a creamy bowl to something you could slice: the perfect substitute for traditional lasagna noodles. Be sure to use yellow coarse-meal polenta for this dish; the white fine-meal polenta is too bland.

POLENTA

- 4 cups low-fat, reduced-sodium chicken broth
- 1/4 teaspoon kosher salt
- 1 1/2 cups coarse polenta

SAUCE

- 1 tablespoon olive oil
- 4 cups sliced mushrooms, stems removed
- 1/4 cup chopped fresh basil
- 2 cups low-sodium store bought marinara sauce

TOPPING

- 1 cup part-skim mozzarella cheese
- 1/4 cup grated fresh Parmesan cheese

1. Coat a 9 × 12-inch baking pan with cooking spray and set aside. In a 3-quart saucepan, bring the chicken broth and salt to a boil. Slowly add in the polenta, reduce the heat to medium, and stir the polenta until it comes away from the sides of the pan, about 20 minutes. (It is not necessary to constantly stir, but do it often enough to ensure a smooth polenta.) Pour the polenta into the prepared pan, spread evenly, and place in the refrigerator for approximately 20 minutes or until it hardens.
2. Preheat the oven to 350°F. Meanwhile, heat the olive oil in a large skillet over high heat. Add the mushrooms and leave undisturbed without stirring for 1 minute. Begin to stir and sauté for about 5 minutes until mushrooms are browned and just begin to give up their moisture. Add in the basil and marinara sauce and simmer for 3 minutes.
3. After the polenta has become hard, remove it from the refrigerator. Spread the mushroom marinara on top of the polenta and top with the mozzarella and Parmesan cheeses.
4. Cover the lasagna and bake for 30 minutes. Uncover and bake for 10–15 minutes more until bubbly and browned. Remove from the oven and let stand 10 minutes before slicing. Cut into squares.

CALORIES	CALORIES FROM FAT	TOTAL FAT	SATURATED FAT	TRANS FAT	CHOLESTEROL	SODIUM	POTASSIUM
90	20	2.0 g	0.9 g	0.0 g	5 mg	210 mg	200 mg

TOTAL CARBOHYDRATE	DIETARY FIBER	SUGARS	PROTEIN	PHOSPHORUS	EXCHANGES/CHOICES:
12 g	1 g	2 g	4 g	80 mg	1 Starch

YOUR CHOICE OF ANY MASTER PROTEIN

See page 8.

....

ORANGE

Serves: 1 | Serving size: 1 orange

1 small orange

1. Peel orange and serve alongside lasagna and master protein.

EXCHANGES / CHOICES
1 Fruit

Calories 45; Calories from Fat 0; Total Fat 0.0 g; Saturated Fat 0.0 g; Trans Fat 0.0 g; Cholesterol 0 mg; Sodium 0 mg; Potassium 170 mg; Total Carbohydrate 11 g; Dietary Fiber 2 g; Sugars 9 g; Protein 1 g; Phosphorus 15 mg

NO NOODLE SPINACH LASAGNA

Serves: 18 | Serving size: 2 × 3-inch square
Prep time: 30 minutes | Cook time: 35 minutes for the sauce, 30 minutes for the lasagna

This lasagna was created for those of us who just want to dig in and eat. Make sure your spinach leaves are dried very well. A salad spinner can help here tremendously. I suggest purchasing flat-leaf spinach versus the thicker curly-edged spinach as the flat-leaf variety will release less moisture. If you want to use frozen spinach instead of fresh, feel free to do so, but be sure to really squeeze out all the moisture.

SAUCE

- 1 1/2 tablespoons olive oil, divided use
- 4 cups sliced mushrooms, stems removed
- 1 medium red onion, thinly sliced
- 2 small carrots, diced
- 1 teaspoon dried thyme leaves
- 1/2 teaspoon dried oregano leaves
- 1/4 teaspoon kosher salt
- 1/4 teaspoon freshly ground black pepper
- 1/4 teaspoon red pepper flakes
- 2 cups low-sodium store-bought marinara sauce

FILLING

- 1 cup small curd cottage cheese (1% milk fat)
- 1 cup nonfat ricotta cheese
- 1 teaspoon fresh grated lemon zest

- 4 cups fresh flat-leaf spinach leaves, coarse stems removed, washed and very well dried
- 1 cup shredded part-skim mozzarella cheese
- 1/4 cup grated Parmesan cheese

1. Coat a 9 × 12-inch baking pan with cooking spray. Preheat the oven to 375°F.
2. Heat 1 tablespoon of olive oil in a large skillet over high heat. Add the mushrooms and leave undisturbed for 1 minute. Begin to stir and sauté the mushrooms for 5 minutes until browned and the mushrooms just begin to release moisture. Remove the mushrooms with a slotted spoon from the skillet to a plate and set aside. Lower the heat to medium. Add the onions and sauté for 5–6 minutes until soft. Add the carrots and sauté for 4 minutes until the carrots are soft. Add the thyme, oregano, salt, pepper, and crushed red pepper. Add back the mushrooms. Add the marinara sauce and simmer on medium low heat for 20 minutes.
3. Add the cottage cheese to a blender and process until thick but smooth. Add the cottage cheese, ricotta cheese, and lemon zest to a bowl.

CALORIES	CALORIES FROM FAT	TOTAL FAT	SATURATED FAT	TRANS FAT	CHOLESTEROL	SODIUM	POTASSIUM
70	20	2.5 g	1.1 g	0.0 g	10 mg	160 mg	230 mg

TOTAL CARBOHYDRATE	DIETARY FIBER	SUGARS	PROTEIN	PHOSPHORUS	EXCHANGES/CHOICES:
5 g	1 g	3 g	6 g	110 mg	1 Nonstarchy Vegetable; 1 Protein, lean

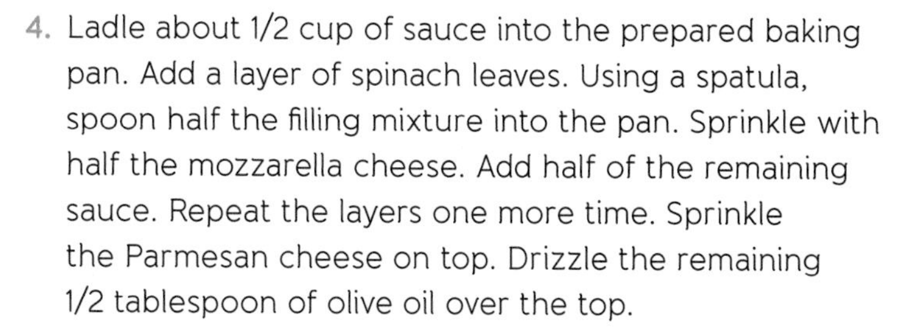

4. Ladle about 1/2 cup of sauce into the prepared baking pan. Add a layer of spinach leaves. Using a spatula, spoon half the filling mixture into the pan. Sprinkle with half the mozzarella cheese. Add half of the remaining sauce. Repeat the layers one more time. Sprinkle the Parmesan cheese on top. Drizzle the remaining 1/2 tablespoon of olive oil over the top.

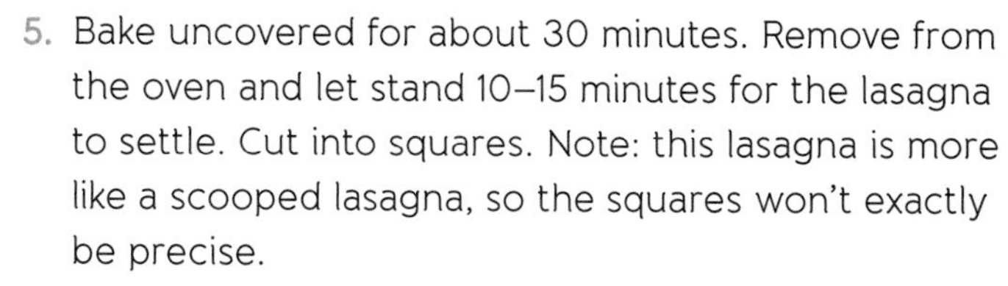

5. Bake uncovered for about 30 minutes. Remove from the oven and let stand 10–15 minutes for the lasagna to settle. Cut into squares. Note: this lasagna is more like a scooped lasagna, so the squares won't exactly be precise.

YOUR CHOICE OF ANY MASTER PROTEIN

See page 8.

• • • • • • • •

PLUMS

Serves: 1 | Serving size: 2 plums

2 small plums

1. Serve plums alongside lasagna and protein.

EXCHANGES / CHOICES
1 Fruit

Calories 60; Calories from Fat 5; Total Fat 0.5 g; Saturated Fat 0.0 g; Trans Fat 0.0 g; Cholesterol 0 mg; Sodium 0 mg; Potassium 210 mg; Total Carbohydrate 15 g; Dietary Fiber 2 g; Sugars 13 g; Protein 1 g; Phosphorus 20 mg

LASAGNA CUPCAKES

Serves: 12 | Serving size: 1 cupcake | Prep time: 15 minutes | Cook time: 20 minutes

I'm not particularly fond of the massive cupcake trend that hit the nation not too long ago, but making lasagna into "cupcakes" is a movement I could get behind. When you want all the elements of lasagna in a low-calorie, very easy to serve way, my Lasagna Cupcakes fit the bill. These are great to bring to a party as they transport beautifully.

- 24 square wonton wrappers
- 3/4 cup low-fat ricotta cheese
- 3/4 cup shredded part-skim mozzarella cheese
- 1 egg, beaten
- 1 teaspoon dried oregano
- 1/4 teaspoon freshly ground black pepper
- 24 fresh basil leaves
- 2 cups low-sodium store-bought marinara sauce
- 1/4 cup grated Parmesan cheese

1. Preheat the oven to 375°F. Coat a 12-cup standard muffin pan with cooking spray.
2. Add one wonton wrapper to the bottom of each cup, pressing down into the center with the pointed ends set up.
3. Mix together the ricotta and mozzarella cheeses, egg, dried oregano, and black pepper. Add a scant tablespoon of the cheese mixture over the wonton wrapper. Lay a basil leaf on top of the cheese. Add a tablespoon of the marinara sauce over the basil leaf. Repeat all the layers one more time ending with sauce. Sprinkle the top of each muffin with Parmesan.
4. Bake the lasagna muffins for 18–20 minutes until bubbly and browned. Remove from the oven and let cool for 5 minutes. Run a knife around each cup to loosen. Remove from the pan and serve.

CALORIES	CALORIES FROM FAT	TOTAL FAT	SATURATED FAT	TRANS FAT	CHOLESTEROL	SODIUM	POTASSIUM
100	25	3.0 g	1.5 g	0.0 g	25 mg	190 mg	180 mg

TOTAL CARBOHYDRATE	DIETARY FIBER	SUGARS	PROTEIN	PHOSPHORUS	EXCHANGES/CHOICES:
14 g	1 g	3 g	7 g	110 mg	1 Starch; 1/2 Fat

SEARED CHICKEN BREASTS

Serves: 4 | Serving size: 3 ounces

1 pound boneless, skinless chicken breasts (remove any tenderloins so chicken lays flat)
1/2 teaspoon kosher salt
1/4 teaspoon freshly ground black pepper
1 1/2 tablespoon olive or vegetable oil

1. Pound the chicken breasts so they are even in thickness. Season the chicken with salt and pepper.
2. Heat the oil in a heavy cast iron skillet over medium-high heat. Add the chicken breasts and sear on both sides for about 5 minutes per side. Be sure to let one side of the chicken thoroughly sear before turning over to the other side. This will ensure even cooking and will prevent sticking.
3. Cover the skillet, lower the heat to low, and cook for about 5-6 minutes until the chicken is cooked through.

EXCHANGES / CHOICES
3 Protein, lean;
1/2 Fat

Calories 170; Calories from Fat 70; Total Fat 8.0 g; Saturated Fat 1.5 g; Trans Fat 0.0 g; Cholesterol 65 mg; Sodium 290 mg; Potassium 200 mg; Total Carbohydrate 0 g; Dietary Fiber 0 g; Sugars 0 g; Protein 24 g; Phosphorus 175 mg

This recipe also in Master Proteins page 9

SPINACH

Serves: 1 | Serving size: 1/2 cup

1/2 cup spinach

1. Steam spinach for 2–3 minutes or until wilted and serve alongside chicken and lasagna cupcakes.

EXCHANGES / CHOICES
1 Nonstarchy Vegetable

Calories 20; Calories from Fat 0; Total Fat 0.0 g; Saturated Fat 0.0 g; Trans Fat 0.0 g; Cholesterol 0 mg; Sodium 65 mg; Potassium 420 mg; Total Carbohydrate 3 g; Dietary Fiber 2 g; Sugars 0 g; Protein 3 g; Phosphorus 50 mg

LASAGNA SOUP

Serves: 9 | Serving size: 1 cup | Prep time: 20 minutes | Cook time: 45 minutes

When trying to think of ways to reduce the amount of noodles in a lasagna, yet still deliver all of its components, I thought, why not soup? Every ingredient typically found in lasagna is here with only four noodles in the recipe. I find the taste of this lasagna soup lighter and you can actually taste each flavor.

1 tablespoon olive oil
4 cups sliced mushrooms
1 medium onion, chopped
2 carrots, peeled and chopped
1 tablespoon whole-wheat flour
6 cups fat-free, low-sodium chicken broth
1 (14.5-ounce) can diced fire-roasted tomatoes
4 curly edged whole-wheat lasagna noodles, broken
1/2 cup sliced fresh basil
3/4 cup nonfat ricotta cheese
3/4 cup shredded mozzarella cheese
1/4 cup grated Parmesan cheese

1. Heat the oil in a large saucepan over high heat. Add the mushrooms and leave undisturbed for 1 minute. Begin to stir and sauté for 5 minutes until mushrooms are browned and just begin to release their liquid. Remove the mushrooms from the pan and set aside.
2. Add in the onions and sauté for 4 minutes. Add in the carrots and sauté for 4 minutes. Add back the mushrooms. Add in the flour and sauté 1 minute until the flour is incorporated into the vegetables. Add in the broth and tomatoes and bring to a boil. Reduce the heat and simmer 15 minutes.
3. Add in the lasagna and raise the heat to medium high. Cook for 6–8 minutes until the noodles are cooked through. Add the basil and cook 1 minute. Ladle the soup into ovenproof bowls. With a spoon, drop ricotta cheese into each bowl. Sprinkle with mozzarella and Parmesan cheese. Set the bowls on a baking sheet and set the oven to broil.
4. Broil the soup, 6 inches from the heat source, just until the cheese is melted. Remove the soup from the oven. With pot holders, place each soup bowl on a plate to serve.

CALORIES	CALORIES FROM FAT	TOTAL FAT	SATURATED FAT	TRANS FAT	CHOLESTEROL	SODIUM	POTASSIUM
140	35	4.0 g	1.6 g	0.0 g	15 mg	320 mg	470 mg
TOTAL CARBOHYDRATE	**DIETARY FIBER**	**SUGARS**	**PROTEIN**	**PHOSPHORUS**	**EXCHANGES/CHOICES:**		
16 g	3 g	5 g	12 g	220 mg	1/2 Starch; 1 Nonstarchy Vegetable; 1 Protein, medium fat		

GREEN BEANS

Serves: 1 | Serving size: 1/2 cup

1/2 cup green beans

1. Steam green beans for 5–7 minutes until tender and crisp and serve alongside pasta and chicken.

EXCHANGES / CHOICES
1 Nonstarchy Vegetable

Calories 20; Calories from Fat 0; Total Fat 0.0 g; Saturated Fat 0.0 g; Trans Fat 0.0 g; Cholesterol 0 mg; Sodium 0 mg; Potassium 90 mg; Total Carbohydrate 5 g; Dietary Fiber 2 g; Sugars 1 g; Protein 1 g; Phosphorus 20 mg

• • • • • • •

ORANGE

Serves: 1 | Serving size: 1 orange

1 small orange

1. Serve orange alongside salad and snow peas.

EXCHANGES / CHOICES
1 Fruit

Calories 45; Calories from Fat 0; Total Fat 0.0 g; Saturated Fat 0.0 g; Trans Fat 0.0 g; Cholesterol 0 mg; Sodium 0 mg; Potassium 170 mg; Total Carbohydrate 11 g; Dietary Fiber 2 g; Sugars 9 g; Protein 1 g; Phosphorus 15 mg

CORN TORTILLA LASAGNA

Serves: 4 | Serving size: 1/4 tortilla | Prep time: 20 minutes | Cook time: 25 minutes

While a majority of the lasagna recipes in this chapter have the traditional ingredients, I've also learned that many homes have other staples on hand that can be put to good use, like tortillas. This is a fun, cake-like lasagna that you cut into wedges. It's inexpensive and a great way to serve fiber-rich beans. Change the beans to any kind you prefer and try blue or yellow corn tortillas.

4 (6-inch) corn tortillas

SAUCE

2 teaspoons olive oil
1/2 cup minced onion
2 garlic cloves, minced
1/2 teaspoon dried oregano
1 cup low-sodium store-bought marinara sauce
1 tablespoon fresh lime juice

1 cup canned cannellini beans, drained and rinsed
1/2 cup shredded part-skim mozzarella cheese
1 tablespoon grated Parmesan cheese

1. Preheat the oven to 350°F. Add the corn tortillas to a baking sheet. Bake the tortillas for 5–7 minutes until lightly toasted.
2. Meanwhile, heat the olive oil in a large skillet over medium heat. Add the onion and sauté for 3 minutes. Add in the garlic and oregano and sauté 1 minute. Add in the marinara sauce, lower the heat and simmer 5 minutes. Add in the lime juice and remove from the heat.
3. Place one toasted tortilla in an 8-inch round cake pan. Spread with some of the sauce, leaving about 1/2 inch all the way around the tortilla exposed. Add cannellini beans. Top with some of the mozzarella cheese. Repeat the layers, ending with the mozzarella cheese. Top entire lasagna with Parmesan cheese.
4. Bake the lasagna for 25 minutes until cheese is melted and tortillas are crisp. Remove from oven and let the lasagna settle for 10 minutes. Cut into wedges to serve.

CALORIES	CALORIES FROM FAT	TOTAL FAT	SATURATED FAT	TRANS FAT	CHOLESTEROL	SODIUM	POTASSIUM
210	50	6.0 g	2.0 g	0.0 g	10 mg	160 mg	460 mg
TOTAL CARBOHYDRATE	**DIETARY FIBER**	**SUGARS**	**PROTEIN**	**PHOSPHORUS**	**EXCHANGES/CHOICES:**		
30g	5 g	5 g	10 g	240 mg	1 1/2 Starch; 1 Nonstarchy Vegetable; 1 Protein, medium fat		

ASPARAGUS

Serves: 1 | Serving size: 6 spears

6 asparagus spears
Pinch lemon zest

1. Steam asparagus spears for 6–8 minutes and top with a pinch of lemon zest.

EXCHANGES / CHOICES
1 Nonstarchy Vegetable

Calories 20; Calories from Fat 0; Total Fat 0.0 g; Saturated Fat 0.0 g; Trans Fat 0.0 g; Cholesterol 0 mg; Sodium 15 mg; Potassium 200 mg; Total Carbohydrate 4 g; Dietary Fiber 2 g; Sugars 1 g; Protein 2 g; Phosphorus 50 mg

LASAGNA ROLL UPS

Serves: 6 | Serving size: 1 roll up | Prep time: 25 minutes | Cook time: 30–35 minutes

My sister and I used to quibble about which square of lasagna we wanted from the casserole dish. We'd invariably pick the same square! Those quarrels were put to an end when my Mom created this recipe. As everyone gets a predetermined portion, there will be no family "fights" about which square each one wants! Each of these roll ups comes out exactly the same and the overall process of creating lasagna is streamlined.

- 6 uncooked whole-wheat lasagna noodles (preferably curly edged)
- 2 teaspoons olive oil
- 3/4 cup nonfat ricotta cheese
- 3/4 cup shredded part-skim mozzarella cheese
- 1 (10-ounce) package chopped frozen spinach, very well drained and squeezed dry
- 1 egg, beaten
- 1 teaspoon dried oregano
- 1/4 teaspoon kosher salt
- 1/4 teaspoon freshly ground black pepper
- Pinch nutmeg
- 2 cups low-sodium store-bought marinara sauce
- 1/4 grated fresh Parmesan cheese

1. Preheat the oven to 375°F. Cook the lasagna noodles according to package directions. Drain and lay into a parchment-lined baking sheet. Drizzle each sheet with olive oil.
2. While the lasagna noodles are cooking, in a bowl, mix together the ricotta and mozzarella cheeses, spinach, egg, oregano, salt, pepper, and nutmeg.
3. Spread about 1/2 cup of the tomato sauce in the bottom of a 9 × 12-inch baking pan. Add a large spoonful of the cheese mixture on one end of a lasagna noodle. Roll up the lasagna noodle, from the short side into a spiral shape. You should have a roll that resembles a fat burrito. Repeat with the remaining noodles. Arrange the noodles, seam side down in the pan. Pour the remaining sauce over all the rolls. Sprinkle with Parmesan.
4. Bake for 30–35 minutes until bubbly and browned.

CALORIES	CALORIES FROM FAT	TOTAL FAT	SATURATED FAT	TRANS FAT	CHOLESTEROL	SODIUM	POTASSIUM
220	50	6.0 g	2.5 g	0.0 g	50 mg	300 mg	470 mg

TOTAL CARBOHYDRATE	DIETARY FIBER	SUGARS	PROTEIN	PHOSPHORUS	EXCHANGES/CHOICES:
26 g	4 g	6 g	16 g	260 mg	1 Starch; 2 Nonstarchy Vegetable; 1 Protein, lean; 1 Fat

STEAMED BROCCOLI

Serves: 1 | Serving size: 1/2 cup

1/2 cup broccoli

1. Steam broccoli for 2–3 minutes until tender and crisp and serve alongside lasagna roll ups and strawberries.

EXCHANGES / CHOICES
1 Nonstarchy Vegetable

Calories 25; Calories from Fat 5; Total Fat 0.5 g; Saturated Fat 0.1 g; Trans Fat 0.0 g; Cholesterol 0 mg; Sodium 30 mg; Potassium 230 mg; Total Carbohydrate 6 g; Dietary Fiber 3 g; Sugars 1 g; Protein 2 g; Phosphorus 50 mg

STRAWBERRIES

Serves: 1 | Serving size: 3/4 cup

3/4 cup strawberries

1. Serve strawberries alongside lasagna roll ups and broccoli.

EXCHANGES / CHOICES
1/2 Fruit

Calories 40; Calories from Fat 5; Total Fat 0.5 g; Saturated Fat 0.0 g; Trans Fat 0.0 g; Cholesterol 0 mg; Sodium 0 mg; Potassium 190 mg; Total Carbohydrate 10 g; Dietary Fiber 2 g; Sugars 6 g; Protein 1 g; Phosphorus 30 mg

SKILLET LASAGNA

Serves: 6 | Serving size: 1 cup | Prep time: 15 minutes | Cook time: 30 minutes

Years ago, I gave a class to a group of people who live on boats. They wanted me to come up with ideas for one-pot meals without the use of an oven. Comfort foods were also a requirement. Needless to say, this Skillet Lasagna worked very well in their tight, cramped galley kitchens. This is somewhat similar to the Lasagna Soup, but thicker and richer.

- 1 (28-ounce) can no-salt-added whole tomatoes
- 1/4 cup water
- 1 tablespoon olive oil
- 1 medium onion, chopped
- 1 large carrot, peeled and diced
- 2 garlic cloves, minced
- 1/2 pound lean ground beef (95%)
- Pinch crushed red pepper flakes
- 4 whole-wheat lasagna noodles, broken
- 3/4 cup small curd, low-fat cottage cheese
- 1/2 cup shredded part-skim mozzarella cheese
- 2 tablespoons grated fresh Parmesan cheese
- 1/4 cup sliced fresh basil

1. Add the tomatoes to a large bowl and crush them coarsely with your hands. Add the water. Set aside.
2. Heat the oil in a large skillet over medium heat. Add the onion and sauté for 4–5 minutes. Add the carrots and sauté for 5 minutes. Add the garlic and sauté 1 minute. Add in the beef and red pepper flakes and sauté 3–4 minutes.
3. Lay the noodles over the beef mixture. Pour the tomato sauce mixture on top. Cover and cook about 15–20 minutes over medium heat or until noodles are soft, stirring occasionally.
4. Add the cottage cheese in dollops over the noodles and then gently mix it in. (You don't have to thoroughly mix in the cottage cheese.) Top with the mozzarella and Parmesan cheeses, cover, and cook 3–4 minutes until the mozzarella cheese melts. Sprinkle the top with fresh basil.

CALORIES	CALORIES FROM FAT	TOTAL FAT	SATURATED FAT	TRANS FAT	CHOLESTEROL	SODIUM	POTASSIUM
210	50	6.0 g	2.3 g	0.1 g	30 mg	240 mg	530 mg

TOTAL CARBOHYDRATE	DIETARY FIBER	SUGARS	PROTEIN	PHOSPHORUS	EXCHANGES/CHOICES:
21 g	4 g	7 g	18 g	235 mg	1/2 Starch; 2 Nonstarchy Vegetable; 2 Protein, lean; 1/2 Fat

ROASTED PEPPER SALAD

Serves: 6 | Serving size: 1 cup
Prep time: 30 minutes | Cook time: 35 minutes

2 large red peppers
2 large yellow or orange peppers
2 large green peppers
2 tablespoons extra-virgin olive oil, divided use
2 teaspoons balsamic vinegar
1 small garlic clove, very finely chopped or crushed

GARNISH
12 black olives, pitted
A handful of small fresh basil leaves

1. Preheat the oven to 400°F. Brush the peppers with 1 tablespoon of the olive oil and arrange them in a shallow roasting pan. Roast for about 35 minutes or until the pepper skins are evenly darkened, turning them 3 or 4 times. Place the peppers in a bowl, cover with plastic wrap, and leave until they are cool enough to handle.
2. Working over a bowl to catch the juice, peel the peppers. Cut them in half and discard the cores and seeds (strain out any seeds that fall into the juice), then cut into thick slices.
3. Measure 1 1/2 tablespoons of the pepper juice into a small bowl (discard the remainder). Add the vinegar and garlic and whisk in the remaining 1 tablespoon of olive oil.
4. Arrange the peppers on a serving platter or on individual salad plates. Drizzle over the dressing and garnish with the olives and basil.

EXCHANGES / CHOICES
2 Nonstarchy Vegetable; 1 Fat

Calories 100; Calories from Fat 50; Total Fat 6.0 g; Saturated Fat 0.8 g; Trans Fat 0.0 g; Cholesterol 0 mg; Sodium 85 mg; Potassium 380 mg; Total Carbohydrate 12 g; Dietary Fiber 3 g; Sugars 6 g; Protein 2 g; Phosphorus 45 mg

This recipe also in Salads page 148

SPINACH

Serves: 1 | Serving size: 1/2 cup

1/2 cup spinach

1. Steam spinach and serve alongside lasagna and salad.

EXCHANGES / CHOICES
1 Nonstarchy Vegetable

Calories 20; Calories from Fat 0; Total Fat 0.0 g; Saturated Fat 0.0 g; Trans Fat 0.0 g; Cholesterol 0 mg; Sodium 65 mg; Potassium 420 mg; Total Carbohydrate 3 g; Dietary Fiber 2 g; Sugars 0 g; Protein 3 g; Phosphorus 50 mg

CHAPTER 4
Meatloaf

THE PRINCIPLES OF MEATLOAF

The ultimate comfort food has to be meatloaf!! What could be easier than mixing everything in one bowl and leaving it to bake? I've had my fair share of meatloaves over the years: everything from very good moist ones to dreadfully dry, boring ones. Meatloaf needs to be flavorful, but subtle; no one wants to be walloped with too much garlic or heavy spices. There are a few principles to follow for the first three meatloaves in this chapter.

The most important part of making a great meatloaf has everything to do with how you handle the ingredients. When you mix your meatloaf, use the gentlest effort to get everything combined. A light hand prevents a compact, dry-tasting meatloaf. Mix it well enough to incorporate all the ingredients, but try not to overmix.

The first three meatloaves are baked without the use of a traditional loaf pan. I've always loved the nice crunchy coating that forms all the way around a meatloaf that's simply shaped and then cooked on a baking sheet. I think you'll love baking your meatloaf this way; the oven hot air has a chance to rotate around, giving the loaf a really nice appearance. Cooking this way also prevents the meat from simply steaming in a pan, which can render the meatloaf tasteless.

I skip the fine breadcrumbs called for in many meatloaf recipes in favor of the thick-cut panko ones. The Pork and Brown Rice Meatloaf is a fine example of how to use high-fiber grains that help bind the meat just as well as the breadcrumbs do. The rice should already be cooked in the recipe, so be sure to make up a batch ahead of time. Brown rice freezes well, so you could prepare more than you need and freeze it for future meatloaf making. Frozen, cooked brown rice is now a convenient staple product found in the freezer section of many major supermarkets.

All three meatloaves create a mellow flavor by sautéing the onion, garlic, and bell pepper instead of adding them raw as many other meatloaf recipes state. These vegetables will absorb the other flavors in the meatloaf and mix better than if you added the vegetables without sautéing them first.

I suggest choosing 1–3 dry spices or herbs, or a combination of both, to add to the mix. For the Classic Meatloaf, all it needs is a sprinkle of Italian seasoning. The Pork and Brown Rice Meatloaf incorporates Asian flavors of curry and ginger, and A Better Turkey Meatloaf is compatible with sage and thyme. Just by changing the choice of spices and herbs, you'll have an entirely different meal all based on the same technique.

For a saucy topping, I've skipped the usual stewed tomatoes and tomato sauce, which I find flat tasting and with an overly sloppy appearance. I like a zestier flavor by combining ketchup, mustard, and just a touch of brown sugar to assist in the browning process. I switched it up in the Pork and Brown Rice Meatloaf by using hoisin sauce, which gives the loaf a really rich look.

Always let the meatloaf rest at least 5–7 minutes prior to slicing. Use a slicing knife instead of a chef's knife to create beautiful, even-looking pieces. Go ahead and master these first three loaves and then we will move on to other types of meatloaves that build on what you've accomplished.

VEGETARIAN MEATLOAVES

When I started eating vegetarian more and more, I was anxious to master the vegetarian meatloaf. When done right, vegetarian meatloaf can be quite comforting.

You'll start by sautéing onions, garlic, and bell peppers, the same way as you did for the previous three recipes. Don't skip this step: the browning of these vegetables is critical for best results. In these vegetarian meatloaves, I added carrots to the mix for extra nutrition and to add a delightful subtle sweetness to the loaf.

These loaves are soft, so they are baked within a pan versus the free-form style of the previous loaves. It's fun to make any of these in individual ramekins as I've done for the Mushroom and Walnut loaf. Be very gentle when slicing these loaves.

I only added a glaze for the Lentil and Brown Rice loaf. It's rich and bold and can be spread on top of the Mushroom and Walnut loaf and the Tofu Meatloaf. I experimented with using a tomato-based glaze, but it just blended in with all the other flavors, so this BBQ balsamic glaze made a much better counterpoint to the relatively mild-flavored loaves.

NONTRADITIONAL MEATLOAVES

These meatloaves will add even more variety to your dinner (or lunch) menus. The mini meatloaves are a perfect example of excellent portion control.

The Bison Meatloaf gives you a chance to try a whole new lean protein you might not have tried. Ground bison or buffalo, as it is called, is not difficult to find and the taste is rich, but without a dense amount of fat. My recipe testers thought this was a perfect loaf to serve at the holidays.

The Stuffed Meatloaf is a great blueprint to stuff with whatever vegetables you like. Feel free to experiment. Visually, it makes a really nice appearance with the filling exposed. I'd fan it out on the dinner plate or serve sliced in a row on a nice platter.

For the ultimate in comfort food, finish your meatloaf making with the Veal and Lamb Meatloaf. It has a satisfying deep flavor and it's a nice change from beef. Treat yourself and pick up New Zealand ground lamb—it's the best!

CLASSIC MEATLOAF

Serves: 6 | Serving size: 3 ounces (approx. 1 1/2 inches thick)
Prep time: 20 minutes | Cook time: 50–55 minutes

Ask anyone about childhood food memories and meatloaf is usually mentioned. We owned a collection of loaf pans when I was growing up, but my mom used them more for baking bread than forming meatloaves. She was the one who taught me to form a meatloaf into an oblong shape on a baking sheet, which let the air circulate all the way around the loaf to produce those crusty edges.

2 teaspoons olive oil
1 small onion, minced
1/3 cup finely minced green or red bell pepper
4 ounces chopped mushrooms
2 garlic cloves, minced
1 teaspoon Italian seasoning
1/4 teaspoon sea salt
1/4 teaspoon freshly ground black pepper
1 pound 95% lean ground beef
1 egg, beaten
1 cup whole-wheat panko breadcrumbs
1 cup fat-free milk
2 teaspoons Worcestershire sauce
1/2 teaspoon liquid smoke (optional)

TOPPING

1/3 cup sugar-free ketchup (such as Walden Farms)
1 1/2 tablespoons Dijon mustard
1 teaspoon brown sugar

1. Preheat the oven to 375°F. Line a baking sheet with parchment paper. Set aside.
2. Heat the oil in a medium skillet over medium heat. Sauté the onion for 3 minutes. Add in the green pepper and mushrooms and sauté for 3 minutes. Add in the garlic, Italian seasoning, salt, and pepper and sauté for 1 minute.
3. Add the onion mixture to a bowl, and let cool for 2 minutes. Add in the beef, egg, breadcrumbs, milk, Worcestershire sauce, and liquid smoke, if using. Mix gently, do not over handle the meat.
4. Place the mixture onto the prepared baking sheet and form into an oblong loaf. Combine the ketchup, mustard, and brown sugar and pour over the meatloaf.
5. Bake the meatloaf for 40–45 minutes until cooked through. Remove from the oven and let the meatloaf rest 5–7 minutes prior to slicing.

CALORIES	CALORIES FROM FAT	TOTAL FAT	SATURATED FAT	TRANS FAT	CHOLESTEROL	SODIUM	POTASSIUM
210	60	7.0 g	2.4 g	0.1 g	75 mg	440 mg	480 mg

TOTAL CARBOHYDRATE	DIETARY FIBER	SUGARS	PROTEIN	PHOSPHORUS	EXCHANGES/CHOICES:
17 g	2 g	5 g	21 g	245 mg	1 Carbohydrate; 3 Protein, lean

BRUSSELS SPROUTS

Serves: 1 | Serving size: 1/2 cup

1/2 cup Brussels sprouts

1. Steam Brussels sprouts for 10–15 minutes, until tender, and serve with meatloaf and strawberries.

EXCHANGES / CHOICES
1 Nonstarchy Vegetable

Calories 30; Calories from Fat 5; Total Fat 0.5 g; Saturated Fat 0.1 g; Trans Fat 0.0 g; Cholesterol 0 mg; Sodium 15 mg; Potassium 250 mg; Total Carbohydrate 6 g; Dietary Fiber 2 g; Sugars 1 g; Protein 2 g; Phosphorus 45 mg

STRAWBERRIES

Serves: 1 | Serving size: 3/4 cup

3/4 cup strawberries

1. Serve strawberries alongside meatloaf and Brussels sprouts.

EXCHANGES / CHOICES
1/2 Fruit

Calories 40; Calories from Fat 5; Total Fat 0.5 g; Saturated Fat 0.0 g; Trans Fat 0.0 g; Cholesterol 0 mg; Sodium 0 mg; Potassium 190 mg; Total Carbohydrate 10 g; Dietary Fiber 2 g; Sugars 6 g; Protein 1 g; Phosphorus 30 mg

PORK AND BROWN RICE MEATLOAF

Serves: 6 | Serving size: 3 ounces (approx. 1 1/2 inches thick)
Prep time: 20 minutes | Cook time: 45–50 minutes + time to cook rice

Brown rice will keep this moist meatloaf together. Be sure to cook up the short grain variety, as its stickier than long grain and will help keep the meatloaf shape better. The curry and ginger here give you a nice refreshing break from traditional Italian seasonings.

- 2 teaspoons olive oil
- 1 small onion, minced
- 1/3 cup finely minced green or red pepper
- 2 garlic cloves, minced
- 1 teaspoon curry powder
- 1/4 teaspoon ground ginger
- 1/4 teaspoon sea salt
- 1/4 teaspoon freshly ground black pepper
- 1 pound 96% lean ground pork
- 1 egg, beaten
- 1/2 cup cooked short grain brown rice
- 3 tablespoons hoisin sauce

1. Preheat the oven to 375°F. Line a baking sheet with parchment paper.
2. Heat the oil in a medium skillet over medium heat. Sauté the onion for 3 minutes. Add in the green pepper and sauté for 3 minutes. Add in the garlic, curry powder, ginger, salt, and pepper and sauté for 1 minute.
3. Add the onion mixture to a bowl, let cool for 2 minutes. Add in the pork, egg, and rice and mix gently, but do not over handle the meat.
4. Place the mixture onto the prepared baking sheet and form into an oblong loaf. Spread the hoisin sauce over the loaf.
5. Bake the meatloaf for 35–40 minutes until the meat is cooked through. Remove the meatloaf from the oven and let rest for 5–7 minutes prior to slicing.

CALORIES	CALORIES FROM FAT	TOTAL FAT	SATURATED FAT	TRANS FAT	CHOLESTEROL	SODIUM	POTASSIUM
170	50	6.0 g	1.6 g	0.0 g	70 mg	280 mg	300 mg

TOTAL CARBOHYDRATE	DIETARY FIBER	SUGARS	PROTEIN	PHOSPHORUS	EXCHANGES/CHOICES:
10 g	1 g	3 g	18 g	175 mg	1/2 Carbohydrate; 2 Protein, lean; 1 Fat

STEAMED BROCCOLI

Serves: 1 | Serving size: 1/2 cup

1/2 cup broccoli

1. Steam broccoli for 2–3 minutes until tender and crisp and serve alongside meatloaf and pineapple.

EXCHANGES / CHOICES
1 Nonstarchy Vegetable

Calories 25; Calories from Fat 5; Total Fat 0.5 g; Saturated Fat 0.1 g; Trans Fat 0.0 g; Cholesterol 0 mg; Sodium 30 mg; Potassium 230 mg; Total Carbohydrate 6 g; Dietary Fiber 3 g; Sugars 1 g; Protein 2 g; Phosphorus 50 mg

• • • • • • •

PINEAPPLE

Serves: 1 | Serving size: 1/2 cup

1/2 cup fresh pineapple

1. Serve pineapple alongside meatloaf and broccoli.

EXCHANGES / CHOICES
1 Fruit

Calories 40; Calories from Fat 0; Total Fat 0.0 g; Saturated Fat 0.0 g; Trans Fat 0.0 g; Cholesterol 0 mg; Sodium 0 mg; Potassium 90 mg; Total Carbohydrate 11 g; Dietary Fiber 1 g; Sugars 8 g; Protein 0 g; Phosphorus 5 mg

A BETTER TURKEY MEATLOAF

Serves: 6 | Serving size: 3 ounces | Prep time: 20 minutes | Cook time: 35–40 minutes

Developing a turkey meatloaf recipe made perfect sense to me; however, many turkey meatloaf recipes can be disappointing, as they are often dry and bland. This meatloaf follows the same exact blueprint as the classic meatloaf recipe and simply changes the choice of meat. The loaf cooks up moist and juicy and makes a delicious, healthy alternative to red meat.

2 teaspoons olive oil
1 small onion, minced
1/3 cup minced green or red pepper
2 garlic cloves, minced
1/2 teaspoon dried thyme leaves
1/2 teaspoon dried sage
1/2 teaspoon sea salt
1/4 teaspoon freshly ground black pepper
1 pound lean ground turkey
1 egg, beaten
1/2 cup whole-wheat panko breadcrumbs
1/2 cup fat-free milk
2 tablespoons grated fresh Parmesan cheese

TOPPING

1/3 cup sugar-free ketchup (such as Walden Farms)
2 tablespoons Dijon mustard
1 teaspoon brown sugar

1. Preheat the oven to 375°F. Line a baking sheet with parchment paper. Set aside.
2. Heat the oil in a medium skillet over medium heat. Sauté the onion for 3 minutes. Add the green pepper and sauté for 3 minutes. Add in garlic, thyme, sage, salt, and pepper and sauté for 1 minute.
3. Add the onion mixture to a large bowl, and let cool for 2 minutes. Add in the turkey, egg, breadcrumbs, milk, and Parmesan cheese. Mix gently, but do not over handle the meat. Combine the ketchup, mustard, and brown sugar and pour over the meatloaf.
4. Place the mixture on the prepared baking sheet. Bake the meatloaf for 35–40 minutes until the meat is cooked through. Remove the meatloaf from the oven and let it rest 5–7 minutes prior to slicing.

CALORIES	CALORIES FROM FAT	TOTAL FAT	SATURATED FAT	TRANS FAT	CHOLESTEROL	SODIUM	POTASSIUM
190	80	9.0 g	2.1 g	0.1 g	85 mg	390 mg	280 mg
TOTAL CARBOHYDRATE	**DIETARY FIBER**	**SUGARS**	**PROTEIN**	**PHOSPHORUS**	**EXCHANGES/CHOICES:**		
10 g	1 g	3 g	19 g	205 mg	1/2 Carbohydrate; 3 Protein, lean; 1/2 Fat		

STEAMED BROCCOLI

Serves: 1 | Serving size: 1/2 cup

1/2 cup broccoli

1. Steam broccoli for 2–3 minutes until tender and crisp and serve alongside meatloaf and cantaloupe.

EXCHANGES / CHOICES
1 Nonstarchy Vegetable

Calories 25; Calories from Fat 5; Total Fat 0.5 g; Saturated Fat 0.1 g; Trans Fat 0.0 g; Cholesterol 0 mg; Sodium 30 mg; Potassium 230 mg; Total Carbohydrate 6 g; Dietary Fiber 3 g; Sugars 1 g; Protein 2 g; Phosphorus 50 mg

• • • • • • • •

CANTALOUPE

Serves: 1 | Serving size: 1/3 cup

1/3 cup cantaloupe, diced
Lime wedge

1. Serve diced cantaloupe melon with a lime wedge.

EXCHANGES / CHOICES
1/2 Fruit

Calories 20; Calories from Fat 0; Total Fat 0.0 g; Saturated Fat 0.0 g; Trans Fat 0.0 g; Cholesterol 0 mg; Sodium 10 mg; Potassium 135 mg; Total Carbohydrate 4 g; Dietary Fiber 0 g; Sugars 4 g; Protein 0 g; Phosphorus 10 mg

MUSHROOM AND WALNUT MEAT LOAF

Serves: 4 | Serving size: 1 ramekin | Prep time: 25 minutes | Cook time: 50–55 minutes

Prepared correctly, mushrooms can be the perfect substitute for meat. Be sure to use a variety of mushrooms in this recipe, as the different flavors and textures make for a more flavorful loaf. These retain their shape well because they are baked in individual ramekin dishes and are perfect for portion control. Feel free to top these with a dollop of barbecue or tomato sauce before baking, if your eating plan allows.

- Cooking spray
- 1 tablespoon olive oil
- 1 large onion, chopped
- 1 pound mixed mushrooms (white, cremini, Portobello, or others) stemmed, cleaned, and finely chopped
- 1/3 cup diced red bell pepper
- 1/3 cup minced rehydrated sun-dried tomatoes
- 1 teaspoon Italian seasoning
- 1/2 teaspoon sea salt
- 1/4 teaspoon freshly ground black pepper
- 1 egg, beaten
- 1 cup panko breadcrumbs
- 1/2 cup fat-free milk
- 1/2 cup finely chopped walnuts

1. Preheat the oven to 350°F. Coat 4 (8-ounce) ramekins with cooking spray. Set the ramekins aside.
2. Heat the oil in a large skillet over medium heat. Sauté the onions and mushrooms for 10 minutes or until richly browned. Add in the red pepper and sun-dried tomatoes and sauté about 8 minutes. Add in the Italian seasoning, salt, and pepper and sauté 1 minute.
3. Add the mushroom mixture to a large bowl, allow to cool for 2 minutes. Add in the egg, breadcrumbs, milk, and walnuts. Mix gently. Divide the mixture among all the ramekins, pressing down on the mixture to fit all the ramekins.
4. Set the ramekins onto a baking sheet and bake in the oven for 30–35 minutes until the top is browned. Run a knife around each ramekin to loosen the loaf.

CALORIES	CALORIES FROM FAT	TOTAL FAT	SATURATED FAT	TRANS FAT	CHOLESTEROL	SODIUM	POTASSIUM
300	140	15.0 g	2.0 g	0.0 g	45 mg	340 mg	1050 mg

TOTAL CARBOHYDRATE	DIETARY FIBER	SUGARS	PROTEIN	PHOSPHORUS	EXCHANGES/CHOICES:
33 g	6 g	10 g	13 g	320 mg	1 Starch; 3 Nonstarchy Vegetable; 1 Protein, lean; 2 1/2 Fat

FRESH SPINACH SALAD

Serves: 1 | Serving size: 1 1/2 cups

1 cup fresh spinach leaves
5 cherry tomatoes, halved
1/4 cup red onion, thinly sliced
1 teaspoon olive oil
1/2 teaspoon lemon juice

1. Combine spinach, tomatoes, and onion slices in a small bowl. Drizzle with olive oil and top with lemon juice.

EXCHANGES / CHOICES
1 Nonstarchy Vegetable; 1 Fat

Calories 70; Calories from Fat 45; Total Fat 5.0 g; Saturated Fat 0.7 g; Trans Fat 0.0 g; Cholesterol 0 mg; Sodium 25 mg; Potassium 360 mg; Total Carbohydrate 7 g; Dietary Fiber 2 g; Sugars 3 g; Protein 2 g; Phosphorus 40 mg

CARROTS

Serves: 1 | Serving size: 1/2 cup

1/2 cup carrots

1. Steam carrots and serve alongside meatloaf and salad.

EXCHANGES / CHOICES
1 Nonstarchy Vegetable

Calories 25; Calories from Fat 0; Total Fat 0.0 g; Saturated Fat 0.0 g; Trans Fat 0.0 g; Cholesterol 0 mg; Sodium 45 mg; Potassium 180 mg; Total Carbohydrate 6 g; Dietary Fiber 2 g; Sugars 3 g; Protein 1 g; Phosphorus 25 mg

LENTIL AND BROWN RICE LOAF

Serves: 4 | Serving size: 1 (1 1/2-inch) slice
Prep time: 25 minutes | Cook time: 50–55 minutes + time to cook rice

A lentil and brown rice loaf was the very first non-meat meatloaf I made, way back in the 1970s. This isn't the original version as that one didn't work out too well! Lots of experimentation later, I believe this is a recipe you'd be happy to serve in place of traditional meatloaf. Making loaves with lentils is tricky, as the legumes can make everything taste flat and mushy. With the addition of sturdy rice, flavorful seasonings, and a tangy topping, this veggie version is a keeper!

- 1 cup brown lentils
- 1/4 teaspoon sea salt
- 2 cups water
- 2 teaspoons olive oil
- 1 large onion, diced
- 1 large carrot, peeled and diced
- 2 garlic cloves, minced
- 1 teaspoon Italian seasoning
- 1/4 teaspoon freshly ground black pepper
- 1/4 cup finely minced parsley
- 1 cup cooked short-grain brown rice
- 2 eggs, beaten
- 4 1/2 ounces low-sodium tomato sauce (about 2/3 cup)
- 3 tablespoons commercial barbecue sauce
- 1/4 cup fresh grated Parmesan cheese

TOPPING

- 3 tablespoons prepared barbeque sauce
- 1 tablespoon balsamic vinegar

1. In a 2-quart saucepan, bring the lentils, salt, and water to a boil. Reduce the heat, cover, and simmer 25 minutes until the lentils are tender. Drain, add the lentils to a bowl, and mash with a potato masher or carefully with an immersion blender, leaving some of the lentils coarse. Set aside.
2. Preheat the oven to 350°F. Coat a 9 × 5-inch loaf pan with cooking spray.
3. Heat the olive oil in a medium skillet over medium heat. Add the onion and sauté for 6–7 minutes. Add the carrots and sauté for 4 minutes. Add the garlic, Italian seasoning, and black pepper and sauté for 1 minute. Add in the parsley and remove from the heat. Add the vegetables to the lentils and let the mixture cool for 2 minutes.
4. Add the remaining ingredients to the lentils and vegetables and mix well. Add the mixture to the prepared pan, patting it down evenly.
5. Combine the topping ingredients. Spread the topping over the lentil loaf. Bake the loaf for 35–40 minutes until browned. Remove from the oven and let stand 5 minutes prior to slicing.

CALORIES	CALORIES FROM FAT	TOTAL FAT	SATURATED FAT	TRANS FAT	CHOLESTEROL	SODIUM	POTASSIUM
250	40	4.5 g	1.4 g	0.0 g	65 mg	380 mg	610 mg

TOTAL CARBOHYDRATE	DIETARY FIBER	SUGARS	PROTEIN	PHOSPHORUS	EXCHANGES/CHOICES:
39 g	9 g	10 g	13 g	270 mg	2 Starch; 1/2 Carbohydrate; 1 Nonstarchy Vegetable; 1 Protein, lean

FRESH SPINACH SALAD

Serves: 1 | Serving size: 1 1/2 cups

1 cup fresh spinach leaves
5 cherry tomatoes, halved
1/4 cup red onion, thinly sliced
1 teaspoon olive oil
1/2 teaspoon lemon juice

1. Combine spinach, tomatoes, and onion slices in a small bowl. Drizzle with olive oil and top with lemon juice.

EXCHANGES / CHOICES
1 Nonstarchy Vegetable; 1 Fat

Calories 70; Calories from Fat 45; Total Fat 5.0 g; Saturated Fat 0.7 g; Trans Fat 0.0 g; Cholesterol 0 mg; Sodium 25 mg; Potassium 360 mg; Total Carbohydrate 7 g; Dietary Fiber 2 g; Sugars 3 g; Protein 2 g; Phosphorus 40 mg

• • • • • • •

STRAWBERRIES

Serves: 1 | Serving size: 3/4 cup

3/4 cup strawberries

1. Serve strawberries alongside meatloaf and salad.

EXCHANGES / CHOICES
1/2 Fruit

Calories 40; Calories from Fat 5; Total Fat 0.5 g; Saturated Fat 0.0 g; Trans Fat 0.0 g; Cholesterol 0 mg; Sodium 0 mg; Potassium 190 mg; Total Carbohydrate 10 g; Dietary Fiber 2 g; Sugars 6 g; Protein 1 g; Phosphorus 30 mg

TOFU MEATLOAF

Serves: 6 | Serving size: 1 (1 1/2-inch) slice | Prep time: 20 minutes | Cook time: 50–55 minutes

When tofu first made its way onto the American food scene, it was everywhere and in everything from hot dogs to ice cream. I truly love the versatility of tofu. This tofu meatloaf combines oats, lentils, and cashews, and produces a soft, but sliceable loaf. It's also delicious served cold the next day stuffed into a lettuce wrap or served on an open-faced sandwich.

- 2 teaspoons olive oil
- 1 small onion, minced
- 1 large carrot, peeled and diced
- 2 garlic cloves, minced
- 1 teaspoon Italian seasoning
- 1/4 teaspoon freshly ground black pepper
- 10 ounces firm tofu, mashed
- 1 1/2 cup rolled oats
- 1 cup cooked brown lentils (follow instructions from the Lentil and Walnut Loaf)
- 1/3 cup finely chopped cashews
- 3 tablespoons lite soy sauce
- 2 tablespoons low-sugar ketchup (such as Walden Farms)
- 1 tablespoon Dijon mustard

1. Coat a 9 × 5-inch loaf pan with cooking spray. Preheat the oven to 375°F.
2. Heat the olive oil in a medium skillet over medium heat. Add the onion and sauté for 5–7 minutes. Add the carrot and sauté for 3 minutes. Add in the garlic, Italian seasoning, and pepper and sauté for 1 minute. Add the vegetables to a large mixing bowl.
3. Add the remaining ingredients to the vegetable mixture and mix well. Add the mixture to the prepared loaf pan, pack well, and bake for 40 minutes until the loaf is browned. Remove from the oven and let the tofu loaf stand 5 minutes prior to slicing.

CALORIES	CALORIES FROM FAT	TOTAL FAT	SATURATED FAT	TRANS FAT	CHOLESTEROL	SODIUM	POTASSIUM
220	70	8.0 g	1.4 g	0.0 g	0 mg	450 mg	390 mg
TOTAL CARBOHYDRATE	**DIETARY FIBER**	**SUGARS**	**PROTEIN**	**PHOSPHORUS**	**EXCHANGES/CHOICES:**		
28 g	6 g	3 g	12 g	250 mg	2 Starch; 1 Protein, medium fat		

FRESH SPINACH SALAD

Serves: 1 | Serving size: 1 1/2 cups

1 cup fresh spinach leaves
5 cherry tomatoes, halved
1/4 cup red onion, thinly sliced
1 teaspoon olive oil
1/2 teaspoon lemon juice

1. Combine spinach, tomatoes, and onion slices in a small bowl. Drizzle with olive oil and top with lemon juice.

EXCHANGES / CHOICES
1 Nonstarchy Vegetable; 1 Fat

Calories 70; Calories from Fat 45; Total Fat 5.0 g; Saturated Fat 0.7 g; Trans Fat 0.0 g; Cholesterol 0 mg; Sodium 25 mg; Potassium 360 mg; Total Carbohydrate 7 g; Dietary Fiber 2 g; Sugars 3 g; Protein 2 g; Phosphorus 40 mg

• • • • • • •

APPLE

Serves: 1 | Serving size: 1 apple

1 small apple

1. Serve apple alongside spinach salad and meatloaf.

EXCHANGES / CHOICES
1 Fruit

Calories 50; Calories from Fat 0; Total Fat 0.0 g; Saturated Fat 0.0 g; Trans Fat 0.0 g; Cholesterol 0 mg; Sodium 0 mg; Potassium 110 mg; Total Carbohydrate 14 g; Dietary Fiber 3 g; Sugars 11 g; Protein 0 g; Phosphorus 10 mg

MINI MEATLOAVES

Serves: 4 | Serving size: 1 mini meatloaf | Prep time: 20 minutes | Cook time: 40–45 minutes

I love to create recipes that illustrate portion control. These mini meatloaves are rich and filling. If you are cooking for one or two people, go ahead and prepare the entire recipe and freeze the leftovers. It's easy to defrost a single serving for lunch or dinner the following week.

2 teaspoons olive oil
1 small onion, diced
1 large carrot, peeled and diced
2 garlic cloves, minced
1 teaspoon dried thyme leaves
1/2 teaspoon rubbed sage
1/2 teaspoon sea salt
1/4 teaspoon freshly ground black pepper
8 ounces 93% lean ground beef
8 ounces 96% lean ground pork
1 cup whole-wheat panko breadcrumbs
1 cup fat-free milk
1 egg, beaten

TOPPING

3 tablespoons low-sugar ketchup (such as Walden Farms)
2 tablespoons balsamic vinegar
1 tablespoon Dijon mustard

1. Preheat the oven to 350°F. Line a baking sheet with parchment paper or nonstick foil.
2. Heat the oil in a large skillet over medium heat. Add the onion and sauté for 5–7 minutes. Add the carrot and sauté for 3 minutes. Add the garlic, thyme, sage, salt, and pepper and cook for 1 minute. Remove the vegetables from the heat and add to a large bowl. Allow to cool for 2 minutes.
3. Add the beef, pork, breadcrumbs, milk, and egg to the vegetables. Mix gently. Form the mixture into 4 football-shaped mini meat loaves. Place the loaves onto the prepared baking sheet. Combine the topping ingredients and spread on top of each loaf.
4. Bake the loaves for 35–40 minutes until well browned.

CALORIES	CALORIES FROM FAT	TOTAL FAT	SATURATED FAT	TRANS FAT	CHOLESTEROL	SODIUM	POTASSIUM
210	60	7.0 g	2.1 g	0.1 g	75 mg	430 mg	410 mg
TOTAL CARBOHYDRATE	**DIETARY FIBER**	**SUGARS**	**PROTEIN**	**PHOSPHORUS**	**EXCHANGES/CHOICES:**		
16 g	2 g	5 g	20 g	225 mg	1 Carbohydrate; 3 Protein, lean		

BISON MEATLOAF

Serves: 6 | Serving size: 1 (1 1/2-inch) slice | Prep time: 25 minutes | Cook time: 60 minutes

The first time I ever ate bison was at a barbecue. The lean meat was reminiscent of roast beef and I was intrigued by its light game flavor. My local butcher had ground bison on sale one day and I took the opportunity to create this bison meatloaf. It has a hearty flavor, yet it is lower in fat content than beef.

- 1 tablespoon olive oil
- 1 large onion, diced
- 8 ounces mushrooms, cleaned, stemmed, and diced
- 1 large carrot, peeled and diced
- 2 garlic cloves, minced
- 1 tablespoon fresh minced thyme
- 1 tablespoon fresh minced sage
- 1 pound lean ground buffalo meat
- 1/2 cup whole-wheat panko breadcrumbs
- 2/3 cup tomato sauce, divided use
- 1 egg, beaten
- 1/2 teaspoon sea salt
- 1/4 teaspoon freshly ground black pepper
- Pinch crushed red pepper flakes

1. Preheat the oven to 350°F. Line a baking sheet with parchment paper or nonstick foil.
2. Heat the oil in a large skillet over medium heat. Add the onion and mushrooms sauté for 5–7 minutes. Add in the carrot and sauté for 3 minutes. Add in the garlic, thyme, and sage and sauté for 1 minute. Remove the vegetables from the heat, add to a large bowl, and allow to cool for 2 minutes.
3. Add the bison meat, panko, 1/2 cup of the tomato sauce, egg, salt, pepper, and crushed red pepper to the vegetables and mix gently. Add the bison mixture to the center of the baking sheet and form into an oblong loaf. Bake the loaf for 30 minutes. Pour over the remaining tomato sauce and continue to bake for 20 minutes.
4. Remove the bison meatloaf from the oven and let stand for 5–10 minutes prior to slicing.

CALORIES	CALORIES FROM FAT	TOTAL FAT	SATURATED FAT	TRANS FAT	CHOLESTEROL	SODIUM	POTASSIUM
180	45	5.0 g	1.2 g	0.0 g	80 mg	380 mg	540 mg

TOTAL CARBOHYDRATE	DIETARY FIBER	SUGARS	PROTEIN	PHOSPHORUS	EXCHANGES/CHOICES:
13 g	3 g	4 g	21 g	205 mg	1/2 Starch; 1 Nonstarchy Vegetable; 3 Protein, lean

STUFFED MEAT LOAF

Serves: 6 | Serving size: 1 (1 1/2-inch) slice | Prep time: 30 minutes | Cook time: 50–55 minutes

Need a recipe to make with your kids? This is it! They will have so much fun rolling the loaf up and over the vegetables. When you slice this loaf after it is cooked, the vegetables peek out over the beef and turkey. Shape the mixture in a rectangle and use the waxed paper as directed, as it will help you to roll the meatloaf into a nice spiral.

2 teaspoons olive oil
1 slice (1/2 ounce) pancetta, diced
1 large onion, chopped
2 carrots, peeled and diced
1 red bell pepper, cored and diced
2 garlic cloves, peeled and minced
1 teaspoon Italian seasoning
1/4 teaspoon sea salt
1/2 teaspoon freshly ground black pepper
1/2 pound 93% lean ground turkey
1/2 pound 93% lean ground beef
1 egg, beaten
1 cup whole-wheat panko breadcrumbs
1/2 cup fat-free milk
1/4 cup tomato sauce

TOPPING

3 tablespoons low-sugar ketchup (such as Walden Farms)
2 tablespoons balsamic vinegar
1 tablespoon Dijon mustard

1. Preheat the oven to 375°F. Line a baking sheet with parchment paper or nonstick foil. Heat the oil and pancetta in a large skillet over medium heat. Add the onion and sauté for 5 minutes. Add the carrots and red pepper and sauté for 4 minutes. Add in the garlic and Italian seasoning, salt, and pepper and sauté for 1 minute. Set aside.
2. In a large bowl, mix together the ground turkey, ground beef, egg, breadcrumbs, milk, and tomato sauce; mix gently.
3. Form the meatloaf into a neat rectangle, about 1/2-inch thick, on top of a sheet of waxed paper. Spread the meatloaf with the vegetables, leaving a 1-inch border all around the sides. Start rolling the meatloaf using the waxed paper to help you lift up the meat from the shorter side. Roll the meatloaf tightly. Place the meatloaf on the prepared baking sheet. Combine the topping ingredients and pour over the meatloaf.
4. Bake the meatloaf for 40–45 minutes until cooked through. Remove the meatloaf from the oven and let stand for 5 minutes prior to slicing.

CALORIES	CALORIES FROM FAT	TOTAL FAT	SATURATED FAT	TRANS FAT	CHOLESTEROL	SODIUM	POTASSIUM
240	80	9.0 g	2.7 g	0.2 g	85 mg	430 mg	500 mg

TOTAL CARBOHYDRATE	DIETARY FIBER	SUGARS	PROTEIN	PHOSPHORUS	EXCHANGES/CHOICES:
20 g	3 g	7 g	20 g	240 mg	1/2 Starch; 2 Nonstarchy Vegetable; 2 Protein, lean; 1 Fat

BROCCOLINI

Serves: 1 | Serving size: 1/2 cup

1/2 cup broccolini

1. Steam broccolini and serve alongside meatloaf and apple slices.

EXCHANGES / CHOICES
1 Nonstarchy Vegetable

Calories 30; Calories from Fat 0; Total Fat 0.0 g; Saturated Fat 0.0 g; Trans Fat 0.0 g; Cholesterol 0 mg; Sodium 20 mg; Potassium 220 mg; Total Carbohydrate 5 g; Dietary Fiber 1 g; Sugars 1 g; Protein 2 g; Phosphorus 45 mg

• • • • • • •

APPLE

Serves: 1 | Serving size: 1 apple

1 small apple

1. Serve apple alongside meatloaf and broccolini.

EXCHANGES / CHOICES
1 Fruit

Calories 50; Calories from Fat 0; Total Fat 0.0 g; Saturated Fat 0.0 g; Trans Fat 0.0 g; Cholesterol 0 mg; Sodium 0 mg; Potassium 110 mg; Total Carbohydrate 14 g; Dietary Fiber 3 g; Sugars 11 g; Protein 0 g; Phosphorus 10 mg

VEAL AND LAMB MEATLOAF

Serves: 6 | Serving size: 1 (1 1/2-inch) slice | Prep time: 20 minutes | Cook time: 55–60 minutes

My friends and recipe testers voted this Veal and Lamb Meatloaf their absolute favorite. This version is great for special occasions as most of us don't eat veal and lamb every day. Be sure to seek out the very best lamb from New Zealand and if possible, have a butcher grind fresh lamb for you. There's nothing like it. Feel free to serve with a nice mustard or BBQ sauce.

1 tablespoon olive oil
1 slice bacon
1 medium onion, chopped
1 cup mushroom slices
1 1/2 carrots, peeled and diced
1/2 cup minced fresh parsley
1 tablespoon minced fresh thyme
2 garlic cloves, minced
1/2 pound lean ground veal
1/2 pound lean ground lamb
1/4 cup egg substitute
3/4 cup whole-wheat panko breadcrumbs
1/2 teaspoon sea salt
1/2 teaspoon freshly ground black pepper

1. Preheat the oven to 375°F. Line a baking sheet with parchment paper or nonstick foil.
2. Heat the oil and bacon in a large skillet over medium heat. Add the onion and mushrooms and sauté until the bacon is lightly crisp. Drain off all but 1 teaspoon fat. Add the carrots and sauté for 3 minutes. Add in the parsley, thyme, and garlic and sauté for 1 minute. Add the vegetables to a large bowl, and allow to cool for 2 minutes.
3. Add the remaining ingredients to the bowl and mix gently. Add the mixture to the prepared baking sheet and form into an oblong loaf. Bake the loaf for 40–45 minutes. Turn on the oven broiler and broil the top of the loaf for 2 minutes. Remove the loaf from the oven and let stand for 5 minutes prior to slicing.

CALORIES	CALORIES FROM FAT	TOTAL FAT	SATURATED FAT	TRANS FAT	CHOLESTEROL	SODIUM	POTASSIUM
160	50	6.0 g	1.9 g	0.0 g	50 mg	300 mg	370 mg
TOTAL CARBOHYDRATE	DIETARY FIBER	SUGARS	PROTEIN	PHOSPHORUS	EXCHANGES/CHOICES:		
12 g	2 g	3 g	16 g	160 mg	1 Carbohydrate; 2 Protein, lean		

CARROTS AND BROCCOLI

Serves: 1 | Serving size: 1 cup

1/2 cup carrots
1/2 cup broccoli

1. Steam carrots and broccoli and serve alongside meatloaf and pear.

EXCHANGES / CHOICES
2 Nonstarchy Vegetable

Calories 50; Calories from Fat 5; Total Fat 0.5 g; Saturated Fat 0.1 g; Trans Fat 0.0 g; Cholesterol 0 mg; Sodium 75 mg; Potassium 410 mg; Total Carbohydrate 12 g; Dietary Fiber 5 g; Sugars 4 g; Protein 2 g; Phosphorus 75 mg

. . . .

PEAR

Serves: 1 | Serving size: 1/2 pear

1/2 small pear

1. Slice pear in half and serve alongside meatloaf and carrots and broccoli.

EXCHANGES / CHOICES
1 Fruit

Calories 40; Calories from Fat 0; Total Fat 0.0 g; Saturated Fat 0.0 g; Trans Fat 0.0 g; Cholesterol 0 mg; Sodium 0 mg; Potassium 85 mg; Total Carbohydrate 11 g; Dietary Fiber 2 g; Sugars 7 g; Protein 0 g; Phosphorus 10 mg

CHAPTER 5
Pasta &
Sauce

THE PRINCIPLES OF PASTA AND SAUCE MAKING

Ahhh… pasta! The very word conjures up good times and sweet memories. And yes, people with diabetes can eat pasta! Only you know what works best for you to manage your blood sugar, but with these intensely flavored dishes, you can get your fill without filling out.

Let's begin with some principles of cooking pasta. Seems easy enough, right? Add pasta to water, let it cook, drain, and you have pasta, right? Well... no. There are some guiding principles that will spell the difference between bland, limp pasta and fantastic, perfectly cooked strands.

1. You'll need to bring a 3–5-quart pot filled with water to a rapid boil. Why so much water and this large pot? The rapidly boiling water will come back to a second rapid boil that much faster after you've added the pasta, and it helps to reduce the pasta sticking to itself as it washes away the starch from the pasta surface.
2. Salt should be added. Even a lightly salted pasta pot will give the pasta the absolute necessary flavor it needs. Otherwise, no matter how much you try to get all the flavor from the sauce, the pasta will taste lifeless and dull. Some of the sodium will go down the sink when the pasta is drained, but enough of it will adhere to make a difference in flavor, so add a few teaspoons. You might even find you'll need to add less sodium overall to the finished dish.
3. Make sure the water is rapidly boiling. There shouldn't just be some surface bubbles. Add the pasta at that point and stir for the first 1–2 minutes. This helps keep the pasta from sticking together.
4. Don't add any oil to the pot. Pasta that's cooked in oily water will become oily itself and the sauce will slide right off, resulting in flavorless pasta.
5. Every shape and strand of pasta will have a different cooking time. Lift a piece of pasta from the pot about 6 minutes into the cooking time and take a taste. You can always cook it longer, but if it's already overlooked there's no going backward. The pasta should always be a bit chewy. I recommend actually undercooking the pasta by about a minute or two, adding it to the sauce, then letting the pasta finish cooking in the sauce for about 1 minute.
6. Once the pasta is cooked, instead of draining it through a conventional strainer,

I recommend you use a big Chinese ladle type strainer or spider (you can get these at any cookware shop). By scooping the pasta out, rather than draining it, you'll retain the shape of the pasta perfectly. Add the scooped and drained pasta immediately to the prepared sauce. Never rinse or allow the pasta to cool (except when we get to the pasta salad recipes; last one in this chapter). Rinsed and cooled pasta prevents the absorption of the sauce because pasta needs a little surface starch for the sauce to adhere to.

7. Save a bit of the hot cooking water and add it to a serving bowl. Let the water sit in the bowl a few minutes and pour the water out. Now you have a nice warm bowl to add your pasta into, which makes everything taste better!
8. As you may notice, the serving size of most of these recipes turns out to be about 1/2 to 3/4 cup of cooked pasta. The standard serving size is usually 2 ounces dry, which translates into about 1 cup cooked. For people with diabetes, this amount may prove challenging for managing blood glucose levels, so I've cut the portion of pasta almost in half. With the sauces so nicely flavored and with the recommended side serving suggestions, this should make a satisfying meal. If there is more sauce to pasta, I'd just recommend sopping up the sauce with the side vegetable suggestions!
9. We tested the pasta shapes with everything from penne to fusilli to shells. All worked but we noticed the smaller the shape, the more we enjoyed the dish. For the strand pastas, choose any of your favorites from linguine to fettuccine to spaghetti and more.

PRINCIPLES OF TOMATO-BASED SAUCES

1. Plum tomatoes are the very best kind of tomato to use. They have a higher proportion of meat to liquid than round tomatoes. In the first three sauce recipes, I use canned tomatoes. In some parts of the country, canned tomatoes may always be superior to fresh, as getting really good fresh tomatoes, even in tomato season, can be a challenge.
2. Always buy whole, canned tomatoes and crush them yourself. Just add them to a deep bowl and use your hands to gently crush them coarsely. This is actually fun; my cooking class students get a real kick out of this step! Or, if you don't wish to get in there with your hands, try using a pastry blender to coarsely chop them, it works really well. Already crushed tomatoes or tomato purée often masks inferior canned tomatoes.
3. Seek out tomatoes in their own liquid, not with added tomato sauce. You probably won't need the liquid anyway, as the tomatoes will provide enough liquid for

the sauce, but hold back a little of it to add just in case.

4. There is no need for thickeners like tomato paste, which give sauces a too sweet flavor and a thickness that's really not necessary. Instead, use the technique of reduction; simmering the sauce for 20–25 minutes until thick. If you are in a rush for sauce, adjust the heat to high and cook until the sauce is thick, about 10 minutes. I usually cook mine in the 20–25-minute range as I'm doing other things to get a meal ready, but both methods will work. As I note in the recipe, always use a skillet rather than a deep pot to prepare the tomato sauces. You want the reduction to be effective and water will evaporate much better by using a skillet rather then a deep pot.
5. Adding fresh herbs is best. I have no objection to dried oregano, thyme, or bay leaves, but don't ever use dried basil! I find that 5 (and definitely no more than 10) basil leaves are plenty. Too many herbs can overwhelm the sauce and perhaps make it taste a little medicinal as well. Feel free to slice them up or use the leaves whole.
6. For the ricotta cheese called for in these recipes, please try to purchase the best you can find. Give it a little stir first in a bowl to increase its creaminess. You can also add it first to a blender or food processor to make it silky smooth.

The tomato sauce recipes are written in a progressive order. Start by mastering marinara, then progress to making a pink sauce, and then finally a vegetable-filled tomato sauce. With these three variations, plus changing up your pasta shapes, and serving different side dishes, you'll have so many dinner options!

PRINCIPLES OF OIL-BASED SAUCES

When growing up, all I knew was a tomato sauce and pasta pairing. Then, I went to Italy. In restaurant after restaurant, I was served simply prepared pasta that was so utterly delicious. It didn't look like there were many ingredients used, but perhaps my eyes deceived me? The secret to minimal ingredients but maximum flavor was the use of a fabulous olive oil-based sauce. Olive oil is the primary flavor. Plus, the addition of herbs and garlic is all that's needed for spectacular flavor. Here are a few guidelines:

1. Use the very best olive oil you can. The oil is not heated on a high flame, so the flavor of the oil will remain.
2. We don't want to overload the dish with too much fat, so the pasta cooking water is added to not only help coat the pasta evenly but to give the final dish a little thickness.
3. Think of an oil-based sauce as a blank canvas. You can go from just oil, garlic, salt, and pepper to adding healthy nuts,

vegetables, and a handful of fresh herbs. But try to keep the essence of oil-based sauces intact and simple.

PRINCIPLES OF BAKED PASTAS

My mom lived with diabetes for 49 years. While she gave up a few foods that wreaked havoc with her blood glucose levels, every week she still prepared a baked pasta. She grew up in an Italian neighborhood in New Jersey and was taught at a young age how to prepare baked ziti, stuffed shells, manicotti, and more. The best part of enjoying her baked pasta dishes was that the pasta was never waterlogged or mushy. Here are her pasta rules to live by:

1. Use a wide shallow baking dish (an oval au gratin dish is perfect). Choose one about 13 inches long and 2 inches deep. This allows the pasta filling to heat quicker, keeping the pasta nice and firm, yet moist.
2. Undercook the pasta slightly. It should be very al dente. And never rinse the pasta; it will only make the casserole mushy.
3. Add cheese, but do so sparingly.

4. Make your own breadcrumbs. This takes no more than a minute or two and the result is infinitely better. Commercial breadcrumbs can taste like chemicals and are often too finely ground, making for a mushy topping.
5. Bake uncovered. Covering the pasta steams it and makes it soggy. Not covering also helps to create an appealing crispy crust everyone loves.
6. No need to let the pasta rest once it's removed from the oven, like you do with lasagna. You want the sauce to be a bit loose.
7. To save time, make up all the components of the recipe ahead of time and store. Then, combine everything just before baking.

PRINCIPLES OF PASTA SALADS

What a really ingenious idea it is to enjoy cool pastas on a hot day. Like a lot of the recipes in this chapter, you'll need a blueprint to follow to ensure you don't end up with heavy, sticky, flavorless pasta salads. Through lots of trial and error, here are the steps to take for the very best results.

1. Make sure to choose the very best pasta, preferably made from 100% semolina or durum wheat. Once pasta cools, you need the sturdiness of a good pasta to help maintain its chewy texture.
2. Choose a pasta shape according to what additional ingredients you'll use. If your dressing is on the chunkier side, choose a heavy pasta like rigatoni. If the dressing is thinner, a smaller shaped pasta such as fusilli will work. If you wish to add some seafood, use shells, as they catch shellfish well.
3. Never overcook the pasta. As a matter of fact, undercook it by a minute.
4. Dressings should be bold tasting. Once a dressing is added to pasta the starch in the pasta actually neutralizes flavors, so start out with a dressing that actually tastes a bit stronger on its own.
5. If adding large leafy fresh herbs, such as basil or mint, just tear them. They won't wilt or bruise this way.
6. After you drain the pasta, toss it with a little olive oil to prevent sticking while it cools. If the pasta is not cooled properly, it will absorb the dressing too fast, resulting in a dull-flavored, dry and sticky pasta salad.
7. After all the ingredients are tossed together, let everything sit for a minimum of 30 minutes and up to 2 hours. Pasta salads aren't exactly appealing past 24 hours, so prepare them and plan on serving them soon.
8. Serve pasta salads cool or at room temperature but never cold. The flavors are not as pronounced in a chilled pasta salad.
9. To finish any pasta dish, a spritz of fresh lemon juice picks up the flavor very nicely!

Classic Italian Marinara page 108

CLASSIC ITALIAN MARINARA

Serves: 10 | Serving size: 1/2 cup | Prep time: 7 minutes | Cook time: 33 minutes

You can make your own marinara sauce at a fraction of the price of commercially bottled sauces. This sauce relies heavily on garlic, but feel free to temper this assertive flavor if you wish. Either cut back on the amount of garlic or slice the garlic instead of mincing it. The more you chop or mince garlic, the more pungent your final dish will be. Larger pieces of garlic, while still flavorful, will release a more subtle taste. This sauce freezes great. Pour into a heavy zip-locked freezer bag and store for up to 6 months.

- 2 tablespoons olive oil
- 5 garlic cloves, minced
- 1 (28-ounce) can good-quality canned tomatoes, preferably packed in its own juice, drained, reserve liquid
- 5 fresh basil leaves with stems, sliced, or you may leave whole
- 10 ounces whole-wheat shaped pasta (penne, shells, fusilli)
- 1/4 teaspoon kosher salt
- 1/4 teaspoon freshly ground black pepper
- 1/4 teaspoon ground red pepper flakes (optional)

- 2 tablespoons freshly grated Parmesan or Pecorino Romano cheese

1. Heat the olive oil and garlic in a large skillet with a lid over low heat (do not use a deep pot, you want the water to quickly evaporate and the sauce to become thick). Cook the garlic for about 6–7 minutes, but do not brown, stirring occasionally.
2. Meanwhile, add the drained tomatoes to a deep bowl. Crush the tomatoes with your hands until coarse. Add the tomatoes and basil to the skillet and simmer for 20–25 minutes until thick. Add some of the reserved liquid from the can of tomatoes, if necessary, if the sauce is too thick.
3. Meanwhile bring a 3–5-quart pot of lightly salted water (fill the pot 2/3 full) to a rolling boil. Add the pasta and stir for the first minute. Continue to cook the pasta approximately 7–8 minutes until al dente. Drain, do not rinse.
4. Add in the salt, pepper, and crushed red pepper, if using, to the tomato sauce. Add the pasta to the sauce, cover, and let the pasta sit in the sauce for 1–2 minutes. Add the pasta to a warmed bowl and sprinkle with cheese. (The sauce can also be frozen. Freeze in a quart container and store for 3–4 months.)

CALORIES	CALORIES FROM FAT	TOTAL FAT	SATURATED FAT	TRANS FAT	CHOLESTEROL	SODIUM	POTASSIUM
150	30	3.5 g	0.6 g	0.0 g	0 mg	250 mg	130 mg
TOTAL CARBOHYDRATE	**DIETARY FIBER**	**SUGARS**	**PROTEIN**	**PHOSPHORUS**	**EXCHANGES/CHOICES:**		
25 g	3 g	2 g	4 g	70 mg	1 1/2 Starch; 1 Nonstarchy Vegetable		

SEARED CHICKEN BREAST

Serves: 4 | Serving size: 3 ounces

1 pound boneless, skinless chicken breasts (remove any tenderloins so chicken lays flat)
1/2 teaspoon kosher salt
1/4 teaspoon freshly ground black pepper
1 1/2 tablespoons olive or vegetable oil

1. Pound the chicken breasts so they are even in thickness. Season the chicken with salt and pepper.
2. Heat the oil in a heavy cast iron skillet over medium-high heat. Add the chicken breasts and sear on both sides for about 5 minutes per side. Be sure to let one side of the chicken thoroughly sear before turning over to the other side. This will ensure even cooking and will prevent sticking.
3. Cover the skillet, lower the heat to low, and cook for about 5–6 minutes until the chicken is cooked through.

EXCHANGES / CHOICES
3 Protein, lean;
1/2 Fat

Calories 170; Calories from Fat 70; Total Fat 8.0 g; Saturated Fat 1.5 g; Trans Fat 0.0 g; Cholesterol 65 mg; Sodium 290 mg; Potassium 200 mg; Total Carbohydrate 0 g; Dietary Fiber 0 g; Sugars 0 g; Protein 24 g; Phosphorus 175 mg

This recipe also in Master Proteins page 9

GREEN BEANS

Serves: 1 | Serving size: 1/2 cup

1/2 cup green beans

1. Steam green beans for 5–7 minutes until tender and crisp and serve alongside pasta and chicken.

EXCHANGES / CHOICES
1 Nonstarchy Vegetable

Calories 20; Calories from Fat 0; Total Fat 0.0 g; Saturated Fat 0.0 g; Trans Fat 0.0 g; Cholesterol 0 mg; Sodium 0 mg; Potassium 90 mg; Total Carbohydrate 5 g; Dietary Fiber 2 g; Sugars 1 g; Protein 1 g; Phosphorus 20 mg

CREAMY PINK SAUCE

Serves: 10 | Serving size: 1/2 | Prep time: 11 minutes | Cook time: 32 minutes

For a twist on Classic Italian Marinara, add smooth ricotta cheese, and you'll have a creamy delicious sauce. This sauce is not quite as bold as the marinara, as the garlic is crushed, not minced, and the amount of fresh basil is reduced. A great sauce to serve over pasta for children—and anyone else, for that matter!

- 1 tablespoon olive oil
- 1 small onion, minced
- 2 garlic cloves, crushed
- 1 (28-ounce) can whole plum tomatoes, drained (reserve a little juice)
- 3 whole fresh basil leaves, cleaned of any grit
- 1/4 teaspoon kosher salt
- 1/4 teaspoon freshly ground black pepper
- 1 cup nonfat ricotta cheese, stirred
- 10 ounces whole-wheat shaped pasta

1. Heat the olive oil in a large skillet with lid over medium heat. Add the onion and sauté for 5–6 minutes until lightly browned. Add the crushed garlic and sauté for 1 minute.
2. Add the tomatoes to a deep bowl and crush them with your hands until coarse. Add the tomatoes and basil to the skillet and bring to a boil. Lower the heat and simmer 20–25 minutes. Add any reserved juice as necessary to make sure the sauce doesn't get too thick.
3. Meanwhile bring a 3–5-quart pot of lightly salted water to a rolling boil (fill the pot 2/3 full). Add the pasta and stir for the first minute. Continue to cook the pasta for 7–8 minutes until al dente. Drain, reserving 1/4 cup of pasta water. Do not rinse the pasta.
4. Add the salt and pepper to the tomato sauce. Mix the ricotta cheese with the reserved pasta water until the ricotta cheese is smooth, then add to the sauce. Add the pasta to the sauce, cover, and let the pasta sit in the sauce for 1 minute. Add the pasta to a warmed bowl and serve.

CALORIES	CALORIES FROM FAT	TOTAL FAT	SATURATED FAT	TRANS FAT	CHOLESTEROL	SODIUM	POTASSIUM
150	20	2.0 g	0.3 g	0.0 g	10 mg	250 mg	180 mg
TOTAL CARBOHYDRATE	**DIETARY FIBER**	**SUGARS**	**PROTEIN**	**PHOSPHORUS**	**EXCHANGES/CHOICES:**		
26 g	4 g	3 g	8 g	120 mg	1 1/2 Starch; 1 Nonstarchy Vegetable		

PAN-GRILLED PORK CHOPS

Serves: 4 | Serving size: 3 ounces

Cooking spray
1 pound boneless pork loin chops, trimmed of fat, brought to room temperature
1/2 teaspoon kosher salt
1/4 teaspoon freshly ground black pepper

1. Coat a nonstick ridged grill pan with cooking spray. Set the pan on high heat until hot, about 2 minutes. Sprinkle the chops with salt and pepper. Add the chops and cook on each side for about 2 minutes per side.
2. Lower the temperature to medium and cook for an additional 3–4 minutes per side or until an internal temperature of 135°F is reached. Remove from the pan and set aside. The internal temperature will reach 145°F as the pork rests.

EXCHANGES / CHOICES
3 Protein, lean

Calories 140; Calories from Fat 30; Total Fat 3.5 g; Saturated Fat 1.4 g; Trans Fat 0.0 g; Cholesterol 55 mg; Sodium 300 mg; Potassium 310 mg; Total Carbohydrate 0 g; Dietary Fiber 0 g; Sugars 0 g; Protein 24 g; Phosphorus 235 mg

STEAMED SPINACH

Serves: 1 | Serving size: 1/2 cup

1/2 cup spinach

1. Serve spinach with pork chop and pink sauce.

EXCHANGES / CHOICES
1 Nonstarchy Vegetable

Calories 20; Calories from Fat 0; Total Fat 0.0 g; Saturated Fat 0.0 g; Trans Fat 0.0 g; Cholesterol 0 mg; Sodium 65 mg; Potassium 420 mg; Total Carbohydrate 3 g; Dietary Fiber 2 g; Sugars 0 g; Protein 3 g; Phosphorus 50 mg

MIXED MUSHROOM SAUCE

Serves: 12 | Serving size: 1/2 cup | Prep time: 15 minutes | Cook time: 36 minutes

This mushroom sauce is my husband's favorite sauce, and it doesn't even include any meat. The addition of a carrot adds a delightful little sweetness that balances out the gamey flavor of the mixed mushrooms.

- 1 tablespoon olive oil
- 1 small onion, minced
- 1 medium carrot, peeled and diced
- 2 garlic cloves, minced
- 10 ounces mixed mushrooms, stemmed and coarsely chopped (use a combination of white button, cremini, Portobello, trumpet, or just use one variety)
- 1 (28-ounce) can plum tomatoes, drained, reserve some juice
- 2 sprigs fresh thyme
- 1/4 teaspoon salt
- 1/4 teaspoon freshly ground black pepper
- 12 ounces whole-wheat shaped pasta

1. Heat the oil in a large skillet with lid over medium heat. Add the onion and carrot and sauté for 5–6 minutes. Add the garlic and mushrooms and sauté for 5 minutes until mushrooms brown.
2. Add the tomatoes to a deep bowl. Crush the tomatoes with your hands until coarse. Add the tomatoes to the skillet with the thyme. Bring to a boil. Lower the heat and simmer for 20–25 minutes. Add some of the reserved liquid from the tomatoes if necessary, if the sauce is too thick.
3. Meanwhile, bring a 3–5-quart pot of lightly salted water to a rolling boil (fill the pot 2/3 full). Add the pasta and stir for the first minute. Cook the pasta for about 7–8 minutes until al dente. Drain, do not rinse.
4. Add the salt and pepper to the sauce. Remove and discard the thyme leaves. Add the pasta, stir, cover, and let the pasta sit in the sauce for 1 minute. Add the pasta to a warmed bowl and serve.

CALORIES	CALORIES FROM FAT	TOTAL FAT	SATURATED FAT	TRANS FAT	CHOLESTEROL	SODIUM	POTASSIUM
130	15	1.5 g	0.2 g	0.0 g	0 mg	200 mg	250 mg
TOTAL CARBOHYDRATE	**DIETARY FIBER**	**SUGARS**	**PROTEIN**	**PHOSPHORUS**	**EXCHANGES/CHOICES:**		
25 g	3 g	3 g	5 g	110 mg	1 1/2 Starch; 1 Nonstarchy Vegetable		

MASTER CHICKEN SEAR

Serves: 4 | Serving size: 1/2 breast or thigh

2 boneless, skinless chicken breasts or 2 boneless, skinless chicken thighs
1/8 teaspoon kosher salt
1/4 teaspoon ground black pepper
1 1/2 tablespoons olive or canola oil

1. Season chicken breasts or chicken thighs with salt and black pepper.
2. In a 12–14-inch heavy skillet, preferably cast iron or stainless (NOT nonstick), heat oil over medium-high heat.
3. Add the chicken and sear until well browned on both sides, about 3–4 minutes per side for the breasts, or 2–3 minutes for the thighs.
4. Transfer the chicken to a plate and tent with foil.
5. Return the chicken and accumulated juices to the skillet and simmer gently until cooked through, about 4–5 minutes.

TO TEST: Chicken should feel firm to the touch. Using closed tongs, press on the center of the chicken. It should feel firm. Alternatively, you may make a very small incision in the center of the meat and check to be sure the meat is cooked through with no traces of pink.

EXCHANGES / CHOICES
3 Protein, lean;
1 Fat

Calories 180; Calories from Fat 90; Total Fat 10.0 g; Saturated Fat 2.0 g; Trans Fat 0.0 g; Cholesterol 85 mg; Sodium 120 mg; Potassium 200 mg; Total Carbohydrate 0 g; Dietary Fiber 0 g; Sugars 0 g; Protein 21 g; Phosphorus 170 mg

This recipe also in Master Proteins page 37

GREEN BEANS

Serves: 1 | Serving size: 1/2 cup

1/2 cup green beans

1. Steam green beans for 5–7 minutes until tender and crisp and serve alongside pasta and chicken.

EXCHANGES / CHOICES
1 Nonstarchy Vegetable

Calories 20; Calories from Fat 0; Total Fat 0.0 g; Saturated Fat 0.0 g; Trans Fat 0.0 g; Cholesterol 0 mg; Sodium 0 mg; Potassium 90 mg; Total Carbohydrate 5 g; Dietary Fiber 2 g; Sugars 1 g; Protein 1 g; Phosphorus 20 mg

GARLIC OIL SAUCE

Serves: 10 | Serving size: 1 tablespoon sauce + 1 ounce of cooked pasta
Prep time: 8 minutes | Cook time: 12 minutes

How can three basic ingredients impart so much flavor? That's what I thought the day I was given a lesson on oil-based sauces in a small town in Italy. When only garlic, olive oil, and parsley were sitting on the large wooden table, I thought surely my instructor was going to fetch more ingredients as we began cooking. I was proven completely wrong and with just these few ingredients, I had one of most memorable meals on vacation.

- 1 heaping tablespoon minced fresh garlic
- 1/4 cup olive oil
- 1/4 teaspoon kosher salt
- 1/4 cup fresh minced parsley
- 10 ounces whole-wheat strand pasta (linguine, spaghetti, angel hair, fettuccine, and more)

1. Bring a 3-quart pot of lightly salted water to a rolling boil.
2. Meanwhile, add the garlic, oil, and salt to a large skillet and sauté over low heat for 3–4 minutes shaking the pan until the garlic just turns golden. Do not overcook. Turn off the heat while the pasta cooks.
3. Add the pasta to the boiling water and cook until al dente, about 6–7 minutes. Drain, reserving a little more than 1/4 cup of the pasta water.
4. Add the pasta, reserved pasta water, and parsley to the garlic oil sauce. Mix well, cover, and let the pasta sit in the sauce for 1 minute. Add the pasta to a warmed bowl.

CALORIES	CALORIES FROM FAT	TOTAL FAT	SATURATED FAT	TRANS FAT	CHOLESTEROL	SODIUM	POTASSIUM
150	50	6.0 g	0.8 g	0.0 g	0 mg	90 mg	45 mg
TOTAL CARBOHYDRATE	**DIETARY FIBER**	**SUGARS**	**PROTEIN**	**PHOSPHORUS**	**EXCHANGES/CHOICES:**		
22 g	4 g	1 g	4 g	75 mg	1 1/2 Starch; 1 Fat		

SEASONED SAUTÉED SHRIMP

Serves: 4 | Serving size: 4 ounces

2 teaspoons chipotle chili powder
1/2 teaspoon dried oregano leaves
1/2 teaspoon sweet paprika
1/4 teaspoon ground cumin
1/4 teaspoon freshly ground black pepper
1/4 teaspoon salt
1 pound peeled and deveined large shrimp
1 tablespoon olive oil

1. In a large bowl, combine the chili powder, oregano, paprika, cumin, black pepper, and salt. Add in the shrimp and toss well.
2. Heat the olive oil on medium heat in a large skillet. Add the shrimp and sauté for 5–7 minutes or until shrimp is cooked through.

EXCHANGES / CHOICES
3 Protein, lean

Calories 130; Calories from Fat 35; Total Fat 4.0 g; Saturated Fat 0.6 g; Trans Fat 0.0 g; Cholesterol 190 mg; Sodium 270 mg; Potassium 300 mg; Total Carbohydrate 1 g; Dietary Fiber 1 g; Sugars 0 g; Protein 24 g; Phosphorus 245 mg

This recipe also in Master Proteins page 9

STEAMED BROCCOLI

Serves: 1 | Serving size: 1/2 cup

1/2 cup broccoli

1. Steam broccoli for 2–3 minutes until tender and crisp and serve alongside shrimp and pasta.

EXCHANGES / CHOICES
1 Nonstarchy Vegetable

Calories 25; Calories from Fat 5; Total Fat 0.5 g; Saturated Fat 0.1 g; Trans Fat 0.0 g; Cholesterol 0 mg; Sodium 30 mg; Potassium 230 mg; Total Carbohydrate 6 g; Dietary Fiber 3 g; Sugars 1 g; Protein 2 g; Phosphorus 50 mg

WALNUT GARLIC SAUCE

Serves: 12 | Serving size: 2 tablespoons sauce + 1 ounce of cooked pasta
Prep time: 10 minutes | Cook time: 15 minutes

After being taught the basic garlic oil sauce, my teacher suggested that we could build on the sauce, without overdoing it. She had some walnuts on hand and lovingly tossed them into the sauce. Now we had yet another delicious sauce with a bit more heft.

- 1/3 cup coarsely chopped walnuts
- 1 heaping tablespoon minced garlic
- 1/4 cup plus 1 tablespoon olive oil
- 1/4 teaspoon salt
- 12 ounces whole-wheat pasta strands (linguine, spaghetti, angel hair, fettuccine, and more)
- 1/4 cup sliced fresh basil
- 1 tablespoon freshly grated Parmesan cheese

1. Add the walnuts to a small skillet and toast over medium heat until aromatic and lightly toasted, about 4 minutes. Set aside. Bring a 3-quart pot of lightly salted water to a rolling boil.
2. Meanwhile, add the garlic, oil, and salt to a large skillet and sauté over low heat for about 3-4 minutes, shaking the pan until the garlic just turns golden. Do not overcook. Turn off the heat while the pasta cooks.
3. Add the pasta to the boiling water and cook until al dente, about 6–7 minutes. Drain and reserve 1/2 cup of the pasta water.
4. Add the drained pasta, reserved pasta water, basil, toasted walnuts, and cheese to the garlic oil sauce. Mix well, cover, and let the pasta sit in the sauce for 1 minute. Add the pasta to a warmed bowl.

CALORIES	CALORIES FROM FAT	TOTAL FAT	SATURATED FAT	TRANS FAT	CHOLESTEROL	SODIUM	POTASSIUM
170	70	8.0 g	1.1 g	0.0 g	0 mg	85 mg	55 mg

TOTAL CARBOHYDRATE	DIETARY FIBER	SUGARS	PROTEIN	PHOSPHORUS	EXCHANGES/CHOICES:
22 g	4 g	1 g	5 g	85 mg	1 1/2 Starch; 1 1/2 Fat

SEASONED BROILED FISH

Serves: 4 | Serving size: 4 ounces

2 teaspoons chipotle chili powder
1/2 teaspoon dried oregano leaves
1/2 teaspoon sweet paprika
1/4 teaspoon ground cumin
1/4 teaspoon freshly ground black pepper
1/4 teaspoon salt
1 pound fish filets, about 1 inch thick
1 tablespoon olive oil

1. Preheat the oven to broil. Line a broiler pan with nonstick foil. In a small ramekin, combine the chili powder, oregano, paprika, cumin, pepper, and salt.
2. Coat both sides of the fish lightly with the seasoning. Drizzle the fish with the olive oil.
3. Broil the fish about 5 minutes per side or until cooked through.

EXCHANGES / CHOICES
3 Protein, lean

Calories 130; Calories from Fat 40; Total Fat 4.5 g; Saturated Fat 0.7 g; Trans Fat 0.0 g; Cholesterol 50 mg; Sodium 230 mg; Potassium 250 mg; Total Carbohydrate 1 g; Dietary Fiber 1 g; Sugars 0 g; Protein 20 g; Phosphorus 130 mg

ASPARAGUS SPEARS

Serves: 1 | Serving size: 6 spears

6 asparagus spears

1. Steam asparagus and serve alongside pasta and fish.

EXCHANGES / CHOICES
1 Nonstarchy Vegetable

Calories 20; Calories from Fat 0; Total Fat 0.0 g; Saturated Fat 0.0 g; Trans Fat 0.0 g; Cholesterol 0 mg; Sodium 15 mg; Potassium 200 mg; Total Carbohydrate 4 g; Dietary Fiber 2 g; Sugars 1 g; Protein 2 g; Phosphorus 50 mg

SPINACH GARLIC SAUCE

Serves: 10 | Serving size: 2 tablespoons sauce + 1 ounce of cooked pasta
Prep time: 10 minutes | Cook time: 15 minutes

Tinged with hot pepper flakes, this zesty sauce elevates spinach to new heights. You can also treat this sauce as a side vegetable without tossing it in pasta. Be sure to use baby spinach leaves, as they are much more tender.

- 4 garlic cloves, peeled and thinly sliced
- 1/4 cup plus 1 tablespoon olive oil
- 6 ounces fresh baby spinach, stems removed if thick and woody
- 1/4 teaspoon kosher salt
- 1/4 teaspoon freshly ground black pepper
- 1/8–1/4 teaspoon crushed red pepper flakes
- 12 ounces whole-wheat pasta strands (linguine, spaghetti, angel hair, or fettuccine)
- 2 tablespoons freshly grated Parmesan cheese

1. Bring a 3-quart pot of lightly salted water to a rolling boil. Meanwhile, heat the garlic and oil in a large skillet over medium-low heat. Sauté the garlic for 3–4 minutes just until it starts to brown a little. Add in the spinach, salt, and pepper and sauté until the spinach just wilts. Turn off the heat as you prepare the pasta.
2. Add the pasta to the pot and cook for 7–8 minutes until al dente. Drain and reserve 3/4 cup of pasta cooking water. Do not rinse the pasta. Add the pasta and 1/2 cup of the pasta water to the garlic sauce and mix well but gently. Add more cooking water, if necessary, so the pasta doesn't appear to be dry.
3. Turn into a warmed serving bowl and top with cheese.

CALORIES	CALORIES FROM FAT	TOTAL FAT	SATURATED FAT	TRANS FAT	CHOLESTEROL	SODIUM	POTASSIUM
160	50	6.0 g	1.0 g	0.0 g	0 mg	100 mg	120 mg

TOTAL CARBOHYDRATE	DIETARY FIBER	SUGARS	PROTEIN	PHOSPHORUS	EXCHANGES/CHOICES:
22 g	4 g	1 g	5 g	85 mg	1 1/2 Starch; 1 Fat

SEASONED SAUTÉED SHRIMP

Serves: 4 | Serving size: 4 ounces

2 teaspoons chipotle chili powder
1/2 teaspoon dried oregano leaves
1/2 teaspoon sweet paprika
1/4 teaspoon ground cumin
1/4 teaspoon freshly ground black pepper
1/4 teaspoon salt
1 pound peeled and deveined large shrimp
1 tablespoon olive oil

1. In a large bowl, combine the chili powder, oregano, paprika, cumin, black pepper, and salt. Add in the shrimp and toss well.
2. Heat the olive oil on medium heat in a large skillet. Add the shrimp and sauté for 5–7 minutes or until shrimp is cooked through.

EXCHANGES / CHOICES
3 Protein, lean

Calories 130; Calories from Fat 35; Total Fat 4.0 g; Saturated Fat 0.6 g; Trans Fat 0.0 g; Cholesterol 190 mg; Sodium 270 mg; Potassium 300 mg; Total Carbohydrate 1 g; Dietary Fiber 1 g; Sugars 0 g; Protein 24 g; Phosphorus 245 mg

This recipe also in Master Proteins page 9

STEAMED BROCCOLI

Serves: 1 | Serving size: 1/2 cup

1/2 cup broccoli

1. Steam broccoli for 2–3 minutes until tender and crisp and serve alongside shrimp and pasta.

EXCHANGES / CHOICES
1 Nonstarchy Vegetable

Calories 25; Calories from Fat 5; Total Fat 0.5 g; Saturated Fat 0.1 g; Trans Fat 0.0 g; Cholesterol 0 mg; Sodium 30 mg; Potassium 230 mg; Total Carbohydrate 6 g; Dietary Fiber 3 g; Sugars 1 g; Protein 2 g; Phosphorus 50 mg

BAKED ZITI

Serves: 12 | Serving size: 3/4 cup | Prep time: 10 minutes | Cook time: 50 minutes

Every Sunday we gathered for dinner around this bubbling casserole. Mom would often invite our next door neighbors over, as Baked Ziti should be shared with others.

Cooking spray
2 teaspoons olive oil
1 medium onion, diced
2 garlic cloves, peeled and minced
1 tablespoon Italian seasoning
5 ounces spicy turkey sausage, diced
1/4 cup dry red wine
1 (28-ounce) can whole plum tomatoes with juices
2 tablespoons fresh minced oregano
8 ounces whole-wheat ziti
1/2 cup nonfat ricotta cheese
1/4 cup grated fresh Pecorino Romano cheese, divided use
Pinch grated fresh nutmeg
3 ounces part-skim mozzarella cheese, cubed

1. Preheat the oven to 425°F. Coat a shallow baking dish, preferably a long oval dish that is no more than 2 inches deep, with cooking spray. Set aside.
2. Heat the olive oil in a large skillet over medium heat. Add the onion and sauté for 3 minutes. Add the garlic, Italian seasoning, and sausage and sauté for 3–4 minutes until sausage is browned. Bring a 3-quart pot of lightly salted water to a boil.
3. Add the red wine to the skillet and continue to cook until the wine evaporates. Add the tomatoes to a deep bowl. Crush the tomatoes with your hands and add them to the pan with all their juices. Cook uncovered on medium-low heat for 20 minutes until thickened. Add in the oregano.
4. Meanwhile, add the ziti to the boiling pot of water and cook for about 8–10 minutes or until just al dente. Mix together the ricotta cheese, half the Romano cheese and nutmeg in a large bowl. Add the cooked ziti and mix well. Add the sausage tomato sauce and the mozzarella. Mix gently. Pour into the prepared baking dish and sprinkle with the remaining Romano cheese. Bake, uncovered, for 20 minutes until lightly browned. Serve immediately.

CALORIES	CALORIES FROM FAT	TOTAL FAT	SATURATED FAT	TRANS FAT	CHOLESTEROL	SODIUM	POTASSIUM
140	35	4.0 g	1.5 g	0.0 g	15 mg	370 mg	230 mg
TOTAL CARBOHYDRATE	**DIETARY FIBER**	**SUGARS**	**PROTEIN**	**PHOSPHORUS**	**EXCHANGES/CHOICES:**		
20 g	2 g	3 g	9 g	150 mg	1 Starch; 1 Nonstarchy Vegetable; 1 Protein, lean		

SPINACH SALAD WITH HOT BACON DRESSING

Serves: 11 | Serving size: 1 1/2 cups
Prep time: 15 minutes | Cook time: 6 minutes

7 cups fresh baby spinach leaves
1 small head romaine lettuce, washed, dried, and broken into bite-sized pieces
10 large white mushrooms, cleaned, peeled, if necessary, stemmed, and sliced

DRESSING
4 slices lean bacon (40% or more less fat), chopped
1 small onion, finely chopped
2 cloves garlic, minced
1/2 cup cider vinegar
1 tablespoon sugar
2 tablespoons tomato paste

1. Toss together the spinach, lettuce, and mushrooms.
2. Cook the bacon in a large heavy skillet over medium heat until crisp. Add the onion and sauté for 2 minutes. Add the garlic, vinegar, sugar, and tomato paste. Stir to blend. Toss salad with dressing and serve.

EXCHANGES / CHOICES
1 Nonstarchy Vegetable

Calories 40; Calories from Fat 10; Total Fat 1.0 g; Saturated Fat 0.3 g; Trans Fat 0.0 g; Cholesterol 0 mg; Sodium 80 mg; Potassium 300 mg; Total Carbohydrate 5 g; Dietary Fiber 1 g; Sugars 3 g; Protein 3 g; Phosphorus 50 mg

This recipe also in Salad page 146

PEAR

Serves: 1 | Serving size: 1/2 pear

1 small pear

1. Serve pear alongside ziti and salad.

EXCHANGES / CHOICES
1 Fruit

Calories 40; Calories from Fat 0; Total Fat 0.0 g; Saturated Fat 0.0 g; Trans Fat 0.0 g; Cholesterol 0 mg; Sodium 0 mg; Potassium 85 mg; Total Carbohydrate 11 g; Dietary Fiber 2 g; Sugars 7 g; Protein 0 g; Phosphorus 10 mg

CREAMY PASTA BAKE

Serves: 12 | Serving size: 3/4 cup | Prep time: 12 minutes | Cook time: 40 minutes

Sometimes, I tire of tomato-based pasta dishes. While this one has tomatoes, they are less of a major player. Thick, evaporated milk stands in for traditional cream, but still produces a robust sauce that seeps into every groove of the pasta. The crunchy topping makes this dish just perfect!

Nonstick cooking spray
2 teaspoons olive oil
1 medium onion, diced
1 large red pepper, cored, seeded, and diced
3 garlic cloves, minced
2 tablespoons fresh minced oregano
1/4 teaspoon kosher salt
1/4 teaspoon freshly ground black pepper
1 (14.5-ounce) can diced tomatoes
1 tablespoon minced fresh thyme
8 ounces whole-wheat shaped pasta (shells, cavatappi, fusilli, penne, ziti, and more)
3/4 cup fat-free evaporated milk
2 tablespoons all-purpose flour
1 cup nonfat ricotta cheese, stirred
2 tablespoons Pecorino Romano cheese

TOPPING

2 slices whole-wheat bread
2 tablespoons Pecorino Romano cheese
1 teaspoon olive oil

1. Preheat the oven to 425°F. Coat a large shallow baking dish with cooking spray, preferably an oval dish that is no deeper than 2 inches. Heat the olive oil in a large skillet over medium heat. Add the onion and sauté for 4 minutes. Add the red peppers and sauté for 3 minutes. Add in the garlic, oregano, salt, and pepper and sauté for 1 minute. Add the tomatoes and fresh thyme and cook for 4 minutes. Set aside.
2. Bring a 3-quart pot of lightly salted water to a boil. Add the pasta and cook for 7–8 minutes or until just al dente. Drain, do not rinse.
3. In a large bowl, mix together the milk and flour until smooth. Add in the ricotta cheese and Pecorino Romano cheese and mix well. Add the cooked pasta to the cheese mixture and mix well. Add in the tomato sauce and mix well. Pour into the prepared baking dish.
4. Add the bread slices to a food processor or blender and process to make coarse crumbs. Mix the crumbs with the Pecorino Romano cheese and olive oil. Top the pasta with the crumbs and bake, uncovered, for 20 minutes until the topping is brown.

CALORIES	CALORIES FROM FAT	TOTAL FAT	SATURATED FAT	TRANS FAT	CHOLESTEROL	SODIUM	POTASSIUM
150	20	2.5 g	0.7 g	0.0 g	10 mg	200 mg	230 mg
TOTAL CARBOHYDRATE	**DIETARY FIBER**	**SUGARS**	**PROTEIN**	**PHOSPHORUS**	**EXCHANGES/CHOICES:**		
25 g	3 g	5 g	8 g	140 mg	1 Starch; 1 Nonstarchy Vegetable; 1 Protein, lean		

BROCCOLI OR BROCCOLINI

Serves: 1 | Serving size: 1/2 cup

1/2 cup broccoli or broccolini

1. Steam broccoli or broccolini and serve alongside pasta and blueberries.

EXCHANGES / CHOICES
1 Nonstarchy Vegetable

Calories 25; Calories from Fat 5; Total Fat 0.5 g; Saturated Fat 0.1 g; Trans Fat 0.0 g; Cholesterol 0 mg; Sodium 30 mg; Potassium 230 mg; Total Carbohydrate 6 g; Dietary Fiber 3 g; Sugars 1 g; Protein 2 g; Phosphorus 50 mg

. . . .

BLUEBERRIES

Serves: 1 | Serving size: 1/3 cup

1/3 cup blueberries

1. Serve blueberries alongside pasta and broccoli.

EXCHANGES / CHOICES
1/2 Fruit

Calories 25; Calories from Fat 0; Total Fat 0.0 g; Saturated Fat 0.0 g; Trans Fat 0.0 g; Cholesterol 0 mg; Sodium 0 mg; Potassium 35 mg; Total Carbohydrate 7 g; Dietary Fiber 1 g; Sugars 5 g; Protein 0 g; Phosphorus 5 mg

MASTER PASTA SALAD

Serves: 12 | Serving size: 1 cup | Prep time: 10 minutes | Cook time: 8 minutes

Here's your blueprint for a pasta salad, but feel free to experiment with the ingredients and see what you like. Choose an herb or champagne vinegar instead of red wine vinegar. Use orange juice instead of lemon juice. Add small blanched broccoli or cauliflower florets. Pack this salad into a container and tote along for a picnic. Since there is no mayonnaise used in the recipe, the salad stands up well in transport.

8 ounces dry whole-wheat shaped pasta
2 teaspoons olive oil

DRESSING

3 tablespoons fresh lemon juice or red wine vinegar
1/4 cup plus 1 tablespoon olive oil
1 garlic clove, minced
1/4 teaspoon sea salt
1/4 teaspoon freshly ground black pepper

VEGETABLES AND HERBS

1 small yellow or orange pepper, thinly sliced
1/2 pint cherry or grape tomatoes, halved
1/4 cup torn basil leaves
1 small shallot, minced
2 tablespoons torn mint leaves
2 tablespoons minced fresh parsley

1. Bring a large pot of lightly salted water to a rolling boil. Add the pasta and cook for 7–8 minutes or until al dente. Drain and add to a bowl. Immediately mix with olive oil, cover, and set in the refrigerator until cooled down (it may still be a bit warm, but that is OK).
2. Whisk together the ingredients for the dressing in a large bowl. Add the vegetables and herbs to the bowl and gently mix. Add in the pasta and mix. Let the pasta stand for 30 minutes prior to serving.

CALORIES	CALORIES FROM FAT	TOTAL FAT	SATURATED FAT	TRANS FAT	CHOLESTEROL	SODIUM	POTASSIUM
130	60	7.0 g	0.9 g	0.0 g	0 mg	75 mg	95 mg
TOTAL CARBOHYDRATE	DIETARY FIBER	SUGARS	PROTEIN	PHOSPHORUS	EXCHANGES/CHOICES:		
16 g	2 g	1 g	3 g	50 mg	1 Starch; 1 Fat		

Baked Ziti page 120

CHAPTER 6
Salads

THE PRINCIPLES OF SALAD MAKING

Small side salads are a nice addition to any meal, but I'm talking about making salad a major event. Before you rummage through your refrigerator, tempted to empty all the contents in your produce drawer into a wooden bowl, let me guide you through several basic principles that will make you a master salad maker.

PICK A THEME

As tempting as it is to just throw all sorts of ingredients together, resist the urge. A good salad needs cohesion, a central theme that brings all the ingredients together. The first five recipes are developed around a specific flavor profile. For example, the Italian Chicken Salad recipe uses flavors that are complementary in Mediterranean cooking. As much as I love tofu, it would be odd to put it in this salad. The Asian Pork Salad and Thai Beef Salad are two more examples of this thematic approach; it would be strange for me to add Parmesan cheese to these.

CHOOSE GREENS

In the summer, sometimes I'll just slice up cucumbers and tomatoes and call it a salad. However, a substantial salad calls for a bed of fluffy fresh greens. I think practically every green variety works in a salad. I recommend combining mild-tasting greens like butter leaf or romaine with sharper, peppery ones, such as spinach or arugula for a balanced taste. For a really nice contrast and to promote deep rich flavor, add whole-leaf herbs and treat them just like greens. Basil and mint leaves are my two favorites. I leave them uncut; just trim the stems and toss them in with the greens. Always wash your greens, even if you buy packaged greens that state the greens have been cleaned. Here are the five steps to ensure that your greens have been cleaned properly:

1. Remove any fasteners or rubber bands that have held the lettuce together. Break off the root ends.
2. Add the leaves to a large bowl or basin filled with cold water and a little salt. The salt will help any tiny insects still clinging to the leaves to become dislodged.
3. Place the leaves in a salad spinner—the best piece of kitchen equipment you'll ever invest in. Spin the leaves until they are dry.

4. Wrap the leaves in several layers of paper towels and press out any remaining moisture. This is key! Any excess moisture in the leaves will only cause a soggy salad.
5. Tear the greens by hand (never cut with a knife) and prepare the salad, or keep the leaves whole, wrapped in the towels, and place in a large plastic bag stored in the refrigerator crisper until you are ready to prepare the salad.

PROTEIN

The addition of protein turns a side salad into a substantial meal. In this chapter, chicken, lean pork, lean beef, fish, and beans provide the protein. The beauty of adding protein is that it's so easy to do. When you have leftover pieces of protein from another meal, toss it right into the greens. In these recipes, the animal proteins are either poached or grilled. Fish and poultry work well with poaching, and heavier meats such as beef and pork benefit from grilling. In both methods, ever-so-subtle flavors are added to the protein; you actually want the proteins to be as much a blank canvas as possible. The salad dressing and other ingredients added to the salad will be the workhorse for adding flavor.

PERFECTLY POACHED

Poaching is submerging food into boiled liquid and letting it cook through, but poaching requires a little finesse! Done right, chicken and thick filets of fish turn out deliciously moist. Done poorly, you end up with hockey pucks. Here's my step-by-step plan to poach fish and chicken to ready them for salads.

1. Always start with a flavorful liquid mixture, don't poach in plain water. You want very subtle flavors to permeate the protein. The result will be a much tastier salad overall. Use a reduced-sodium broth or water, but be sure to add at least one aromatic, such as peppercorns, citrus slices, or onion. For example, if you want to prepare an Asian flavored salad, poach the chicken with the addition of scallion slices and maybe some chopped fresh lemongrass.
2. Add the liquid to a large skillet with high sides and a tight fitting lid. Make sure that lid fits very snugly in the pan. In order for the protein to properly cook through, you need to create lots of gentle steam within the pan that cannot escape.
3. Bring the liquid and the aromatics to a gentle boil, around 160–165°F. No need to have the poaching liquid at a furious boil.
4. Add your poultry or fish and let it poach, uncovered, for 3–4 minutes, well before the liquid ever has a chance to come back to a boil. After 3–4 minutes, cover and remove from the heat source (just slide it to an unused burner). Let the food remain in the poaching liquid for 12–14 minutes.

5. Remove the food with a slotted spoon, discard the poaching liquid. Then let cool enough to handle. Slice, cube, shred or flake the protein as desired and add to your salad.

PERFECTLY GRILLED

Pork and lean cuts of beef can easily dry out. That's because the pork and beef raised today is much leaner than many years ago. Still, with a few tips, your pork and beef can be juicy and succulent.

1. Purchase bone-in pork chops when you can. There is nothing wrong with boneless chops, except that a more watchful eye is needed to make sure you don't overcook them. Purchase the very best pork you can find. It's worth it to buy organically raised meat as it is more tender and flavorful. For beef, the bone isn't as crucial, as beef usually contains more fat than pork and that extra bit of fat helps keep the meat juicy even without a bone.
2. Use a little bit of salt and pepper on the surface as you grill. It helps create a flavorful crust and will brown the meat to a beautiful color. This will make your final salad even more appealing.
3. Bring the pork and beef to room temperature for 30 minutes prior to cooking. Cold meat will cause the outside to cook too quickly.
4. Start with a hot pan to get the surface of pork and beef crusty and golden brown. Then switch to a medium heat to continue the cooking. The meat will be juicier this way.
5. Cook the pork to an internal temperature of 135°F. Remove the pork from the heat source and let it rest. As it rests, the internal temperature will rise to 145°F, ensuring a perfectly cooked piece of pork. For steaks, the finger test is a good one. When it feels soft, it's still rare; when it feels firm, it's well done. Somewhere in between should be the amount of "done" you will like.

TEXTURE

It's the crunch, coupled with a few creamy counterpoint ingredients, that makes a great salad. The single most important factor in warding off salad boredom is to combine hard, raw vegetables with soft greens, and rough textured topping, such as nuts, with a smooth dressing. Here are a few things to keep in mind:

1. Keep all salad ingredients bite-sized. Nothing is more disconcerting than trying to maneuver a large chunk of tomato on a fork, let alone trying to fit it in your mouth! You want to get as many vegetables on your fork, so that you have a variety of flavors that work together for one great taste.

2. Consider adding a small amount of crunchy toppings such as nuts and seeds. If your food plan will allow it, a small amount of smooth, sharp cheese, such as blue cheese, or a slice of fresh avocado really make the salad shine.
3. Find the right balance of crunchy vegetables. Add too many raw vegetables and your salad will take forever to eat. Too few vegetables and you risk sacrificing good nutrition, plus the texture will quickly become plain and boring.

SALAD DRESSING

I cannot recall the last time I used a bottled salad dressing, as I always make my own. It's easy and inexpensive. Here is my 3-step formula to creating a perfect salad dressing:

1. Choose your oil: Sure you could forgo the oil in a dressing, but it's the oil that will help the dressing adhere to the greens rather than ending up in the bottom of the bowl. For calorie and fat gram savings, just use enough oil to coat the greens very lightly. Stick with the most flavorful oils to get the most bang for your buck. Olive, grapeseed, walnut, peanut, avocado, and sesame oils are the ones I recommend most. These spoil faster than plain vegetable oil, so buy in small quantities. If necessary, keep them in the refrigerator to prolong their shelf life.
2. Choose your acid: Vinegars and citrus juices are your choices. Although you can never go wrong with red wine vinegar or lemon juice, consider champagne vinegar and lime or orange juices for a change. The purpose of including acids is to "wake-up" the greens and bring out their garden-fresh flavor. But don't overdo it — too much acid throws the balance of the dressing off and makes a salad literally hard to swallow!
3. Flavor enhancers: You could simply whisk together oil and vinegar, add dashes of salt and pepper and you would have a good dressing. A great dressing takes advantage of adding the third component to a salad dressing—the flavor enhancers. The amount of enhancers you add is entirely your choice, so go ahead and experiment. Mustard, honey, chopped fresh herbs, minced garlic, chopped shallots, and low-sodium soy sauce can all be added to a basic oil-vinegar base in varying degrees. Your flavor enhancer can tie the salad theme together. For example, in the Thai Beef Salad, peanut oil and lime juice are enhanced with fish sauce and chili purée. These ingredients make perfect sense given the Asian theme of the salad.

Feel free to make up any of the salad dressings in this chapter in quantity and store in an airtight container in the refrigerator for up to one week.

The last five recipes in this chapter are created as side salads; however, add any protein and you'll have five more main-dish salads. The Roasted Pepper Salad is a great springboard for other recipes. Once you learn how to prepare homemade roasted peppers, you can add them to egg dishes, homemade sandwiches, and pizzas, slice them into main dish soups and stews, or chop them and add them to a salad dressing. The Spinach Salad with Hot Bacon Dressing is a perfect example of how to add interest to a salad. Cool greens and warm dressing make for a delicious contrast. The Garden Salad is an all-purpose salad that you can serve every day, just switch up the greens and change around the dressing ingredients for added interest. These five last salad recipes are perfect blueprints—with a few simple switches, so you can have an entirely new salad to enjoy.

Garlicky Tomato Salad page 144, with **Seasoned Sauteed Shrimp** page 145

ITALIAN CHICKEN SALAD

Serves: 6 | Serving size: 1 cup | Prep time: 10 minutes | Cook time: 22 minutes

I remember the first time I ate a chicken salad without mayonnaise. Honestly, it took a while to get used to. Gradually, I switched over completely to chicken salads made with olive oil and vinegar. To change this salad up, substitute pine nuts for the walnuts, use chopped fresh oregano and basil instead of dried, use a roasted red pepper instead of a fresh one, or add sliced rehydrated sun-dried tomatoes to the mix.

1 quart reduced sodium, low-fat chicken broth or water
4 peppercorns
3 slices fresh lemon or orange
1/2 small onion, cut into wedges
1 pound boneless, skinless chicken breasts
1 tablespoon olive oil
1/2 cup chopped walnuts
1 red pepper, diced
1 teaspoon dried oregano
1/2 teaspoon dried basil
1 (15-ounce) can artichoke hearts, drained and halved
10 pitted Kalamata olives, sliced
2 tablespoons minced fresh parsley

DRESSING
3 tablespoons olive oil
1 tablespoon fresh lemon juice
1 tablespoon red wine vinegar
1 garlic clove, minced
1/2 teaspoon sugar
1/2 teaspoon salt
1/4 teaspoon black pepper

6 cups mixed greens

1. Bring the broth or water to a simmer in a large skillet with tight-fitting lid. Add the peppercorns, lemons, and onions and simmer for 10 minutes. Add the chicken and cook for 4 minutes, uncovered. Cover, remove from the heat and let the chicken stand in the water for 12–14 minutes. Remove the chicken from the skillet with a slotted spoon and place on a plate and refrigerate until cool enough to handle. Discard poaching liquid.
2. Heat the oil in a skillet over medium heat. Add the walnuts and sauté for 2 minutes. Add the red pepper, oregano, and basil and sauté for 3 minutes. Remove from the heat and let cool.
3. Meanwhile, in a salad bowl, combine the artichoke hearts, olives, and parsley.
4. Combine all dressing ingredients. Add the walnut mixture to the salad. Cut the chicken into 1-inch cubes and add to the salad. Pour over the dressing. Toss well and serve over mixed greens.

CALORIES	CALORIES FROM FAT	TOTAL FAT	SATURATED FAT	TRANS FAT	CHOLESTEROL	SODIUM	POTASSIUM
290	170	19.0 g	2.5 g	0.0 g	45 mg	450 mg	430 mg

TOTAL CARBOHYDRATE	DIETARY FIBER	SUGARS	PROTEIN	PHOSPHORUS	EXCHANGES/CHOICES:
10 g	4 g	2 g	20 g	175 mg	2 Nonstarchy Vegetable; 2 Protein, lean; 3 Fat

PEACHES

Serves: 1 | Serving size: 1/2 cup

1/2 cup peaches

1. Serve peaches alongside salad and crackers.

EXCHANGES / CHOICES
1/2 Fruit

Calories 30; Calories from Fat 0; Total Fat 0.0 g; Saturated Fat 0.0 g; Trans Fat 0.0 g; Cholesterol 0 mg; Sodium 0 mg; Potassium 150 mg; Total Carbohydrate 7 g; Dietary Fiber 1 g; Sugars 6 g; Protein 1 g; Phosphorus 15 mg

• • • • • • •

CRACKERS

Serves: 1 | Serving size: 1 ounce

1 ounce baked crackers, such as Wheat Thins or Triscuits

1. Serve crackers alongside salad and peaches.

EXCHANGES / CHOICES
1 Starch; 1 Fat

Calories 130; Calories from Fat 40; Total Fat 4.5 g; Saturated Fat 0.8 g; Trans Fat 0.1 g; Cholesterol 0 mg; Sodium 180 mg; Potassium 105 mg; Total Carbohydrate 20 g; Dietary Fiber 3 g; Sugars 2 g; Protein 3 g; Phosphorus 95 mg

ASIAN PORK AND PLUM SALAD

Serves: 8 | Serving size: 1 cup | Prep time: 10 minutes | Cook time: 10 minutes

Combining fruit and lean proteins together was something my mother always used to do in her cooking. She'd often add fruit to a soup or stew; she even added fruit on top of homemade pizza! By having her fruit with her meal rather than eating fruit all by itself, she was better able to control her blood sugar levels.

Nonstick cooking spray
1 1/2 pounds lean boneless pork loin chops, trimmed, brought to room temperature
1/2 teaspoon kosher salt
1/2 teaspoon freshly ground black pepper

SALAD
1 (11-ounce) can mandarin oranges (in its own juice), drained
2 small red plums, pitted and sliced
4 scallions, thinly sliced
1/2 cup sliced canned water chestnuts, drained
1 pound romaine lettuce, washed, dried, cored, and chopped

DRESSING
1/3 cup low-fat mayonnaise
3 tablespoons creamy peanut butter
1 tablespoon water
2 teaspoons reduced-sodium soy sauce
1 garlic clove, minced
1 teaspoon minced fresh ginger or 1/2 teaspoon ground ginger

2 tablespoons chopped unsalted, roasted cashews

1. Coat a nonstick ridged grill pan with nonstick cooking spray and set over high heat until hot, about 2 minutes. Sprinkle the pork chops with salt and pepper. Add the pork chops to grill pan and cook on each side, about 2 minutes per side. Lower the temperature to medium and cook for an additional 3–4 minutes per side or until an internal temperature of 135°F is reached. Remove from the pan and set aside. The internal temperature will reach 145°F as the pork rests.
2. Meanwhile, combine all ingredients for the salad. Whisk together the dressing ingredients.
3. Slice the pork into thin strips (discard bone if using bone-in chops). Toss into the salad. Add the dressing to the salad and toss. Top the salad with cashews.

CALORIES	CALORIES FROM FAT	TOTAL FAT	SATURATED FAT	TRANS FAT	CHOLESTEROL	SODIUM	POTASSIUM
200	70	8.0 g	1.8 g	0.0 g	40 mg	330 mg	520 mg

TOTAL CARBOHYDRATE	DIETARY FIBER	SUGARS	PROTEIN	PHOSPHORUS	EXCHANGES/CHOICES:
11 g	3 g	5 g	22 g	240 mg	1 Carbohydrate; 3 Protein, lean

WHOLE-WHEAT CRACKERS

Serves: 1 | Serving size: 1 ounce

1 ounce baked crackers such as Triscuits or Wheat Thins

1. Serve crackers alongside salad and Greek yogurt.

EXCHANGES / CHOICES
1 Starch ; 1 Fat

Calories 130; Calories from Fat 40; Total Fat 4.5 g; Saturated Fat 0.8 g; Trans Fat 0.1 g; Cholesterol 0 mg; Sodium 180 mg; Potassium 105 mg; Total Carbohydrate 20 g; Dietary Fiber 3 g; Sugars 2 g; Protein 3 g; Phosphorus 95 mg

• • • • • • •

GREEK YOGURT

Serves: 1 | Serving size: 4 ounces

4 ounces fat-free plain and raspberry jam Greek yogurt

1. Serve yogurt alongside salad and crackers.

EXCHANGES / CHOICES
1/2 Milk, fat-free

Calories 70; Calories from Fat 0; Total Fat 0.0 g; Saturated Fat 0.0 g; Trans Fat 0.0 g; Cholesterol 0 mg; Sodium 45 mg; Potassium 160 mg; Total Carbohydrate 5 g; Dietary Fiber 1 g; Sugars 5 g; Protein 11 g; Phosphorus 155 mg

SPICY BLACK BEAN SALAD

Serves: 8 | Serving size: 1 cup | Prep time: 15 minutes

This no-cook salad stands up well; it will last about 3–4 days in the refrigerator. You can also use this salad as a salsa. I've also filled up endive spears with this salad and served it as an appetizer for dinner parties.

- 3 (15-ounce) cans black beans, or 3 cups cooked dried black beans
- 1 red onion, minced
- 1 cup corn (fresh, cut from the cob, or frozen, thawed)
- 3 large ripe tomatoes, seeded and chopped
- 1 medium red pepper, diced
- 1 medium yellow pepper, diced
- 1 cup peeled, diced jicama
- 1/2 cup chopped fresh cilantro
- 2 small jalapeño peppers, seeded and minced
- 3 garlic cloves, minced
- 2 tablespoons lemon or lime juice
- 1 1/2 teaspoons ground cumin
- 1 tablespoon red wine vinegar
- 1/3 cup olive oil
- 1/2 teaspoon kosher salt
- 1/4 teaspoon freshly ground black pepper

1. Place the canned beans in a large colander and rinse well under cold running water. Drain thoroughly.
2. In a large mixing bowl, combine the beans with remaining ingredients and toss gently until mixed. Cover and refrigerate for 1 hour prior to serving.

CALORIES	CALORIES FROM FAT	TOTAL FAT	SATURATED FAT	TRANS FAT	CHOLESTEROL	SODIUM	POTASSIUM
260	90	10.0 g	1.4 g	0.0 g	0 mg	240 mg	700 mg

TOTAL CARBOHYDRATE	DIETARY FIBER	SUGARS	PROTEIN	PHOSPHORUS	EXCHANGES/CHOICES:
35 g	11 g	7 g	10 g	180 mg	1 1/2 Starch; 2 Nonstarchy Vegetable; 1 Protein, lean; 1 Fat

FRESH SPINACH SALAD

Serves: 1 | Serving size: 1 1/2 cups

1 cup fresh spinach leaves
5 cherry tomatoes halved
1/4 cup sliced red onion
1/4 teaspoon olive oil
1/2 teaspoon lemon juice

1. Combine spinach, tomatoes, and red onion in a small bowl. Drizzle olive oil over salad and top with lemon juice.

EXCHANGES / CHOICES
1 Nonstarchy Vegetable

Calories 20; Calories from Fat 0; Total Fat 0.0 g; Saturated Fat 0.0 g; Trans Fat 0.0 g; Cholesterol 0 mg; Sodium 15 mg; Potassium 200 mg; Total Carbohydrate 4 g; Dietary Fiber 2 g; Sugars 1 g; Protein 2 g; Phosphorus 50 mg

THAI BEEF SALAD

Serves: 6 | Serving size: 3/4 cup | Prep time: 10 minutes | Cook time: 12 minutes + 10 minutes for standing

This recipe is courtesy of the chefs at the Peninsula Hotel in Bangkok. Sitting at the terrace restaurant of a grand hotel, I ordered the beef salad. After one bite, I asked our waiter to summon the chef so I could know what all these fabulous exotic tastes were. When I explained what I did for a living, the chef was more than happy to introduce me to the world of chiles, fish sauce, and more.

4 ounces udon noodles

1 pound flank steak, trimmed of excess fat, brought to room temperature
1/4 teaspoon kosher salt
1/4 teaspoon freshly ground black pepper

DRESSING
3 tablespoons peanut oil
3 tablespoons lime juice
1/2 tablespoon fish sauce
1 tablespoon brown sugar
1/4 teaspoon chili puree with garlic

VEGETABLES
1 cup sliced red onion
1 cup thinly sliced red pepper
1 cup thinly sliced cucumber
1/3 cup chopped scallions

4 cups romaine torn lettuce leaves
1/4 cup chopped unsalted peanuts

1. Cook the noodles according to package directions. Drain and set aside.
2. Sprinkle both sides of the beef with salt and pepper. Coat an outdoor grill rack with cooking spray and set the rack 6 inches above the heat source. Set the grill to medium high. Alternatively, coat an indoor grill pan with cooking spray and set it on medium-high heat. Place the beef on the rack and grill for about 6–7 minutes per side. Remove the beef to plate, cover loosely, and let stand for 10 minutes. Cut the beef diagonally across the grain into thin slices.
3. Combine all the dressing ingredients. Add the beef, red onion, red pepper, cucumbers, scallions, and udon noodles. Add the dressing and toss well. Serve on lettuce and top with peanuts.

CALORIES	CALORIES FROM FAT	TOTAL FAT	SATURATED FAT	TRANS FAT	CHOLESTEROL	SODIUM	POTASSIUM
300	140	15.0 g	3.3 g	0.0 g	40 mg	450 mg	480 mg
TOTAL CARBOHYDRATE	**DIETARY FIBER**	**SUGARS**	**PROTEIN**	**PHOSPHORUS**	**EXCHANGES/CHOICES:**		
21 g	3 g	7 g	20 g	220 mg	1 Starch; 1 Nonstarchy Vegetable; 2 Protein, lean; 2 Fat		

SNOW PEAS

Serves: 1 | Serving size: 1/2 cup

1/2 cup snow peas

1. Steam snow peas and serve alongside salad and orange.

EXCHANGES / CHOICES
1 Nonstarchy Vegetable

Calories 35; Calories from Fat 0; Total Fat 0.0 g; Saturated Fat 0.0 g; Trans Fat 0.0 g; Cholesterol 0 mg; Sodium 0 mg; Potassium 190 mg; Total Carbohydrate 6 g; Dietary Fiber 2 g; Sugars 3 g; Protein 3 g; Phosphorus 45 mg

• • • • • • •

ORANGE

Serves: 1 | Serving size: 1 orange

1 small orange

1. Serve orange alongside salad and snow peas.

EXCHANGES / CHOICES
1 Fruit

Calories 45; Calories from Fat 0; Total Fat 0.0 g; Saturated Fat 0.0 g; Trans Fat 0.0 g; Cholesterol 0 mg; Sodium 0 mg; Potassium 170 mg; Total Carbohydrate 11 g; Dietary Fiber 2 g; Sugars 9 g; Protein 1 g; Phosphorus 15 mg

SWORDFISH SALAD WITH SALSA DRESSING

Serves: 4 | Serving size: 1 cup | Prep time: 10 minutes | Cook time: 12 minutes

On my first date with my husband, he ordered swordfish. All these years later, he still requests this salad once a month. If swordfish is not a favorite of yours, use salmon, halibut, haddock, or sea bass, all of which work wonderfully well in this dish.

- 1 pound swordfish steaks
- 1/2 cup fresh orange juice
- 2 tablespoons olive oil
- 1 tablespoon fresh lemon juice
- 1/4 teaspoon cayenne pepper

SALSA

- 1 medium orange, peeled, sectioned, and chopped into 1-inch pieces
- 1 cup diced fresh or canned (in its own juice) pineapple chunks
- 1/2 cup peeled, diced mango
- 1 jalapeño pepper, seeded and minced
- 3 tablespoons orange juice
- 1 tablespoon diced red pepper
- 1 tablespoon minced cilantro

- 1 1/2 tablespoons olive oil
- 2 tablespoons red wine vinegar
- 1 teaspoon sugar
- 4 cups salad greens
- 2 tablespoons toasted slivered almonds

1. In a nonreactive pan, place the swordfish with the orange juice, olive oil, lemon juice, and cayenne pepper and marinate for 15 minutes.
2. Coat an outdoor grill with cooking spray and set the rack 6 inches from the heat source. Set the heat to medium-high. Alternatively, coat an indoor grill pan with cooking spray and place it on medium-high heat.
3. Grill the swordfish on each side for about 12–15 minutes, until opaque in the center. Remove the swordfish from the grill and allow to cool. Cut into 1-inch pieces.
4. Combine all ingredients for the salsa. Toss the swordfish with the salsa.
5. Combine the olive oil, red wine vinegar, and sugar. Whisk together well. Toss the greens with the dressing. Pile the swordfish salad on top of the lettuce. Top with almonds.

CALORIES	CALORIES FROM FAT	TOTAL FAT	SATURATED FAT	TRANS FAT	CHOLESTEROL	SODIUM	POTASSIUM
310	130	14.0 g	2.5 g	0.0 g	45 mg	115 mg	700 mg

TOTAL CARBOHYDRATE	DIETARY FIBER	SUGARS	PROTEIN	PHOSPHORUS	EXCHANGES/CHOICES:
20 g	3 g	15 g	25 g	350 mg	1 Fruit; 1 Nonstarchy Vegetable; 3 Protein, lean; 1 1/2 Fat

ZUCCHINI

Serves: 1 | Serving size: 1/2 cup

1/2 cup zucchini

1. Steam zucchini and serve alongside salad and Greek yogurt.

EXCHANGES / CHOICES
Free food

Calories 15; Calories from Fat 5; Total Fat 0.5 g; Saturated Fat 0.1 g; Trans Fat 0.0 g; Cholesterol 0 mg; Sodium 0 mg; Potassium 240 mg; Total Carbohydrate 2 g; Dietary Fiber 1 g; Sugars 2 g; Protein 1 g; Phosphorus 35 mg

• • • • • • •

GREEK YOGURT

Serves: 1 | Serving size: 1/2 cup

1/2 cup Greek yogurt

1. Serve alongside salad and zucchini.

EXCHANGES / CHOICES
1/2 Milk, fat-free

Calories 60; Calories from Fat 5; Total Fat 0.5 g; Saturated Fat 0.1 g; Trans Fat 0.0 g; Cholesterol 10 mg; Sodium 40 mg; Potassium 105 mg; Total Carbohydrate 7 g; Dietary Fiber 0 g; Sugars 5 g; Protein 9 g; Phosphorus 115 mg

GARLICKY TOMATO SALAD

Serves: 10 | Serving size: 1 cup | Prep time: 10 minutes

Plum and cherry tomatoes taste good year-round, so you can enjoy this salad anytime. In the summer, feel free to substitute yellow or heirloom tomatoes. Grilled shrimp is superb in this salad, so add it if you want to turn this into a main dish. Try this with sliced mint leaves in place of the basil or use half mint and half basil.

1 large head butter lettuce, large leaves torn into smaller pieces
2 large or 4 small ripe plum tomatoes, sliced
20 cherry tomatoes, halved

GARLIC VINAIGRETTE

1 large garlic clove, very finely chopped
2 teaspoons red wine vinegar
1/2 teaspoon Dijon mustard
2 tablespoons olive oil
1/4 teaspoon kosher salt
1/4 teaspoon freshly ground black pepper

16 fresh basil leaves, thinly sliced
1 tablespoon toasted pumpkin seeds
1 tablespoon sunflower seeds

1. Place a layer of lettuce leaves on a serving platter or on four plates and arrange the sliced tomatoes. Place the cherry tomatoes on top.
2. Whisk together the ingredients for the dressing and pour over the tomatoes.
3. Scatter the basil leaves and the pumpkin and sunflower seeds over the tomatoes and serve at once.

CALORIES	CALORIES FROM FAT	TOTAL FAT	SATURATED FAT	TRANS FAT	CHOLESTEROL	SODIUM	POTASSIUM
120	80	9.0 g	1.3 g	0.0 g	0 mg	140 mg	520 mg
TOTAL CARBOHYDRATE	**DIETARY FIBER**	**SUGARS**	**PROTEIN**	**PHOSPHORUS**	**EXCHANGES/CHOICES:**		
8 g	3 g	4 g	3 g	105 mg	1 Nonstarchy Vegetable; 2 Fat		

SEASONED SAUTÉED SHRIMP

Serves: 4 | Serving size: 4 ounces

2 teaspoons chipotle chili powder
1/2 teaspoon dried oregano leaves
1/2 teaspoon sweet paprika
1/4 teaspoon ground cumin
1/4 teaspoon freshly ground black pepper
1/4 teaspoon salt
1 pound peeled and deveined large shrimp
1 tablespoon olive oil

1. In a large bowl, combine the chili powder, oregano, paprika, cumin, black pepper, and salt. Add in the shrimp and toss well.
2. Heat the olive oil on medium heat in a large skillet. Add the shrimp and sauté for 5–7 minutes or until shrimp is cooked through.

EXCHANGES / CHOICES
3 Protein, lean

Calories 130; Calories from Fat 35; Total Fat 4.0 g; Saturated Fat 0.6 g; Trans Fat 0.0 g; Cholesterol 190 mg; Sodium 270 mg; Potassium 300 mg; Total Carbohydrate 1 g; Dietary Fiber 1 g; Sugars 0 g; Protein 24 g; Phosphorus 245 mg

This recipe also in Master Proteins page 9

SPINACH

Serves: 1 | Serving size: 1/2 cup

1/2 cup spinach

1. Steam spinach and serve alongside salad and shrimp.

EXCHANGES / CHOICES
1 Nonstarchy Vegetable

Calories 20; Calories from Fat 0; Total Fat 0.0 g; Saturated Fat 0.0 g; Trans Fat 0.0 g; Cholesterol 0 mg; Sodium 65 mg; Potassium 420 mg; Total Carbohydrate 3 g; Dietary Fiber 2 g; Sugars 0 g; Protein 3 g; Phosphorus 50 mg

SPINACH SALAD WITH HOT BACON DRESSING

Serves: 11 | Serving size: 1 1/2 cups | Prep time: 15 minutes | Cook time: 6 minutes

I learned very early on, for a great dressing such as this, make sure you cook the bacon in a heavy, perfectly flat-bottomed skillet for best results. The crispy pieces of bacon are crucial to making this salad a winner. The addition of romaine lettuce with the spinach cuts down on an overly peppery flavor coming from the spinach and will make the flavors more balanced.

7 cups fresh baby spinach leaves
1 small head romaine lettuce, washed, dried, and broken into bite-sized pieces
10 large white mushrooms, cleaned, peeled, if necessary, stemmed, and sliced

DRESSING

4 slices lean bacon (40% or more less fat), chopped
1 small onion, finely chopped
2 cloves garlic, minced
1/2 cup cider vinegar
1 tablespoon sugar
2 tablespoons tomato paste

1. Toss together the spinach, lettuce, and mushrooms.
2. Cook the bacon in a large heavy skillet over medium heat until crisp. Add the onion and sauté for 2 minutes. Add the garlic, vinegar, sugar, and tomato paste. Stir to blend. Toss salad with dressing and serve.

CALORIES	CALORIES FROM FAT	TOTAL FAT	SATURATED FAT	TRANS FAT	CHOLESTEROL	SODIUM	POTASSIUM
40	10	1.0 g	0.3 g	0.0 g	0 mg	80 mg	300 mg
TOTAL CARBOHYDRATE	**DIETARY FIBER**	**SUGARS**	**PROTEIN**	**PHOSPHORUS**	**EXCHANGES/CHOICES:**		
5 g	1 g	3 g	3 g	50 mg	1 Nonstarchy Vegetable		

MASTER CHICKEN SEAR

Serves: 4 | Serving size: 1/2 breast or thigh

2 boneless, skinless chicken breasts or 2 boneless, skinless chicken thighs
1/8 teaspoon kosher salt
1/4 teaspoon ground black pepper
1 1/2 tablespoons olive or canola oil

1. Season chicken breasts or chicken thighs with salt and black pepper.
2. In a 12–14-inch heavy skillet, preferably cast iron or stainless (NOT nonstick), heat oil over medium-high heat.
3. Add the chicken and sear until well browned on both sides, about 3–4 minutes per side for the breasts, or 2–3 minutes for the thighs.
4. Transfer the chicken to a plate and tent with foil.
5. Return the chicken and accumulated juices to the skillet and simmer gently until cooked through, about 4–5 minutes.

TO TEST: Chicken should feel firm to the touch. Using closed tongs, press on the center of the chicken. It should feel firm. Alternately, you may make a very small incision in the center of the meat and check to be sure the meat is cooked through with no traces of pink.

EXCHANGES / CHOICES
3 Protein, lean;
1 Fat

Calories 180; Calories from Fat 90; Total Fat 10.0 g; Saturated Fat 2.0 g; Trans Fat 0.0 g; Cholesterol 85 mg; Sodium 120 mg; Potassium 200 mg; Total Carbohydrate 0 g; Dietary Fiber 0 g; Sugars 0 g; Protein 21 g; Phosphorus 170 mg

This recipe also in Master Proteins page 37

BAKED POTATO WITH NONFAT GREEK YOGURT

Serves: 1 | Serving size: 1 potato

1 small (6-ounce) baked potato
1 tablespoon nonfat Greek yogurt

1. Bake potato in a 400°F oven for 45–55 minutes or until the internal temperature reaches 210°F. Top baked potato with Greek yogurt.

EXCHANGES / CHOICES
2 Starch

Calories 140; Calories from Fat 0; Total Fat 0.0 g; Saturated Fat 0.0 g; Trans Fat 0.0 g; Cholesterol 0 mg; Sodium 20 mg; Potassium 760 mg; Total Carbohydrate 30 g; Dietary Fiber 3 g; Sugars 2 g; Protein 5 g; Phosphorus 115 mg

ROASTED PEPPER SALAD

Serves: 6 | Serving size: 1 cup | Prep time: 30 minutes | Cook time: 35 minutes

Bell peppers are so tasty when they are raw, so why ever mess with them by roasting them? It's because fire does something incredibly magical to a pepper—it transforms its flavor and texture into something juicier, sweeter, and more versatile than before it stepped into the flames. Roasted peppers jazz up pasta, eggs, soups, stews, homemade pizza, and many more everyday foods.

- 2 large red peppers
- 2 large yellow or orange peppers
- 2 large green peppers
- 2 tablespoons extra virgin olive oil, divided use
- 2 teaspoons balsamic vinegar
- 1 small garlic clove, very finely chopped or crushed
- 12 black olives, pitted
- Handful of small fresh basil leaves

1. Preheat the oven to 400°F. Brush the peppers with 1 tablespoon of the olive oil and arrange them in a shallow roasting pan. Roast for about 35 minutes or until the pepper skins are evenly darkened, turning them 3 or 4 times. Place the peppers in a bowl, cover with plastic wrap, and leave until they are cool enough to handle.
2. Working over a bowl to catch the juice, peel the peppers. Cut them in half and discard the cores and seeds (strain out any seeds that fall into the juice), then cut into thick slices.
3. Measure 1 1/2 tbsp. of the pepper juice into a small bowl (discard the remainder). Add the vinegar and garlic and whisk in the remaining 1 tablespoon of olive oil.
4. Arrange the peppers on a serving platter or on individual salad plates. Drizzle with dressing and garnish with the olives and basil.

CALORIES	CALORIES FROM FAT	TOTAL FAT	SATURATED FAT	TRANS FAT	CHOLESTEROL	SODIUM	POTASSIUM
100	50	6.0 g	0.8 g	0.0 g	0 mg	85 mg	380 mg
TOTAL CARBOHYDRATE	**DIETARY FIBER**	**SUGARS**	**PROTEIN**	**PHOSPHORUS**	**EXCHANGES/CHOICES:**		
12 g	3 g	6 g	2 g	45 mg	2 Nonstarchy Vegetable; 1 Fat		

SEASONED SAUTÉED SHRIMP

Serves: 4 | Serving size: 4 ounces

2 teaspoons chipotle chili powder
1/2 teaspoon dried oregano leaves
1/2 teaspoon sweet paprika
1/4 teaspoon ground cumin
1/4 teaspoon freshly ground black pepper
1/4 teaspoon salt
1 pound peeled and deveined large shrimp
1 tablespoon olive oil

1. In a large bowl, combine the chili powder, oregano, paprika, cumin, black pepper, and salt. Add in the shrimp and toss well.
2. Heat the olive oil on medium heat in a large skillet. Add the shrimp and sauté for 5–7 minutes or until shrimp is cooked through.

EXCHANGES / CHOICES
3 Protein, lean

Calories 130; Calories from Fat 35; Total Fat 4.0 g; Saturated Fat 0.6 g; Trans Fat 0.0 g; Cholesterol 190 mg; Sodium 270 mg; Potassium 300 mg; Total Carbohydrate 1 g; Dietary Fiber 1 g; Sugars 0 g; Protein 24 g; Phosphorus 245 mg

This recipe also in Master Proteins page 9

CRACKERS

Serves: 1 | Serving size: 1 ounce

1 ounce whole-wheat crackers (such as Triscuits or Wheat Thins)

1. Serve crackers alongside salad and shrimp.

EXCHANGES / CHOICES
1 Starch; 1 Fat

Calories 130; Calories from Fat 45; Total Fat 5.0 g; Saturated Fat 1.0 g; Trans Fat 0.0 g; Cholesterol 0 mg; Sodium 50 mg; Potassium 85 mg; Total Carbohydrate 19 g; Dietary Fiber 3 g; Sugars 0 g; Protein 3 g; Phosphorus 85 mg

GARDEN SALAD WITH BALSAMIC VINAIGRETTE

Serves: 8 | Serving size: 1 cup | Prep time: 7 minutes | Cook time: 4 minutes

Ever have a really good garden salad in a restaurant? All you need is a zesty dressing, a few vegetables, and a crunchy topping. This basic recipe gives you everything you need to know—so go ahead and enjoy a healthy and delicious salad every day.

NUTS

3/4 cup walnuts
2 tablespoons sugar

DRESSING

1/4 cup balsamic vinegar
1 garlic clove, minced
1 teaspoon coarse Dijon mustard
1 teaspoon honey or sugar
3 tablespoons olive oil
1/4 teaspoon sea salt
1/4 teaspoon freshly ground black pepper

SALAD

5 cups mixed greens
1 cup halved cherry tomatoes
2 large carrots, peeled and grated
1/2 medium red onion, thinly sliced

1. To make the walnuts, in a small sauté pan or skillet over medium-high heat, toss the walnuts with the sugar for 3 to 4 minutes or until the sugar melts and caramelizes. Watch that the nuts do not burn. Remove the nuts from the pan and let cool.
2. In a large bowl, combine dressing ingredients and whisk well.
3. Add the salad ingredients to the dressing and quickly toss together. Serve in individual plates, top with the nuts.

CALORIES	CALORIES FROM FAT	TOTAL FAT	SATURATED FAT	TRANS FAT	CHOLESTEROL	SODIUM	POTASSIUM
160	120	13.0 g	1.4 g	0.0 g	0 mg	105 mg	250 mg

TOTAL CARBOHYDRATE	DIETARY FIBER	SUGARS	PROTEIN	PHOSPHORUS	EXCHANGES/CHOICES:
11 g	2 g	7 g	3 g	65 mg	1/2 Carbohydrate; 1 Nonstarchy Vegetable; 2 1/2 Fat

SEARED CHICKEN BREASTS

Serves: 4 | Serving size: 3 ounces

1 pound boneless, skinless chicken breasts, remove any tenderloins so chicken lays flat
1/2 teaspoon kosher salt
1/4 teaspoon freshly ground black pepper
1 1/2 tablespoons olive or vegetable oil

1. Pound the chicken breasts if necessary so they are even in thickness. Season the chicken with salt and pepper.
2. Heat the oil in a heavy cast iron skillet over medium-high heat. Add the chicken breasts and sear on both sides for about 5 minutes per side. Be sure to let one side of the chicken thoroughly sear before turning over to the other side. This will ensure even cooking and will prevent sticking.
3. Cover the skillet, lower the heat to low, and cook for about 5–6 minutes until the chicken is cooked through.

EXCHANGES / CHOICES
3 Protein, lean;
1/2 Fat

Calories 170; Calories from Fat 70; Total Fat 8.0 g; Saturated Fat 1.5 g; Trans Fat 0.0 g; Cholesterol 65 mg; Sodium 290 mg; Potassium 200 mg; Total Carbohydrate 0 g; Dietary Fiber 0 g; Sugars 0 g; Protein 24 g; Phosphorus 175 mg

This recipe also in Master Proteins page 9

RASPBERRIES

Serves: 1 | Serving size: 1/2 cup

1/2 cup raspberries

1. Serve raspberries alongside salad and chicken.

EXCHANGES / CHOICES
1/2 Fruit

Calories 30; Calories from Fat 5; Total Fat 0.5 g; Saturated Fat 0.0 g; Trans Fat 0.0 g; Cholesterol 0 mg; Sodium 0 mg; Potassium 95 mg; Total Carbohydrate 7 g; Dietary Fiber 4 g; Sugars 3 g; Protein 1 g; Phosphorus 20 mg

BASIC CREAMY DRESSING

Serves: 16 | Serving size: 1 tablespoon | Prep time: 5 minutes

I've given you the basic formula for a great vinaigrette, but you might be in the mood for something creamier. Here is a master recipe for creating a creamy dressing. Toss aside the bottled ranch dressing in favor of your own.

- 1/2 cup low-fat buttermilk
- 2 tablespoons nonfat mayonnaise
- 2 tablespoons plain nonfat Greek yogurt
- 1 tablespoon fresh lemon juice
- 2 teaspoons grated Parmesan cheese
- 1/2 teaspoon lite soy sauce
- 1 garlic clove, finely minced
- 1/4 teaspoon freshly ground black pepper
- 1/8 teaspoon cayenne pepper

1. In a blender, purée all the ingredients until smooth. Add to an airtight container and store in the refrigerator for up to 4 days.
2. For a little variation, try adding 1/4 fresh avocado or 2 tablespoons unsweetened, unflavored almond milk in place of the yogurt.

CALORIES	CALORIES FROM FAT	TOTAL FAT	SATURATED FAT	TRANS FAT	CHOLESTEROL	SODIUM	POTASSIUM
5	0	0.0 g	0.1 g	0.0 g	0 mg	35 mg	20 mg

TOTAL CARBOHYDRATE	DIETARY FIBER	SUGARS	PROTEIN	PHOSPHORUS	EXCHANGES/CHOICES:
1 g	0 g	1 g	1 g	10 mg	Free food

Roasted Pepper Salad page 148

CHAPTER 7
Soups

THE PRINCIPLES OF SOUP MAKING

For me, a bowl of soup makes everything right in the world. There isn't another dish on the planet that creates all its magic by simmering quietly as you sit patiently in anticipation of its goodness. That's why I believe soup can be part of the perfect meal; the effort is small compared to the enormous payoff of bold, satisfying flavor. Preparing soup is a like building a house; it needs a solid foundation and detailed finishes. So let's start at the beginning with the root of all soup—the stock.

STOCK MAKING

I didn't grow up using canned stock; in fact when I was 12, making stock from scratch was the first cooking lesson my mother taught me. I remember thinking how easy it was to start with some basic ingredients that we always had in our refrigerator. Put some carrots, celery, onions, or whatever else was in the fridge into a large pot with water; walk away and return later to a golden-hued vat of homemade stock that smelled heavenly. At the time, canned stocks were just making their debut, but I'm grateful that I learned how to make it the old-fashioned way. Is homemade stock absolutely necessary for soup? No, in fact there are several low-sodium and organic stock brands in the supermarket that are quite good.

THE SOLID FOUNDATIONS

STOCK

1. Start with a good amount of chicken parts (about 4 pounds). Don't skimp on this! Even if you don't consume dark meat chicken on a regular basis, you must add it in order to produce a rich, flavorful stock. Never remove the skin from the chicken. You'll be removing the excess fat from the stock later. You can also use 4 pounds of necks and backs; your store's butcher often has them available even if they are not packaged and on display. Just ask. I often see people trying to prepare chicken broth with the leftover bones from consuming a chicken dinner. Broth made with mostly bones and very little meat will sadly just taste like bones. It won't be rich and your soup will not have that rounded, full-bodied taste.
2. Three simple vegetables are all you need to add to produce perfect chicken broth—an onion, carrots, and celery. Leave the onion

unpeeled as it will impart a richer flavor. The carrots too can remained unpeeled, just be sure to thoroughly wash them. Coarsely chop the vegetables; no need to be precise with size of the cuts. If you are inclined, add some garlic as well. I use it sometimes in stock, but only when I know my soup will be able to handle the garlic's pungency.

3. Finally, add a few sprigs of fresh parsley, a few peppercorns, and a bay leaf. This trio helps provide a fresh, clean stock with a slight spicy taste from the peppercorns and is essential to creating a flavorful stock.
4. Once all the ingredients are in the pot, bring to a boil, remove any surface scum with a flat ladle, and turn the heat down to a simmer. It's really important to keep the heat low. If your stock remains at a temperature higher than a simmer, the fat can become so thoroughly dispersed in the liquid and will be difficult to remove. Keeping the stock above a simmer can cause a greasy, cloudy stock.
5. When it's time to strain the stock, the best piece of equipment for this is a chinois, or a conical shaped strainer. It's not necessary to have one, but it makes straining stock a snap. Whatever strainer you use, strain it through a piece of cheesecloth so that your stock will be clear. Pressing down on the vegetables helps extract more flavor.
6. Make stock well ahead of the time. This way you can refrigerate overnight and skim off all the visible fat the next day. There are quicker methods of removing the fat so you don't have to wait through the overnight chilling process, but I still find this is the best method to obtain clean, clear stock.

THE SEASONING VEGETABLES

Once the stock is made, you will start building the soup. All soups and stews should begin with at least these two seasoning vegetables; onion and garlic. Most of the recipes in this chapter include them both. The other two seasoning vegetables I recommend are carrots and celery. I use all-purpose yellow onions, but feel free to try a red onion. Always sauté the onion at least 3 minutes. I typically sauté the onions with the garlic, celery, or carrots to save some time. You can sauté the onions alone at first, then add the other seasoning vegetables. Just don't sauté garlic by itself as it will burn and turn bitter.

THE DETAILS

Great stock and a few seasoning vegetables are all you need to form the base of all soups and stews. Your choice of adding beans, meats, poultry, seafood, canned tomatoes, rice, pasta, more vegetables, milk, herbs, or more spices is what makes the soup or stew creative and uniquely yours. Keep all these ingredients on hand and you will be ready and able to whip up something special for your friends and family.

BROTH SOUPS

The first three recipes in this chapter build on how to prepare fresh chicken stock. The Old-Fashioned Chicken and Rice Soup is actually two recipes in one. I give you the master plan to make chicken stock and then the full chicken and rice soup recipe. Once you've mastered this soup, you can create many variations by adding beans, pasta, other grains such as quinoa and couscous, or adding different fresh herbs or fresh chilies. This is a staple soup that should have a permanent place in your repertoire. The Thai Shrimp Soup is a simple brothy soup that relies heavily on the stock base to carry a few bold herbs, shrimp, and rice noodles. The variations are endless: substitute scallops, cubed chicken, cubed tofu, or try brown rice instead of rice noodles. Use the Lemon and Asparagus Soup as a blueprint to prepare any "cream" based soup, such as broccoli or mushroom.

BEAN SOUPS

Once you master the simple Tuscan Bean Soup, you'll be able to master the rest. They all start out with great broth and a sauté of seasoning vegetables. Then beans, tomatoes, additional vegetables, and herbs and spices are used. One soup is puréed, one adds in a grain, and one relies on using Indian spices, but they all stem from the same method as the Tuscan Bean Soup. Here are a few pointers:

1. Use BPA-free canned beans and drain and rinse the beans. You are certainly welcome to cook your own beans from scratch. I still buy dried lentils because they cook quickly, as you will see in the Indian Lentil Soup.
2. Use whole canned or diced tomatoes but never crushed tomatoes in these soups. Crushed tomatoes will not give you the delightful rough texture that makes soups so deliciously hearty. Crushing your own canned whole tomatoes is actually fun and easy and, trust me, they will taste infinitely better than pre-crushed tomatoes.
3. Use fresh herbs in the soup as I call for them. The fresh herbs will provide a spring-like flavor and help bring together all the neutral ingredients such as the stock and beans. You can use dried if you wish, but the flavor will not be as intense.

STEWS

I included only two recipes for stew. Once you learn these two basic methods, you are well on your way to making substitutions to create many different types of stews. In the Classic Beef Stew, you will start out browning the beef so it creates a flavorful base. Once the meat is removed, mushrooms will be sautéed in this delicious leftover flavor. The mushrooms are removed and will be added back later. Onions and garlic get a chance to sauté in both meat and mushroom juices. The meat is added back, along with some liquid, and all is left to develop a rich stew. It's important to keep the heat very low during this first simmer. The classic carrots and potatoes are added next. The mushrooms are added back later along with peas so they retain their shape and texture. Use this same blueprint to prepare a pork, chicken, or turkey stew.

The second recipe, Braised Beef Stew, is a quicker version of the classic. It starts out the same way as the classic, but it's more like a long-simmering stir fry than the more involved Classic Beef Stew. This is a great way to get beef stew flavor, without all the additional effort to add more ingredients. So, when you don't have time for the full-fledged version, this is an excellent alternative.

OLD-FASHIONED CHICKEN AND RICE SOUP

Serves: 12 | Serving size: 1 cup | Prep time: 15 minutes for the stock + 15 minutes for the soup
Cook time: 2 1/2 hours for the stock + 20 minutes for the soup | Chill time: 8 hours or overnight

Honestly, if all you tackle is this recipe, you'll be a master soup maker in no time! This recipe includes two techniques in one: a basic chicken stock, and an all-purpose chicken and rice soup. Master the stock and you'll always have a rich broth that is perfect for so many soups and stews. Resist grabbing canned and boxed broth in favor of this step-by-step guide to making perfect broth.

CHICKEN STOCK

- 1 (4-pound) chicken, cut into parts, washed
- 2 large onions, quartered, unpeeled
- 4 medium carrots, unpeeled, cut into chunks
- 4 large celery stalks, coarsely chopped
- 6 sprigs fresh parsley
- 6 black peppercorns
- 3 bay leaves

ALL-PURPOSE SEASONING

- 2 teaspoons onion powder
- 2 teaspoons garlic powder
- 2 teaspoons dried oregano
- 2 teaspoons dried basil
- 2 teaspoons ground coriander
- 1 teaspoon turmeric
- 1 teaspoon sweet paprika
- 1 teaspoon freshly ground black pepper

SOUP

- 2 teaspoons olive oil
- 1 large onion, chopped
- 2 large carrots, peeled and sliced diagonally into 1/2-inch pieces
- 1 large celery stalk, sliced diagonally into 1/2-inch pieces
- 1 tablespoon all-purpose seasoning
- 1 cup long-grain brown Basmati rice
- 1/2 teaspoon kosher salt
- 1/4 teaspoon freshly ground black pepper
- 2 tablespoons minced fresh parsley
- 2 teaspoons minced fresh thyme

1. **PREPARE THE STOCK.** Put the chicken parts into a heavy stockpot. Add the onions, carrots, and celery stalks. Add in 3 quarts of water and bring to a boil. Skim the surface and remove any gray residue.
2. Add the parsley, peppercorns, and bay leaves. Partially cover the pan and simmer on low heat for 2–2 1/2 hours. Remove the chicken parts and set aside to cool.
3. Line a large colander with cheesecloth and strain the broth, pressing on the solids. Discard the vegetables and reserve all of the stock. Add the stock to a large container and refrigerate overnight.
4. Remove the stock from the refrigerator. Spoon off any accumulated solidified fat and discard the fat. Your stock should be clear.

CALORIES	CALORIES FROM FAT	TOTAL FAT	SATURATED FAT	TRANS FAT	CHOLESTEROL	SODIUM	POTASSIUM
170	50	6.0 g	1.4 g	0.0 g	30 mg	140 mg	310 mg

TOTAL CARBOHYDRATE	DIETARY FIBER	SUGARS	PROTEIN	PHOSPHORUS	EXCHANGES/CHOICES:
15 g	2 g	2 g	14 g	165 mg	1 Starch; 2 Protein, lean

5. **PREPARE THE ALL-PURPOSE SEASONING.** Combine all the ingredients for the all-purpose seasoning. Transfer to a small coffee or spice grinder until well blended. You'll need 1 tablespoon for this recipe.
6. **PREPARE THE SOUP.** In a large pot, heat the olive oil. Add the onion and sauté for 5 minutes. Add in the carrots, celery, and all-purpose seasoning and sauté for 3 minutes. Add the rice and continue to cook for 2 minutes. Add in the reserved stock and bring to a boil. Reduce the heat and simmer for 6–7 minutes.
7. While the rice is cooking, remove and discard all the bones from the chicken parts. Cut about 1 pound of the chicken meat into small pieces for the soup. Save any remaining chicken for another use. Wrap the leftover chicken in an airtight container and keep in the refrigerator for up to 2–3 days.
8. Stir the cooked chicken into the soup and cook for 3 minutes. Season with salt and freshly ground black pepper. Sprinkle the soup with the parsley and thyme.

FRESH SPINACH SALAD

Serves: 1 | Serving size: 1 1/2 cups

1 cup fresh spinach leaves
5 cherry tomatoes, halved
1/4 cup sliced red onion
1 teaspoon olive oil
1/2 teaspoon lemon juice

1. Combine spinach, tomatoes, and red onion to a small bowl. Drizzle olive oil over salad and top with lemon juice.

EXCHANGES / CHOICES
1 Nonstarchy Vegetable; 1 Fat

Calories 70; Calories from Fat 45; Total Fat 5.0 g; Saturated Fat 0.7 g; Trans Fat 0.0 g; Cholesterol 0 mg; Sodium 25 mg; Potassium 360 mg; Total Carbohydrate 7 g; Dietary Fiber 2 g; Sugars 3 g; Protein 2 g; Phosphorus 40 mg

• • • • • • •

WHOLE-GRAIN CRACKERS

Serves: 1 | Serving size: 1 ounce

1 ounce whole-grain crackers

1. Serve crackers alongside soup and salad.

EXCHANGES / CHOICES
1 Starch; 1 Fat

Calories 130; Calories from Fat 45; Total Fat 5.0 g; Saturated Fat 1.0 g; Trans Fat 0.0 g; Cholesterol 0 mg; Sodium 50 mg; Potassium 85 mg; Total Carbohydrate 19 g; Dietary Fiber 3 g; Sugars 0 g; Protein 3 g; Phosphorus 85 mg

TUSCAN BEAN SOUP

Serves: 9 | Serving size: 1 cup | Prep time: 10 minutes | Cook time: 28 minutes

This Tuscan Bean Soup was one of the first soups I learned in a cooking class on a farm in Italy. I simplified it by using canned beans (the original recipe calls for using dried beans), which I think are perfectly fine. This is similar to minestrone soup, minus the pasta. Be sure to add the balsamic vinegar, it really draws out the flavor of the vegetables and makes the chickpeas taste even richer.

- 1 tablespoon olive oil
- 1 onion, diced
- 2 stalks celery, diced
- 2 carrots, diced
- 4 cloves garlic, minced
- 2 teaspoons minced fresh rosemary
- 5 cups low-sodium chicken stock
- 1 (14-ounce) can chopped tomatoes
- 2 (16-ounce) cans chickpeas, rinsed and drained
- 2 tablespoons minced basil
- 1 to 2 tablespoons balsamic vinegar

1. In a saucepot over medium heat, heat the olive oil. Add the onions, celery, and carrots and sauté for 5 minutes. Add the garlic and rosemary and sauté 1 minute. Add the remaining ingredients, except the fresh basil and vinegar. Bring to a boil. Reduce heat and simmer, partially covered for 20 minutes.
2. Add the vinegar and basil and cook for 2 minutes. Top each bowl with fresh grated Parmesan cheese, if desired.

CALORIES	CALORIES FROM FAT	TOTAL FAT	SATURATED FAT	TRANS FAT	CHOLESTEROL	SODIUM	POTASSIUM
140	25	3.0 g	0.4 g	0.0 g	0 mg	210 mg	460 mg

TOTAL CARBOHYDRATE	DIETARY FIBER	SUGARS	PROTEIN	PHOSPHORUS	EXCHANGES/CHOICES:
22 g	6 g	6 g	7 g	145 mg	1 Starch; 1 Nonstarchy Vegetable; 1 Protein, lean

GARDEN SALAD WITH BALSAMIC VINAIGRETTE

Serves: 8 | Serving size: 1 cup | Prep time: 7 minutes | Cook time: 4 minutes

3/4 cup walnuts
2 tablespoons sugar

DRESSING
1/4 cup balsamic vinegar
1 garlic clove, minced
1 teaspoon coarse Dijon mustard
1 teaspoon honey or sugar
3 tablespoons olive oil
1/4 teaspoon sea salt
1/4 teaspoon freshly ground black pepper

SALAD
5 cups mixed greens
1 cup halved cherry tomatoes
2 large carrots, peeled and grated
1/2 medium red onion, thinly sliced

1. In a small sauté pan or skillet over medium-high heat, toss the walnuts with the sugar for 3 to 4 minutes or until the sugar melts and caramelizes. Watch that the nuts do not burn. Remove the nuts from the pan and let cool.
2. In a large bowl, combine dressing ingredients and whisk well.
3. Add the salad ingredients to the dressing and quickly toss together. Serve on individual plates, top with the nuts.

EXCHANGES / CHOICES
1/2 Carbohydrate; 1 Nonstarchy Vegetable; 2 1/2 Fat

Calories 160; Calories from Fat 120; Total Fat 13.0 g; Saturated Fat 1.4 g; Trans Fat 0.0 g; Cholesterol 0 mg; Sodium 105 mg; Potassium 250 mg; Total Carbohydrate 11 g; Dietary Fiber 2 g; Sugars 7 g; Protein 3 g; Phosphorus 65 mg

This recipe also in Salads page 150

INDIAN LENTIL SOUP

Serves: 4 | Serving size: 1 1/4 cups | Prep time: 5 minutes | Cook time: 40 minutes

Through the years, I've experimented with all kinds of flavoring for lentil soup, and finally decided that I like this Indian version best. While the soup base is quite tasty, my favorite part is the topping! Ginger-tinged yogurt provides the perfect topper for this hearty soup. Serve a spoonful on top for presentation, but then swirl it right into the soup to create even more flavor.

1 tablespoon olive oil
1 large onion, chopped
3 garlic cloves, minced
2 teaspoons salt-free Tandoori seasoning*
1 (15-ounce) can no-salt-added diced tomatoes
2 1/2 cups water
1/2 cup brown lentils, picked over and rinsed

TOPPING

1/2 cup plain fat-free yogurt
1 teaspoon peeled, grated fresh ginger
1 teaspoon fresh lemon juice
1/2 teaspoon sugar

**Salt-free Tandoori seasoning is available at www.penzeys.com. Also look for it in your grocer's spice aisle.*

1. Heat the olive oil in a large saucepan over medium heat. Add the onions and garlic and sauté for about 6–8 minutes until the onion is golden. Add in the Tandoori seasoning and sauté for 1 minute.
2. Add in the tomatoes with their juice, water, and lentils. Bring to a boil, lower the heat, cover, and simmer on low heat for about 30 minutes until lentils are tender.
3. For the topping, combine the yogurt, ginger, lemon juice, and sugar. Add a dollop of the ginger yogurt mixture to each bowl of soup.

CALORIES	CALORIES FROM FAT	TOTAL FAT	SATURATED FAT	TRANS FAT	CHOLESTEROL	SODIUM	POTASSIUM
170	35	4.0 g	0.6 g	0.0 g	0 mg	65 mg	620 mg
TOTAL CARBOHYDRATE	**DIETARY FIBER**	**SUGARS**	**PROTEIN**	**PHOSPHORUS**	**EXCHANGES/CHOICES:**		
27 g	8 g	9 g	9 g	210 mg	1 Starch; 2 Nonstarchy Vegetable; 1 Protein, lean		

FRESH SPINACH SALAD

Serves: 1 | Serving size: 1 1/2 cups

1 cup fresh spinach leaves
5 cherry tomatoes, halved
1/4 cup red onion, thinly sliced
1 teaspoon olive oil
1/2 teaspoon lemon juice

1. Combine spinach, tomatoes, and onion slices in a small bowl. Drizzle with olive oil and top with lemon juice.

EXCHANGES / CHOICES
1 Nonstarchy Vegetable; 1 Fat

Calories 70; Calories from Fat 45; Total Fat 5.0 g; Saturated Fat 0.7 g; Trans Fat 0.0 g; Cholesterol 0 mg; Sodium 25 mg; Potassium 360 mg; Total Carbohydrate 7 g; Dietary Fiber 2 g; Sugars 3 g; Protein 2 g; Phosphorus 40 mg

MOROCCAN BEAN AND VEGETABLE SOUP WITH FARRO

Serves: 20 | Serving size: 1 cup | Prep time: 20 minutes | Cook time: 1 hour and 20 minutes

The beauty of this recipe is that it makes a lot! Farro is an ancient Roman grain that has been cultivated for over 400 years. Fortunately, it's become very popular in the U.S. and it's easier to find in major supermarkets. Just follow the package directions for cooking. If you want to use brown rice or another whole grain instead, feel free to substitute.

3 tablespoons olive oil
4 cups sliced onions (2 large onions)
2 garlic cloves, minced
1/2 teaspoon ground cumin
1/4 teaspoon ground coriander
1/4 teaspoon cayenne pepper
2 quarts low-sodium, fat-free chicken broth
3 cups peeled and thinly sliced carrots (about 5 large carrots)
2 cups sliced zucchini (about 1 large or 2 medium)
2 cups sliced yellow squash (about 1 large and 2 medium)
4 cups thinly sliced peeled russet potatoes (4 medium potatoes)
1/4 cup fresh lemon juice
1/2 cup chopped fresh cilantro
1 (14.5-ounce) can no-salt-added canned chickpeas, drained and rinsed
1 (14.5-ounce) can diced no-salt-added canned tomatoes
1 cup uncooked farro, cooked (makes approximately 2 cups cooked farro)

1. Heat the oil in large 5-quart saucepan over medium-high heat. Add the onion and garlic and sauté for 3 minutes. Add in the cumin, coriander, and cayenne and cook for 1 minute. Add in the broth, carrots, zucchini, yellow squash, and potatoes and bring to a boil. Turn down the heat to simmer and cover for 1 hour.
2. Remove the pan from the heat and add the lemon juice and cilantro. Transfer in batches to a food processor, blender, or use a hand-held immersion blender and puree until smooth. Return the pureed soup to a saucepan and add in the chickpeas, tomatoes, and cooked farro. Simmer for 2 minutes.

CALORIES	CALORIES FROM FAT	TOTAL FAT	SATURATED FAT	TRANS FAT	CHOLESTEROL	SODIUM	POTASSIUM
140	25	3.0 g	0.4 g	0.0 g	0 mg	80 mg	530 mg

TOTAL CARBOHYDRATE	DIETARY FIBER	SUGARS	PROTEIN	PHOSPHORUS	EXCHANGES/CHOICES:
23 g	4 g	4 g	6 g	135 mg	1 Starch; 1 Nonstarchy Vegetable; 1/2 Fat

SEASONED BROILED FISH

Serves: 4 | Serving size: 4 ounces

2 teaspoons chipotle chili powder
1/2 teaspoon dried oregano leaves
1/2 teaspoon sweet paprika
1/4 teaspoon ground cumin
1/4 teaspoon freshly ground black pepper
1/4 teaspoon salt
1 pound fish filets, about 1-inch thick
1 tablespoon olive oil

1. Preheat the oven to broil. Line a broiler pan with nonstick foil. In a small ramekin, combine the chili powder, oregano, paprika, cumin, pepper, and salt.
2. Coat both sides of the fish lightly with the seasoning. Drizzle the fish with the olive oil.
3. Broil the fish about 5 minutes per side or until cooked through.

EXCHANGES / CHOICES
3 Protein, lean;
1 1/2 Fat

Calories 210; Calories from Fat 110; Total Fat 12.0 g; Saturated Fat 2.4 g; Trans Fat 0.0 g; Cholesterol 60 mg; Sodium 230 mg; Potassium 440 mg; Total Carbohydrate 1 g; Dietary Fiber 1 g; Sugars 0 g; Protein 22 g; Phosphorus 295 mg

This recipe also in Master Proteins page 9

CANTALOUPE

Serves: 1 | Serving size: 1/2 cup

1/2 cup cantaloupe

1. Serve cantaloupe alongside soup and broiled fish.

EXCHANGES / CHOICES
1/2 Fruit

Calories 20; Calories from Fat 0; Total Fat 0.0 g; Saturated Fat 0.0 g; Trans Fat 0.0 g; Cholesterol 0 mg; Sodium 10 mg; Potassium 135 mg; Total Carbohydrate 4 g; Dietary Fiber 0 g; Sugars 4 g; Protein 0 g; Phosphorus 10 mg

ZUPPA DI CECI (CHICKPEA SOUP)

Serves: 6 | Serving size: 1 cup | Prep time: 15 minutes | Cook time: 20 minutes

Garlic, beans, herbs, and onions shine and become amazing in this classic soup. This recipe relies heavily on lots of garlic, fresh sage, and basil—accept no substitutes, as the herbs are what make this a winner. The soup also freezes very well.

- 2 tablespoons olive oil, divided use
- 1 large celery stalk, finely chopped
- 1 large onion, finely chopped
- 1 small sprig fresh rosemary, finely chopped
- 6 sage leaves, finely chopped
- 4 garlic cloves, finely minced
- 1 (28-ounce) can no-salt-added whole tomatoes
- 2 (15-ounce) cans no-salt-added chickpeas, drained and rinsed
- 1 1/4 cups water, divided use
- 4 tablespoons finely chopped fresh basil
- 1/2 teaspoon ground black pepper
- 1 tablespoon fresh lemon juice

1. Heat 1 tablespoon olive oil in a large saucepan over medium heat. Add the celery, onion, rosemary, and sage and sauté for about 8 minutes. Add in the garlic and sauté for 2 minutes.
2. Add the can of tomatoes to a large bowl. With your hands, crush the tomatoes, leaving the tomatoes slightly coarse. Add the tomatoes with the juices to the pan.
3. Puree one can of the chickpeas in a food processor or blender with 1/4 cup of the water until smooth, but still thick. Add the pureed chickpeas and the other can of whole chickpeas to the soup. Add in the remaining water, the basil and black pepper and bring the soup to a boil. Lower the heat and simmer for 15 minutes.
4. Add in the lemon juice and remove the soup from the heat and serve with a drizzle of olive oil over each individual bowl.

CALORIES	CALORIES FROM FAT	TOTAL FAT	SATURATED FAT	TRANS FAT	CHOLESTEROL	SODIUM	POTASSIUM
180	45	5.0 g	0.7 g	0.0 g	0 mg	25 mg	470 mg

TOTAL CARBOHYDRATE	DIETARY FIBER	SUGARS	PROTEIN	PHOSPHORUS	EXCHANGES/CHOICES:
27 g	7 g	7 g	8 g	150 mg	1 Starch; 2 Nonstarchy Vegetable; 1 Fat

FRESH SPINACH SALAD

Serves: 1 | Serving size: 1 1/2 cups

1 cup fresh spinach leaves
5 cherry tomatoes, halved
1/4 cup red onion, thinly sliced
1 teaspoon olive oil
1/2 teaspoon lemon juice

1. Combine spinach, tomatoes, and onion slices in a small bowl. Drizzle with olive oil and top with lemon juice.

EXCHANGES / CHOICES
1 Nonstarchy Vegetable; 1 Fat

Calories 70; Calories from Fat 45; Total Fat 5.0 g; Saturated Fat 0.7 g; Trans Fat 0.0 g; Cholesterol 0 mg; Sodium 25 mg; Potassium 360 mg; Total Carbohydrate 7 g; Dietary Fiber 2 g; Sugars 3 g; Protein 2 g; Phosphorus 40 mg

....

ZUCCHINI

Serves: 1 | Serving size: 1/2 cup

1/2 cup zucchini

1. Steam zucchini and serve alongside soup and salad.

EXCHANGES / CHOICES
Free food

Calories 15; Calories from Fat 5; Total Fat 0.5 g; Saturated Fat 0.1 g; Trans Fat 0.0 g; Cholesterol 0 mg; Sodium 0 mg; Potassium 240 mg; Total Carbohydrate 2 g; Dietary Fiber 1 g; Sugars 2 g; Protein 1 g; Phosphorus 35 mg

CLASSIC BEEF STEW

Serves: 6 | Serving size: 1 cup | Prep time: 20 minutes | Cook time: 2 hours

You don't need cold weather to enjoy a great beef stew. There are so many new renditions of beef stew, but if you can make this classic version really well, that's all you'll need. Although button mushrooms can be used, try and seek out cremini mushrooms as the stew will taste more full-bodied.

- 2 tablespoons all-purpose flour or whole-wheat pastry flour
- 1 tablespoon Italian seasoning
- 3 tablespoons olive oil
- 2 pounds top round, cut into 3/4-inch cubes
- 1 1/2 pounds cremini mushrooms, cleaned, stemmed, and quartered
- 4 cups reduced-sodium, low-fat chicken broth, divided use
- 1 large onion, coarsely chopped
- 3 garlic cloves, minced
- 2 large russet potatoes
- 3 medium carrots, peeled
- 1 cup frozen peas
- 1 tablespoon fresh minced thyme
- 1 tablespoon red wine vinegar
- 1/4 to 1/2 teaspoon freshly ground black pepper

1. Combine the all-purpose flour with the Italian seasoning. Heat the olive oil in a large Dutch oven over medium heat. Dredge the beef cubes lightly in the flour mixture and add the beef, in batches to keep the beef in one layer, until well browned on each side.
2. Remove the beef from the pan and deglaze the pan with 1/4 cup chicken broth. Add in the mushrooms and sauté for about 4 minutes until well browned. Remove the mushrooms from the pan and deglaze with another 1/4 cup of the broth. Add the onions and garlic and sauté for 4 minutes. Return the beef to the pot, add the remaining chicken broth, and bring to a boil. Partially cover, lower the heat to simmer, and cook for 45 minutes, stirring occasionally.
3. Peel and cut the potatoes into 3/4-inch pieces. Cut the carrots into 1/2-inch pieces. Add the potatoes and carrots to the stew and continue to cook for another 45 minutes or until vegetables are tender. Add in the reserved mushrooms, peas, and thyme. Season with red wine vinegar and black pepper.

CALORIES	CALORIES FROM FAT	TOTAL FAT	SATURATED FAT	TRANS FAT	CHOLESTEROL	SODIUM	POTASSIUM
250	60	7.0 g	1.5 g	0.0 g	45 mg	290 mg	980 mg

TOTAL CARBOHYDRATE	DIETARY FIBER	SUGARS	PROTEIN	PHOSPHORUS	EXCHANGES/CHOICES:
24 g	3 g	5 g	25 g	285 mg	1 Starch; 2 Nonstarchy Vegetable; 3 Protein, lean

WHOLE-WHEAT ROLL

Serves: 1 | Serving size: 1 roll

1 whole-wheat roll

1. Serve roll alongside stew.

EXCHANGES / CHOICES
1 Starch

Calories 90; Calories from Fat 15; Total Fat 1.5 g; Saturated Fat 0.3 g; Trans Fat 0.0 g; Cholesterol 0 mg; Sodium 170 mg; Potassium 70 mg; Total Carbohydrate 16 g; Dietary Fiber 1 g; Sugars 2 g; Protein 2 g; Phosphorus 60 mg

BRAISED BEEF STEW

Serves: 3 | Serving size: 1 cup | Prep time: 15 minutes | Cook time: 55 minutes

This Braised Beef Stew is Classic Beef Stew's little cousin. With just beef and onion as the main ingredients, you'd think something was missing, but behold the magic of simplicity. When you don't have the pantry stocked with ingredients, or the time to spare, this braised version comes in handy. Try preparing this with pork as well.

2 tablespoons all-purpose or whole-wheat pastry flour
1/4 teaspoon kosher salt
1/4 teaspoon freshly ground black pepper
1 pound top round, cut into 3/4-inch cubes
2 tablespoons peanut oil
1 cup sliced onion
1 tablespoon finely minced garlic
1/4 teaspoon crushed red chili flakes
2 cups low-sodium, fat-free chicken broth
Juice of 1 lime

1. Combine the flour, salt, and pepper on a plate, in a bowl, or plastic bag. Add the beef and coat the beef. Heat the oil in a large deep skillet over medium-high heat.
2. Dredge the beef cubes lightly in the flour mixture and add the beef, in batches to keep the beef in one layer, until well browned on each side. Remove the beef from the pan with a slotted spoon and add the onion. Sauté the onion on medium heat for about 7–8 minutes until very soft. Add in the garlic and chili flakes and sauté for 1 minute. Add in the broth and lower the heat to simmer. Simmer for 25–30 minutes or until the meat is very tender. Add in the lime juice.

CALORIES	CALORIES FROM FAT	TOTAL FAT	SATURATED FAT	TRANS FAT	CHOLESTEROL	SODIUM	POTASSIUM
310	130	14.0 g	3.1 g	0.0 g	80 mg	290 mg	530 mg

TOTAL CARBOHYDRATE	DIETARY FIBER	SUGARS	PROTEIN	PHOSPHORUS	EXCHANGES/CHOICES:
10 g	1 g	2 g	35 g	280 mg	1/2 Starch; 1 Nonstarchy Vegetable; 4 Protein, lean; 1 Fat

BROCCOLINI

Serves: 1 | Serving size: 1/2 cup

1/2 cup broccolini

1. Steam broccolini and serve alongside stew and noodles.

EXCHANGES / CHOICES
1 Nonstarchy Vegetable

Calories 30; Calories from Fat 0; Total Fat 0.0 g; Saturated Fat 0.0 g; Trans Fat 0.0 g; Cholesterol 0 mg; Sodium 20 mg; Potassium 220 mg; Total Carbohydrate 5 g; Dietary Fiber 1 g; Sugars 1 g; Protein 2 g; Phosphorus 45 mg

• • • • • • •

WHOLE-WHEAT NOODLES

Serves: 1 | Serving size: 1/2 cup

1/2 cup whole-wheat noodles

1. Cook noodles according to package directions. Pour stew over noodles and serve along with the broccolini.

EXCHANGES / CHOICES
1 1/2 Starch

Calories 100; Calories from Fat 5; Total Fat 0.5 g; Saturated Fat 0.1 g; Trans Fat 0.0 g; Cholesterol 0 mg; Sodium 5 mg; Potassium 35 mg; Total Carbohydrate 21 g; Dietary Fiber 2 g; Sugars 1 g; Protein 4 g; Phosphorus 70 mg

THAI SHRIMP SOUP

Serves: 6 | Serving size: 1 cup | Prep time: 5 minutes | Cook time: 25 minutes

This soup is typically served in Thailand. Every ingredient in this soup has a strong purpose that forms a massive explosion of flavor. You'll get heat, citrus, and herb flavors in every bite. You shouldn't have trouble finding lemongrass, but if you can't obtain it, just use the grated zest of one lemon in its place.

6 cups low-fat, reduced-sodium chicken broth (use the Chicken Stock recipe in Old Fashioned Chicken and Rice Soup, page 160)
3 stalks fresh lemongrass, lower part only, sliced diagonally into 3 pieces and slightly crushed
Zest of 1 lime
1 small serrano pepper, seeded and diced
4 ounces rice noodles
1 pound large peeled and deveined shrimp, tails removed
2 tablespoons fresh lime juice
4 scallions, white part only, minced
1/4 cup minced fresh cilantro
1 small red Thai chili pepper, minced

1. Add the broth, lemongrass, lime zest, and diced serrano pepper to a large saucepot over high heat. Bring to a boil, add the rice noodles, lower the heat, cover, and simmer for 20 minutes.
2. Strain the broth and return the broth the saucepot. Add in the shrimp and simmer on low heat for 3-5 minutes until shrimp are just cooked through. Stir in the lime juice.
3. Garnish each bowl with scallions, cilantro, and chili pepper.

CALORIES	CALORIES FROM FAT	TOTAL FAT	SATURATED FAT	TRANS FAT	CHOLESTEROL	SODIUM	POTASSIUM
150	5	0.5 g	0.1 g	0.0 g	90 mg	135 mg	450 mg
TOTAL CARBOHYDRATE	**DIETARY FIBER**	**SUGARS**	**PROTEIN**	**PHOSPHORUS**	**EXCHANGES/CHOICES:**		
20 g	1 g	1 g	15 g	200 mg	1 Starch; 1 Nonstarchy Vegetable; 1 Protein, lean		

FRESH SPINACH SALAD

Serves: 1 | Serving size: 1 1/2 cups

1 cup fresh spinach leaves
5 cherry tomatoes, halved
1/4 cup red onion, thinly sliced
1 teaspoon olive oil
1/2 teaspoon lemon juice

1. Combine spinach, tomatoes, and onion slices in a small bowl. Drizzle with olive oil and top with lemon juice.

EXCHANGES / CHOICES
2 Nonstarchy Vegetable

Calories 50; Calories from Fat 5; Total Fat 0.5 g; Saturated Fat 0.1 g; Trans Fat 0.0 g; Cholesterol 0 mg; Sodium 75 mg; Potassium 410 mg; Total Carbohydrate 12 g; Dietary Fiber 5 g; Sugars 4 g; Protein 2 g; Phosphorus 75 mg

• • • • • • •

MANDARIN ORANGES

Serves: 1 | Serving size: 1/2 cup

1/2 cup mandarin oranges

1. Serve mandarin oranges alongside soup and salad.

EXCHANGES / CHOICES
1 Fruit

Calories 45; Calories from Fat 0; Total Fat 0.0 g; Saturated Fat 0.0 g; Trans Fat 0.0 g; Cholesterol 0 mg; Sodium 5 mg; Potassium 170 mg; Total Carbohydrate 12 g; Dietary Fiber 1 g; Sugars 11 g; Protein 1 g; Phosphorus 10 mg

LEMON ASPARAGUS SOUP

Serves: 12 | Serving size: 1 cup | Prep time: 20 minutes | Cook time: 30 minutes

Asparagus has an assertive flavor, but it's nicely tempered in a soup. Potatoes and asparagus work well together and they make a perfect pair. When buying asparagus, settle on stalks that are medium in width. If the stalks are a little too thick-stemmed, peel them. Otherwise, the stems are quite tasty, so leave them in the soup. Although you can find asparagus year round, I'd wait until spring to make this, when asparagus are young and sweet.

- 1 tablespoon olive oil
- 1 small leek, bottom portion only, washed and chopped
- 1 medium onion, chopped
- 2 garlic cloves, minced
- 2 pounds asparagus, stems trimmed, sliced into 2-inch pieces
- 2 large russet potatoes, peeled and cubed
- 6 cups fat-free, low-sodium chicken broth
- 1 tablespoon lemon pepper seasoning
- 1/2 cup half and half
- grated zest of 1 fresh lemon
- 1/4 cup toasted chopped pistachio nuts

1. Heat the olive oil in a large saucepan over medium heat. Add the leek, onion, and garlic and sauté for about 7–9 minutes until vegetables are soft. Add in the asparagus, potatoes, and broth. Bring to a boil, lower the heat to medium and cook, covered, until potatoes are tender, about 15–17 minutes.
2. Ladle the soup into a food processor or blender and process until the soup is smooth, working in batches if necessary. Return the soup to the saucepan and add in the lemon pepper seasoning and half and half. Heat through for 1 minute.
3. Garnish each bowl with lemon zest and pistachio nuts.

CALORIES	CALORIES FROM FAT	TOTAL FAT	SATURATED FAT	TRANS FAT	CHOLESTEROL	SODIUM	POTASSIUM
110	30	3.5 g	1.1 g	0.0 g	5 mg	170 mg	510 mg

TOTAL CARBOHYDRATE	DIETARY FIBER	SUGARS	PROTEIN	PHOSPHORUS	EXCHANGES/CHOICES:
17 g	2 g	3 g	5 g	120 mg	1 Starch; 1 Nonstarchy Vegetable; 1/2 Fat

SEASONED BROILED FISH

Serves: 4 | Serving size: 4 ounces

2 teaspoons chipotle chili powder
1/2 teaspoon dried oregano leaves
1/2 teaspoon sweet paprika
1/4 teaspoon ground cumin
1/4 teaspoon freshly ground black pepper
1/4 teaspoon salt
1 pound fish filets, about 1 inch thick
1 tablespoon olive oil

1. Preheat the oven to broil. Line a broiler pan with nonstick foil. In a small ramekin, combine the chili powder, oregano, paprika, cumin, pepper, and salt.
2. Coat both sides of the fish lightly with the seasoning. Drizzle the fish with the olive oil.
3. Broil the fish about 5 minutes per side or until cooked through.

EXCHANGES / CHOICES
3 Protein, lean;
1 1/2 Fat

Calories 210; Calories from Fat 110; Total Fat 12.0 g; Saturated Fat 2.4 g; Trans Fat 0.0 g; Cholesterol 60 mg; Sodium 230 mg; Potassium 440 mg; Total Carbohydrate 1 g; Dietary Fiber 1 g; Sugars 0 g; Protein 22 g; Phosphorus 295 mg

GREEN BEANS

Serves: 1 | Serving size: 1/2 cup

1/2 cup green beans

1. Steam green beans and serve alongside soup and fish.

EXCHANGES / CHOICES
1 Nonstarchy Vegetable

Calories 20; Calories from Fat 0; Total Fat 0.0 g; Saturated Fat 0.0 g; Trans Fat 0.0 g; Cholesterol 0 mg; Sodium 0 mg; Potassium 90 mg; Total Carbohydrate 5 g; Dietary Fiber 2 g; Sugars 1 g; Protein 1 g; Phosphorus 20 mg

WALNUT CREAM SOUP TOPPING

Serves: 4 | Serving size: 1 tablespoon
Prep time: 5 minutes

To make any of the soups in this chapter extra special, a little dollop of this cream will do the trick. Substitute hazelnut or almond oil for the walnut and switch up the nuts to any of your favorite varieties.

2 tablespoons nonfat cream cheese, softened
1 tablespoon walnut oil
1 tablespoon finely chopped walnuts
Dash nutmeg

1. In a small bowl, mix all ingredients. Store in an airtight container in the refrigerator for up to 3 days

EXCHANGES / CHOICES
1 Fat

Calories 50; Calories from Fat 40; Total Fat 4.5 g; Saturated Fat 0.4 g; Trans Fat 0.0 g; Cholesterol 0 mg; Sodium 55 mg; Potassium 30 mg; Total Carbohydrate 1 g; Dietary Fiber 0 g; Sugars 0 g; Protein 1 g; Phosphorus 50 mg

CASHEW CREAM SOUP TOPPING

Serves: 16 | Serving size: 1 tablespoon
Prep time: 5 minutes

Here's a dairy-free topping for your soup that tastes like rich cream. The method is super simple, as the cashews just need to soak overnight and then be puréed the next day. Cashews are the best nuts for this, but almonds work as well. Make sure your nuts are raw, not roasted or salted.

1 cup raw cashews
Cold water to cover
1 teaspoon fresh lemon juice
1/4 teaspoon sea salt

1. Place the cashews in a bowl. Pour cold water over the cashews and set aside to soak overnight. Drain the cashews.
2. Add the cashews to a blender or food processor. Add fresh water just to cover the cashews by one inch. Add the lemon juice and salt. Purée until very smooth.

EXCHANGES / CHOICES
1 Fat

Calories 50; Calories from Fat 35; Total Fat 4.0 g; Saturated Fat 0.8 g; Trans Fat 0.0 g; Cholesterol 0 mg; Sodium 35 mg; Potassium 60 mg; Total Carbohydrate 3 g; Dietary Fiber 0 g; Sugars 1 g; Protein 2 g; Phosphorus 55 mg

Tuscan Bean Soup page 162

CHAPTER 8
Stir Fry

THE PRINCIPLES OF STIR FRY

Stir fry usually comes to mind as the perfect one-pot meal; however, many people think preparing a stir fry is a license to just throw everything that's in the refrigerator crisper bin into the pot! Really good stir fry follows a structure, to ensure your finished dish doesn't end up a watery mess. Before I give you the Master Stir Fry, let's take a look at equipment, choice of oil, level of heat, and more.

1. I recommend a wok. It can be a traditional round-bottomed wok or a flat-bottomed wok that's traditionally called a wok pan. Just make sure your wok of choice is deep. The sloping sides of a real wok are ideal to get vegetables nice and crisp. The issue with just a large pan without sloping sides is that the vegetables cook in only one layer, which produces excess water from all the steaming going on. Woks are inexpensive, and trust me, the results are worth it.
2. Choose an oil that can withstand high heat. I like peanut oil the most, but if you have an allergy to peanuts, I would recommend a plain vegetable oil. The oil doesn't necessarily have to contain a lot of flavor, as the ingredients will provide plenty of flavor on their own.
3. Make sure your heat is kept high. For the most part, the heat is kept high so the cooking time is quick. You'll produce less water when the ingredients are tossed about quickly on high heat.
4. Slice, dice, and chop your stir fry ingredients first, then bring everything over to the stove and begin cooking. The preparation may take a bit more time, but once you get the hang of the Master Recipe, you'll be able to get dinner on the table in no time!

THE MASTER CHICKEN STIR FRY

This first recipe is really a master recipe for the remaining stir fry recipes. The format is the same: a protein is stir fried first in a hot wok to develop a crust. Then aromatic herbs and spices, usually fresh, are stir fried quickly to perfume the entire pan. A few vegetables are added; do not add a mountain of vegetables. If you do, they will cook at different rates and will produce a watery stir fry. My rule is no more than four vegetables and no more than two colors. Then, the cooked protein is added back in, followed by a finishing sauce. In each of the stir fry recipes in this chapter, I'll add

a few different ingredients just to add variety to the dish. But once you get the hang of the framework, you'll learn to cook these without even looking at the recipe!

The sauce is a super-basic one. Use it for at least the first three recipes, or all ten recipes, so you don't have to reinvent the wheel. However, for the beef, pork, and shrimp stir fry dishes, the sauce is even more simplified, as these proteins are hearty enough on their own and need few enhancements.

Think of a stir fry in four components: a protein, seasoning herbs and spices, vegetables, and a sauce.

INDIAN STIR FRY

Indian flavors are bold and flavorful, and when you tire of the traditional Asian soy-based stir fry, you can turn to these for a change of pace. These versions rely more on ground spices and herbs and skip some of the steps found in the Master Recipe. I'd recommend learning the Master Recipe first before trying these versions.

MASTER CHICKEN STIR FRY

Serves: 5 | Serving size: 1 cup | Prep time: 15 minutes | Cook time: 12 minutes

1 pound boneless, skinless chicken breasts, cut into 1/2-inch × 1-inch strips
1 tablespoon lite soy sauce
1 tablespoon rice vinegar
2 teaspoons cornstarch or arrowroot

MASTER SAUCE

3/4 cup low-sodium, fat-free chicken broth
2 tablespoons hoisin sauce
1/2 tablespoon lite soy sauce
1 teaspoon chili purée with garlic
1 tablespoon cornstarch or arrowroot

VEGETABLES

1 tablespoon vegetable or peanut oil, divided use
3 garlic cloves, minced
1 tablespoon peeled, grated ginger
1 medium red pepper, cored, seeded, and thinly sliced
2 celery stalks, thinly sliced
1 cup broccoli florets
1/4 cup low-sodium, fat-free broth

1. In a medium-sized bowl, combine the chicken with the soy sauce, rice vinegar, and cornstarch. Set aside to marinate at room temperature for 15 minutes.
2. In another bowl, combine all the ingredients for the sauce. Set aside.
3. Heat half the vegetable oil in a large wok over high heat. When hot, turn the heat to medium high and add the chicken. Stir fry for 5 minutes or until the chicken is cooked through. (You do not need to continuously stir the chicken as you want the chicken to develop a crust and sear.) Remove the chicken from the wok to a plate and set aside.
4. Add the remaining oil to the wok. Add in the garlic and ginger and stir fry for 30 seconds. Add the red pepper, celery, and broccoli and stir fry for 30 seconds. Add the broth, cover, and steam 3 minutes.
5. Add the chicken and stir fry for 1 minute. Add in the sauce and cook for 1 minute, coating the chicken and vegetables with the sauce. Serve immediately.

CALORIES	CALORIES FROM FAT	TOTAL FAT	SATURATED FAT	TRANS FAT	CHOLESTEROL	SODIUM	POTASSIUM
180	45	5.0 g	1.1 g	0.0 g	55 mg	390 mg	400 mg

TOTAL CARBOHYDRATE	DIETARY FIBER	SUGARS	PROTEIN	PHOSPHORUS	EXCHANGES/CHOICES:
10 g	2 g	4 g	21 g	185 mg	1/2 Carbohydrate; 1 Nonstarchy Vegetable; 3 Protein, lean

BROWN RICE

Serves: 1 | Serving size: 1/2 cup

1/2 cup brown rice

1. Cook brown rice according to package directions and serve alongside stir fry and orange slices.

EXCHANGES / CHOICES
1 1/2 Starch

Calories 110; Calories from Fat 10; Total Fat 1.0 g; Saturated Fat 0.2 g; Trans Fat 0.0 g; Cholesterol 0 mg; Sodium 0 mg; Potassium 40 mg; Total Carbohydrate 22 g; Dietary Fiber 2 g; Sugars 0 g; Protein 3 g; Phosphorus 80 mg

. . . .

ORANGE

Serves: 1 | Serving size: 1 orange

1 small orange

1. Slice orange and serve alongside stir fry and brown rice.

EXCHANGES / CHOICES
1 Fruit

Calories 45; Calories from Fat 0; Total Fat 0.0 g; Saturated Fat 0.0 g; Trans Fat 0.0 g; Cholesterol 0 mg; Sodium 0 mg; Potassium 170 mg; Total Carbohydrate 11 g; Dietary Fiber 2 g; Sugars 9 g; Protein 1 g; Phosphorus 15 mg

CRISPY TOFU STIR FRY

Serves: 6 | Serving size: 1 cup | Prep time: 10 minutes | Freeze time: 24 hours | Cook time: 15 minutes

Unlike animal proteins, tofu is better when you rid it of its "mushy" characteristics. Please be aware that the first step in this recipe calls for freezing the tofu overnight. This process makes the tofu even firmer and more receptive to the flavors you will add to it.

- 14 ounces extra-firm tofu, cut in 3/4-inch slices, then cut into 2-inch triangles
- 2 tablespoons vegetable or peanut oil, divided use
- 1/2 teaspoon salt
- 1/2 teaspoon black pepper
- 1 tablespoon peeled, grated ginger
- 3 garlic cloves, minced
- 1 pound asparagus, peeled and cut diagonally into 2-inch lengths
- 3 ounces shiitake mushrooms, stemmed and caps cleaned, thinly sliced

MASTER SAUCE

- 3/4 cup low-sodium, fat-free chicken broth
- 2 tablespoons hoisin sauce
- 1/2 tablespoon lite soy sauce
- 1 teaspoon chili purée with garlic
- 1 tablespoon cornstarch or arrowroot

1. Freeze the tofu triangles, uncovered, on a cookie sheet overnight. In the morning, set the frozen tofu in the refrigerator to thaw. Before cooking, dry the tofu with paper towels to remove any excess surface moisture.
2. When ready to stir fry, heat 1 tablespoon of the oil in a large wok. Add the tofu, in batches, and season with salt and pepper. Turn the tofu every 3 minutes for a total cooking time of 10 minutes. Remove the tofu from the pan.
3. Heat the remaining oil in the wok. Add the ginger and garlic and stir fry for 30 seconds. Add the asparagus and mushrooms and stir fry for 3–4 minutes until asparagus is tender, but still bright green.
4. Combine all the Master Sauce ingredients in a bowl.
5. Add back the tofu and add the sauce and cook 1 minute, coating the tofu and vegetables with the sauce.

CALORIES	CALORIES FROM FAT	TOTAL FAT	SATURATED FAT	TRANS FAT	CHOLESTEROL	SODIUM	POTASSIUM
140	80	9.0 g	0.8 g	0.0 g	0 mg	380 mg	230 mg
TOTAL CARBOHYDRATE	**DIETARY FIBER**	**SUGARS**	**PROTEIN**	**PHOSPHORUS**	**EXCHANGES/CHOICES:**		
9 g	1 g	3 g	8 g	125 mg	1/2 Carbohydrate; 1 Nonstarchy Vegetable; 1 Protein, lean; 1 Fat		

BROWN RICE

Serves: 1 | Serving size: 1/2 cup

1/2 cup brown rice

1. Cook brown rice according to package directions and serve alongside stir fry and orange slices.

EXCHANGES / CHOICES
1 1/2 Starch

Calories 110; Calories from Fat 10; Total Fat 1.0 g; Saturated Fat 0.2 g; Trans Fat 0.0 g; Cholesterol 0 mg; Sodium 0 mg; Potassium 40 mg; Total Carbohydrate 22 g; Dietary Fiber 2 g; Sugars 0 g; Protein 3 g; Phosphorus 80 mg

• • • • • • •

ORANGE

Serves: 1 | Serving size: 1 orange

1 small orange

1. Slice orange and serve alongside stir fry and brown rice.

EXCHANGES / CHOICES
1 Fruit

Calories 45; Calories from Fat 0; Total Fat 0.0 g; Saturated Fat 0.0 g; Trans Fat 0.0 g; Cholesterol 0 mg; Sodium 0 mg; Potassium 170 mg; Total Carbohydrate 11 g; Dietary Fiber 2 g; Sugars 9 g; Protein 1 g; Phosphorus 15 mg

ALL VEGGIE STIR FRY

Serves: 5 | Serving size: 1 cup | Prep time: 15 minutes | Cook time: 15 minutes

I paired this with the Master Chicken Sear; however, any of the Master Proteins will also work. Go ahead and choose your favorite! Resist the temptation to use all the leftovers from your refrigerator crisper drawer. Keep it simple. Use no more than two colors of vegetables and no more than 3–4 vegetables total.

MASTER SAUCE

3/4 cup low-sodium, fat-free chicken broth
2 tablespoons hoisin sauce
1/2 tablespoon lite soy sauce
1 teaspoon chili purée with garlic
1 tablespoon cornstarch or arrowroot

2 large carrots, peeled and sliced on a diagonal 1/4-inch thick
2 teaspoons vegetable or peanut oil
3 garlic cloves, minced
1 tablespoon peeled, grated fresh ginger
2 large celery stalks, sliced on a diagonal 1/4-inch thick
2 cups trimmed snow peas

1. Prepare the Master Sauce in a bowl and set aside.
2. Bring a large pot of water to a boil. Add the carrots and cook 1 minute. Turn off the heat and let the carrots stand in the water for 2–3 minutes. Drain the carrots and set aside.
3. Heat the oil in a large wok or heavy skillet over medium-high heat. Add the garlic and ginger and stir fry for 30 seconds. Add the celery and stir fry for 1 minute. Add the snow peas and stir fry for 2 minutes. Add in the carrots and stir fry for 1 minute.
4. Add the Master Sauce to the pan and cook for 1 minute until sauce is thickened.

CALORIES	CALORIES FROM FAT	TOTAL FAT	SATURATED FAT	TRANS FAT	CHOLESTEROL	SODIUM	POTASSIUM
70	20	2.0 g	0.4 g	0.0 g	0 mg	250 mg	260 mg
TOTAL CARBOHYDRATE	**DIETARY FIBER**	**SUGARS**	**PROTEIN**	**PHOSPHORUS**	**EXCHANGES/CHOICES:**		
11 g	2 g	5 g	2 g	45 mg	1/2 Carbohydrate; 1 Nonstarchy Vegetable		

MASTER CHICKEN SEAR

Serves: 4 | Serving size: 1/2 breast or thigh

2 boneless, skinless chicken breasts or 2 boneless, skinless chicken thighs
1/8 teaspoon kosher salt
1/4 teaspoon ground black pepper
1 1/2 tablespoons olive or canola oil

1. Season chicken breasts or chicken thighs with salt and black pepper.
2. In a 12–14-inch heavy skillet, preferably cast iron or stainless (NOT nonstick) heat oil over medium-high heat.
3. Add the chicken and sear until well browned on both sides, about 3-4 minutes per side for the breasts, or 2–3 minutes for the thighs.
4. Transfer the chicken to a plate and tent with foil.
5. Return the chicken and accumulated juices to the skillet and simmer gently until cooked through, about 4–5 minutes.

TO TEST: Chicken should feel firm to the touch. Using closed tongs, press on the center of the chicken. It should feel firm. Alternatively, you may make a very small incision in the center of the meat and check to be sure the meat is cooked through with no traces of pink.

EXCHANGES / CHOICES
3 Protein, lean;
1 Fat

Calories 180; Calories from Fat 90; Total Fat 10.0 g; Saturated Fat 2.0 g; Trans Fat 0.0 g; Cholesterol 85 mg; Sodium 120 mg; Potassium 200 mg; Total Carbohydrate 0 g; Dietary Fiber 0 g; Sugars 0 g; Protein 21 g; Phosphorus 170 mg

This recipe also in Master Proteins page 37

PEACHES

Serves: 1 | Serving size: 1/2 cup

1/2 cup sliced peaches

1. Serve peaches alongside stir fry and chicken.

EXCHANGES / CHOICES
1/2 Fruit

Calories 30; Calories from Fat 0; Total Fat 0.0 g; Saturated Fat 0.0 g; Trans Fat 0.0 g; Cholesterol 0 mg; Sodium 0 mg; Potassium 150 mg; Total Carbohydrate 7 g; Dietary Fiber 1 g; Sugars 6 g; Protein 1 g; Phosphorus 15 mg

BEEF STIR FRY WITH ONIONS

Serves: 6 | Serving size: 1 cup | Prep time: 20 minutes | Cook time: 15 minutes

- 1 pound flank steak, partially frozen, thinly sliced across the grain into 1/4-inch slices
- 2 tablespoons lite soy sauce
- 1 tablespoon rice vinegar
- 2 teaspoons arrowroot or cornstarch
- 1 tablespoon vegetable or peanut oil, divided use
- 2 garlic cloves, minced
- 1 tablespoon peeled, fresh grated ginger
- 2 scallions, finely minced
- 1 large yellow onion, halved, peeled and sliced in 1/2-inch pieces
- 1 1/2 cups broccoli florets
- 1/3 cup low-fat, reduced-sodium chicken broth
- 1 tablespoon hoisin or oyster sauce

1. In a medium-sized bowl, combine the beef, soy sauce, rice vinegar, and arrowroot and mix well. Set aside to marinate for 15 minutes at room temperature.
2. Heat 2 teaspoons of the oil in a large wok or heavy skillet over medium-high heat. Add the beef and stir fry for 2 minutes. Remove the beef from the wok and set aside.
3. Add the remaining oil to the pan. Add the garlic, ginger, and scallions. Stir fry for 20 seconds. Add in the onions and stir fry for 5–6 minutes until onions are soft. Add in the broccoli, cover, and steam for 2 minutes.
4. Add the broth and hoisin to the pan and cook, uncovered, for 2 minutes until some of the liquid evaporates. Add back the beef and cook 1 minute.

CALORIES	CALORIES FROM FAT	TOTAL FAT	SATURATED FAT	TRANS FAT	CHOLESTEROL	SODIUM	POTASSIUM
160	50	6.0 g	1.9 g	0.0 g	40 mg	300 mg	350 mg

TOTAL CARBOHYDRATE	DIETARY FIBER	SUGARS	PROTEIN	PHOSPHORUS	EXCHANGES/CHOICES:
8 g	1 g	3 g	17 g	150 mg	1 Nonstarchy Vegetable; 2 Protein, lean; 1 Fat

GARDEN SALAD WITH BALSAMIC VINAIGRETTE

Serves: 8 | Serving size: 1 cup
Prep time: 7 minutes | Cook time: 4 minutes

3/4 cup walnuts
2 tablespoons sugar

DRESSING
1/4 cup balsamic vinegar
1 garlic clove, minced
1 teaspoon coarse Dijon mustard
1 teaspoon honey or sugar
3 tablespoons olive oil
1/4 teaspoon sea salt
1/4 teaspoon freshly ground black pepper

SALAD
5 cups mixed greens
1 cup halved cherry tomatoes
2 large carrots, peeled and grated
1/2 medium red onion, thinly sliced

1. In a small sauté pan or skillet over medium-high heat, toss the walnuts with the sugar for 3 to 4 minutes or until the sugar melts and caramelizes. Watch that the nuts do not burn. Remove the nuts from the pan and let cool.
2. In a large bowl, combine dressing ingredients and whisk well.
3. Add the salad ingredients to the dressing and quickly toss together. Serve on individual plates, top with the nuts.

Exchanges / Choices
1/2 Carbohydrate; 1 Nonstarchy Vegetable; 2 1/2 Fat

Calories 160; Calories from Fat 120; Total Fat 13.0 g; Saturated Fat 1.4 g; Trans Fat 0.0 g; Cholesterol 0 mg; Sodium 105 mg; Potassium 250 mg; Total Carbohydrate 11 g; Dietary Fiber 2 g; Sugars 7 g; Protein 3 g; Phosphorus 65 mg

This recipe also in Salads page 150

BROWN RICE

Serves: 1 | Serving size: 1/2 cup

1/2 cup brown rice

1. Cook brown rice according to package directions and serve alongside stir fry and salad.

EXCHANGES / CHOICES
1 1/2 Starch

Calories 110; Calories from Fat 10; Total Fat 1.0 g; Saturated Fat 0.2 g; Trans Fat 0.0 g; Cholesterol 0 mg; Sodium 0 mg; Potassium 40 mg; Total Carbohydrate 22 g; Dietary Fiber 2 g; Sugars 0 g; Protein 3 g; Phosphorus 80 mg

PORK STIR FRY

Serves: 6 | Serving size: 1 cup | Prep time: 10 minutes + freezing time | Cook time: 7 minutes

Pork and citrus juices have a natural affinity for each other and the tangy flavor really complements the slightly salty flavor of the soy sauce. I'm going to skip marinating the pork; this stir fry, while rich and flavorful, is also lighter than the chicken and beef versions, which makes it perfect for serving during the warmer months.

- 1 tablespoon peanut oil, divided use
- 1 pound lean boneless pork tenderloin, partially frozen, sliced into thin strips
- 2 garlic cloves, minced
- 1 tablespoon peeled and finely grated fresh ginger
- 2 scallions, thinly sliced
- 2 cups fresh snow peas, trimmed
- 1/4 cup low-fat, reduced-sodium chicken broth
- Juice of 1/2 large lime
- 2 tablespoons lite soy sauce

1. Heat 2 teaspoons of the peanut oil in a wok over high heat. Add the pork and stir fry for about 3–4 minutes until browned. Remove the pork with a slotted spoon to a plate and set aside.
2. Add the remaining oil to the pan and add the garlic, ginger, and scallions. Stir fry for 30 seconds. Add the snow peas and stir fry for 30 seconds. Add the broth and cover for 1 minute.
3. Add back the pork and stir fry 30 seconds. Add in the lime juice and soy sauce and serve.

CALORIES	CALORIES FROM FAT	TOTAL FAT	SATURATED FAT	TRANS FAT	CHOLESTEROL	SODIUM	POTASSIUM
180	50	6.0 g	1.6 g	0.0 g	60 mg	360 mg	480 mg
TOTAL CARBOHYDRATE	**DIETARY FIBER**	**SUGARS**	**PROTEIN**	**PHOSPHORUS**	**EXCHANGES/CHOICES:**		
5 g	1 g	2 g	24 g	230 mg	1 Nonstarchy Vegetable; 3 Protein, lean		

BROWN RICE

Serves: 1 | Serving size: 1/2 cup

1/2 cup brown rice

1. Cook brown rice according to package directions and serve alongside stir fry and carrots.

EXCHANGES / CHOICES
1 1/2 Starch

Calories 110; Calories from Fat 10; Total Fat 1.0 g; Saturated Fat 0.2 g; Trans Fat 0.0 g; Cholesterol 0 mg; Sodium 0 mg; Potassium 40 mg; Total Carbohydrate 22 g; Dietary Fiber 2 g; Sugars 0 g; Protein 3 g; Phosphorus 80 mg

• • • • • • •

CARROTS

Serves: 1 | Serving size: 1/2 cup

1/2 cup carrots

1. Steam carrots and serve alongside brown rice and stir fry.

EXCHANGES / CHOICES
1 Nonstarchy Vegetable

Calories 25; Calories from Fat 0; Total Fat 0.0 g; Saturated Fat 0.0 g; Trans Fat 0.0 g; Cholesterol 0 mg; Sodium 45 mg; Potassium 180 mg; Total Carbohydrate 6 g; Dietary Fiber 2 g; Sugars 3 g; Protein 1 g; Phosphorus 25 mg

SHRIMP STIR FRY

Serves: 6 | Serving size: 1 cup | Prep time: 15 minutes | Cook time: 5 minutes

Shrimp stir fry begs for a little heat, so I'm going to add chili paste with garlic in this one. The Master Marinade (page 184) works well for the shrimp as they need a little moisture, so they don't become hard really fast on high heat. I'll use the same seasoning vegetables, although I'll cut down on the amount of ginger used, so as not to overwhelm the flavor.

SHRIMP

1 pound extra-large shrimp, peeled and deveined

2 tablespoons lite soy sauce

1 tablespoon rice vinegar

2 teaspoons cornstarch or arrowroot

1 tablespoon peanut oil, divided use

VEGETABLES

2 garlic cloves, minced

2 teaspoons peeled and finely grated ginger

2 scallions, sliced

1 1/2 pounds bok choy, leaves and stems chopped into 1-inch pieces

1 teaspoon chili paste with garlic

1 teaspoon dark sesame oil

1 teaspoon lite soy sauce

1. Add the shrimp to a large bowl with the soy sauce, rice vinegar, and cornstarch and mix well. Let the shrimp marinate for 15 minutes at room temperature.
2. Heat 2 teaspoons of the peanut oil in a large wok or heavy skillet over medium-high heat. Add the shrimp and stir fry for 2–3 minutes or until shrimp is almost cooked through. Remove the shrimp from the pan and set aside.
3. Add the remaining peanut oil to the pan. Add in the garlic, ginger, and scallions and stir fry for 30 seconds. Add in the bok choy and stir fry for 2 minutes until the cabbage wilts.
4. Add back the shrimp and drizzle with the chili paste, sesame oil, and soy sauce. Serve immediately.

CALORIES	CALORIES FROM FAT	TOTAL FAT	SATURATED FAT	TRANS FAT	CHOLESTEROL	SODIUM	POTASSIUM
100	30	3.5 g	0.5 g	0.0 g	80 mg	330 mg	400 mg
TOTAL CARBOHYDRATE	**DIETARY FIBER**	**SUGARS**	**PROTEIN**	**PHOSPHORUS**	**EXCHANGES/CHOICES:**		
5 g	1 g	2 g	12 g	150 mg	1 Nonstarchy Vegetable; 1 Protein, lean; 1/2 Fat		

WHOLE-WHEAT COUSCOUS

Serves: 1 | Serving size: 1/2 cup

1/2 cup whole-wheat couscous

1. Cook couscous according to package directions. Serve alongside stir fry and broccoli.

EXCHANGES / CHOICES
1 Starch

Calories 90; Calories from Fat 5; Total Fat 0.5 g; Saturated Fat 0.0 g; Trans Fat 0.0 g; Cholesterol 0 mg; Sodium 0 mg; Potassium 45 mg; Total Carbohydrate 19 g; Dietary Fiber 3 g; Sugars 0 g; Protein 3 g; Phosphorus 20 mg

• • • • • • •

BROCCOLI WITH RED PEPPER

Serves: 1 | Serving size: 1/2 cup

1/4 cup broccoli
1/4 cup chopped red pepper

1. Steam broccoli and red pepper together for three minutes or until tender.

EXCHANGES / CHOICES
1 Nonstarchy Vegetable

Calories 30; Calories from Fat 5; Total Fat 0.5 g; Saturated Fat 0.1 g; Trans Fat 0.0 g; Cholesterol 0 mg; Sodium 30 mg; Potassium 250 mg; Total Carbohydrate 6 g; Dietary Fiber 3 g; Sugars 1 g; Protein 2 g; Phosphorus 55 mg

INDIAN SALMON STIR FRY

Serves: 5 | Serving size: 1 cup | Prep time: 15 minutes | Cook time: 15 minutes

In this stir fry, I give you alternative flavors instead of the traditional Asian ones. Asian flavors are bold and flavorful, but turn to this recipe for a change of pace.

- 1 tablespoon vegetable oil, divided use
- 2 teaspoons cumin seeds
- 1 teaspoon brown mustard seeds
- 1/2 teaspoon ground turmeric
- 1 pound skinless salmon filet, cut into 1-inch cubes
- 1 large onion, halved, peeled, and sliced into 1/2-inch slices
- 2 garlic cloves, minced
- 1 tablespoon peeled, grated fresh ginger
- 1–2 finely minced hot green chili peppers (optional)
- 1 cup halved cherry tomatoes

1. Heat 2 teaspoons of the oil in a wok or heavy skillet over medium-high heat. Add the cumin, mustard seeds, and turmeric and stir fry for 1 minute until seeds begin to pop. Add the salmon and stir fry quickly but gently for about 3–4 minutes. Remove the salmon from the pan and set aside.
2. Add the remaining oil to the pan. Lower the heat to medium. Add the onion and stir fry for about 6–7 minutes until onions are soft. Add in the garlic, ginger, and chili pepper and stir fry for 1 minute. Add in the cherry tomatoes and stir fry for 1–2 minutes until cherry tomatoes just begin to soften. Add back the salmon and stir fry very gently for 1 minute.

CALORIES	CALORIES FROM FAT	TOTAL FAT	SATURATED FAT	TRANS FAT	CHOLESTEROL	SODIUM	POTASSIUM
200	90	10.0 g	1.7 g	0.0 g	50 mg	65 mg	540 mg
TOTAL CARBOHYDRATE	**DIETARY FIBER**	**SUGARS**	**PROTEIN**	**PHOSPHORUS**	**EXCHANGES/CHOICES:**		
8 g	2 g	3 g	19 g	270 mg	2 Nonstarchy Vegetable; 2 Protein, lean; 1 1/2 Fat		

BROWN RICE

Serves: 1 | Serving size: 1/2 cup

1/2 cup brown rice

1. Cook brown rice according to package directions and serve alongside stir fry and spinach.

EXCHANGES / CHOICES
1 1/2 Starch

Calories 110; Calories from Fat 10; Total Fat 1.0 g; Saturated Fat 0.2 g; Trans Fat 0.0 g; Cholesterol 0 mg; Sodium 0 mg; Potassium 40 mg; Total Carbohydrate 22 g; Dietary Fiber 2 g; Sugars 0 g; Protein 3 g; Phosphorus 80 mg

. . . .

SPINACH

Serves: 1 | Serving size: 1/2 cup

1/2 cup spinach

1. Steam spinach and serve alongside stir fry and brown rice.

EXCHANGES / CHOICES
1 Nonstarchy Vegetable

Calories 20; Calories from Fat 0; Total Fat 0.0 g; Saturated Fat 0.0 g; Trans Fat 0.0 g; Cholesterol 0 mg; Sodium 65 mg; Potassium 420 mg; Total Carbohydrate 3 g; Dietary Fiber 2 g; Sugars 0 g; Protein 3 g; Phosphorus 50 mg

CHICKPEA STIR FRY

Serves: 5 | Serving size: 1 cup | Prep time: 5 minutes | Cook time: 12 minutes

My favorite Indian spice is garam masala, which is a blend of five spices: peppercorns, cinnamon, turmeric, cloves, and cumin. Think of it as your all-purpose seasoning for Indian dishes. Chickpeas are the primary bean used in Indian cooking, but this can be made with lentils, another Indian favorite.

- 1 tablespoon vegetable oil
- 1 medium onion, halved, peeled and cut into 1/2-inch slices
- 2 garlic cloves, minced
- 1 tablespoon peeled, grated fresh ginger
- 1/2 teaspoon ground cumin
- 1/2 teaspoon ground turmeric
- 1/2 teaspoon ground cardamom
- 1/2 teaspoon garam masala
- 1/4 teaspoon sea salt
- 1/4 teaspoon freshly ground black pepper
- 2 (15-ounce) cans chickpeas, drained and rinsed
- 3 cups baby spinach
- 2 tablespoons water
- Juice of 1/2 lemon

1. Heat the oil in a large wok or heavy skillet over medium heat. Add the onions and stir fry for 6–7 minutes until onions are soft. Add in the garlic and ginger. Stir fry for 1 minute. Add in the cumin, turmeric, cardamom, garam masala, salt, and pepper. Stir fry for 30 seconds.
2. Add the chickpeas and stir fry for 2 minutes. Add in the spinach and water, cover the pan and let steam for 1–2 minutes until spinach is just wilted. Add the lemon juice, stir gently, and serve.

CALORIES	CALORIES FROM FAT	TOTAL FAT	SATURATED FAT	TRANS FAT	CHOLESTEROL	SODIUM	POTASSIUM
210	45	5.0 g	0.5 g	0.0 g	0 mg	300 mg	460 mg
TOTAL CARBOHYDRATE	**DIETARY FIBER**	**SUGARS**	**PROTEIN**	**PHOSPHORUS**	**EXCHANGES/CHOICES:**		
32 g	9 g	7 g	10 g	190 mg	1 1/2 Starch; 1 Nonstarchy Vegetable; 1 Protein, lean; 1/2 Fat		

BLUEBERRIES

Serves: 1 | Serving size: 1/2 cup

1/2 cup blueberries

1. Serve blueberries alongside stir fry.

EXCHANGES / CHOICES
1/2 Fruit

Calories 25; Calories from Fat 0; Total Fat 0.0 g; Saturated Fat 0.0 g; Trans Fat 0.0 g; Cholesterol 0 mg; Sodium 0 mg; Potassium 35 mg; Total Carbohydrate 7 g; Dietary Fiber 1 g; Sugars 5 g; Protein 0 g; Phosphorus 5 mg

TEMPEH AND SUGAR SNAP PEA STIR FRY

Serves: 6 | Serving size: 1 cup | Prep time: 15 minutes | Marinate time: 1 hour | Cook time: 13 minutes

Tempeh is a fermented soy product that's meatier than tofu. Tempeh holds its shape very well and tastes more like meat than tofu does. Tempeh is sold in the refrigerated case in your market. Keep it no longer than one week for best freshness. I've marinated the tempeh first to give it much more flavor.

- 10 ounces tempeh, cut into 1-inch pieces
- 2 tablespoons good-quality balsamic vinegar
- 1 1/2 tablespoons garlic-flavored olive oil, divided use
- 1/4–1/2 teaspoon red pepper flakes
- 1/4 teaspoon sea salt
- 1/4 teaspoon freshly ground black pepper
- 1 small onion, halved and thinly sliced
- 2 cloves garlic, finely minced
- 1 red bell pepper, cored, seeded, and thinly sliced
- 2 cups trimmed fresh sugar snap or snow peas
- 2 tablespoons low-sodium vegetable broth

1. In a medium bowl, combine the tempeh, balsamic vinegar, 2 teaspoons of the garlic-flavored oil, red pepper flakes, salt, and black pepper. Let the mixture stand for 1 hour at room temperature.
2. Heat the remaining oil in a large skillet or wok over medium-high heat. Add the tempeh and stir fry for 3–4 minutes or until golden brown. Remove the tempeh from the pan and set aside. Add the onion and minced garlic and stir fry for 3 minutes. Add the red pepper and stir fry for 3 minutes. Add the sugar snap peas and vegetable broth and cover. Steam for 3 minutes just until the peas turn bright green. Add back the tempeh and gently stir.

CALORIES	CALORIES FROM FAT	TOTAL FAT	SATURATED FAT	TRANS FAT	CHOLESTEROL	SODIUM	POTASSIUM
160	80	9.0 g	1.5 g	0.0 g	0 mg	105 mg	320 mg

TOTAL CARBOHYDRATE	DIETARY FIBER	SUGARS	PROTEIN	PHOSPHORUS	EXCHANGES/CHOICES:
11 g	2 g	12 g	10 g	155 mg	1/2 Carbohydrate; 1 Nonstarchy Vegetable; 1 Protein, lean; 1 Fat

BROWN RICE

Serves: 1 | Serving size: 1/2 cup

1/2 cup brown rice

1. Cook brown rice according to package directions and serve alongside stir fry and orange slices.

EXCHANGES / CHOICES
1 1/2 Starch

Calories 110; Calories from Fat 10; Total Fat 1.0 g; Saturated Fat 0.2 g; Trans Fat 0.0 g; Cholesterol 0 mg; Sodium 0 mg; Potassium 40 mg; Total Carbohydrate 22 g; Dietary Fiber 2 g; Sugars 0 g; Protein 3 g; Phosphorus 80 mg

. . . .

ORANGE

Serves: 1 | Serving size: 1 orange

1 small orange

1. Slice orange and serve alongside stir fry and brown rice.

EXCHANGES / CHOICES
1 Fruit

Calories 45; Calories from Fat 0; Total Fat 0.0 g; Saturated Fat 0.0 g; Trans Fat 0.0 g; Cholesterol 0 mg; Sodium 0 mg; Potassium 170 mg; Total Carbohydrate 11 g; Dietary Fiber 2 g; Sugars 9 g; Protein 1 g; Phosphorus 15 mg

SAUSAGE STIR FRY

Serves: 6 | Serving size: 1 cup | Prep time: 10 minutes | Cook time: 14 minutes

In this stir fry, I use lean turkey sausage as the main protein and combine it with multicolored peppers. This stir fry is reminiscent of the classic sausage and peppers but with a whole lot less fat and calories. Try to buy a zesty turkey sausage for great flavor. I also spiced this up a bit with the addition of red pepper flakes.

- 1 tablespoon vegetable oil, divided use
- 10 ounces turkey sausage (preferably Italian flavored), cut into 1/2-inch slices
- 3 garlic cloves, minced
- 1 small red onion, halved and thinly sliced
- 2 teaspoons Italian seasoning
- 1/4 teaspoon red pepper flakes
- 1 small red bell pepper, cored, seeded, and thinly sliced
- 1 small yellow pepper, cored, seeded, and thinly sliced
- 1 small green pepper, cored, seeded, and thinly sliced
- 1 (14.5-ounce) can diced canned tomatoes, drained
- Pinch allspice

1. Heat half the oil in a large wok or heavy skillet over medium-high heat. Add the sausage and stir fry for 4 minutes until sausage is browned. Remove the sausage from the pan and set aside.
2. Add the remaining oil to the pan and add the garlic and onions and stir fry for 3 minutes. Add in the Italian seasoning, red pepper flakes, and all the peppers. Stir fry for 4 minutes until peppers soften. Add in the tomatoes and allspice, lower the heat and simmer, uncovered, for 3 minutes. Add back the sausage and stir gently.

CALORIES	CALORIES FROM FAT	TOTAL FAT	SATURATED FAT	TRANS FAT	CHOLESTEROL	SODIUM	POTASSIUM
130	60	7.0 g	1.3 g	0.2 g	35 mg	290 mg	320 mg

TOTAL CARBOHYDRATE	DIETARY FIBER	SUGARS	PROTEIN	PHOSPHORUS	EXCHANGES/CHOICES:
9 g	2 g	3 g	9 g	110 mg	2 Nonstarchy Vegetable; 1 Protein, lean; 1 Fat

WHOLE-WHEAT NOODLES

Serves: 1 | Serving size: 1/2 cup

1/2 whole-wheat noodles

1. Cook pasta according to package directions. Serve alongside stir fry and salad.

EXCHANGES / CHOICES
1 1/2 Starch

Calories 100; Calories from Fat 5; Total Fat 0.5 g; Saturated Fat 0.1 g; Trans Fat 0.0 g; Cholesterol 0 mg; Sodium 5 mg; Potassium 35 mg; Total Carbohydrate 21 g; Dietary Fiber 2 g; Sugars 1 g; Protein 4 g; Phosphorus 70 mg

• • • • • • •

FRESH SPINACH SALAD

Serves: 1 | Serving size: 1 1/2 cups

1 cup fresh spinach leaves
5 cherry tomatoes, halved
1/4 cup red onion, thinly sliced
1 teaspoon olive oil
1/2 teaspoon lemon juice

1. Combine spinach, tomatoes, and onion slices in a small bowl. Drizzle with olive oil and top with lemon juice.

EXCHANGES / CHOICES
1 Nonstarchy Vegetable; 1 Fat

Calories 70; Calories from Fat 45; Total Fat 5.0 g; Saturated Fat 0.7 g; Trans Fat 0.0 g; Cholesterol 0 mg; Sodium 25 mg; Potassium 360 mg; Total Carbohydrate 7 g; Dietary Fiber 2 g; Sugars 3 g; Protein 2 g; Phosphorus 40 mg

CHAPTER 9

Tacos

THE PRINCIPLES OF TACO MAKING

Whether it's rolled or folded, the taco is the epitome of the perfect meal—lean protein, smart carbohydrates, and healthy fats all stuffed together as one. While there are endless varieties of tacos and several methods to put a taco together, here are my basic principles.

THE TORTILLA

Tortillas were born of necessity! Mexicans created masa, a moist dough made from ground lime-soaked corn kernels. The masa was shaped into discs and toasted. The result was a good-tasting, portable tortilla. I opt for using corn tortillas as they are healthier than tortillas made from white flour. They are also smaller, so we can keep the calories and carbohydrates under control.

I give instructions in every taco recipe to toast the tortilla in an ungreased skillet. I find this gives the tortilla a nice flavor and the method is quick. If you want to increase the volume of any recipe and use more tortillas, stack them in foil and heat at 350°F for about 15 minutes. Be sure not to keep heating a tortilla longer than necessary or it will become hard and brittle.

There are very good tortillas on the market these days. You can even freeze them for later use. They will last a few months.

SEASONING MIX

I've repeated the same seasoning mix throughout most of the recipes. This way, you can make up a batch of the mix anytime and you'll always have that part of the recipe ready when you are set to make tacos. There is absolutely no need to purchase premixed seasonings. They are often loaded with unnecessary sodium. My basic mix is chili powder, oregano, paprika, cumin, salt, and pepper. The key to a really great-tasting taco is to not overpower the flavor with too many seasonings.

Be sure to use ground spices that aren't more than a year old for best results. You can make a big batch of the seasoning mix, place in a freezer bag and store in the freezer. You can keep the mix for up to a year without sacrificing too much flavor.

A few of the seasoning mixes in this chapter call for chipotle chili powder. This type of chili powder is slightly smoky, yet has a pleasant fruity undertone. If you can't find it, regular

chili powder is fine. If you could grind your own cumin from cumin seeds, all the better. Simply add the cumin seeds to a coffee or spice grinder and grind to a powder. Cumin in absolutely heavenly ground by your own hand! Choose either sweet paprika or smoked. Always use freshly ground black pepper.

THE SAUCE

For the first three recipes—beef, chicken, and pork tacos—I created a gently spiced tomato-onion sauce, which is an excellent complement to these lean proteins. Using fresh tomatoes and chiles as a base, these sauces can be made ahead of time and kept in the refrigerator for a week or frozen for up to 6 months. I used mild Anaheim chiles for both the beef and chicken tacos, but switched it up and used jalapeños for the pork tacos. Feel free to use any fresh chiles you like. If you wish to use dried chiles, just soak them for 10 minutes in very hot water to rehydrate, and then use as you would fresh chiles.

The seasonings of ginger, cloves, and cinnamon may at first seem odd in a sauce, but they really complement the spices in the seasoning mix quite well, so don't omit them.

This sauce is very versatile and can be used beyond taco making. Simmer whole breasts of chicken, lean pork loin chops, or beef filet in the sauce for a fantastic main meal.

Some of the other tacos are actually better off without an actual sauce. In these cases, you will find the main protein is just lightly tossed in seasonings and then quickly cooked.

GARNISHES

Many would argue that the garnishes are what makes a taco. I think all a good taco needs is a sturdy protein coated with great spices and a fresh tortilla with clean and simple garnishes.

So I just offer up lettuce, tomatoes, and some sour cream for the most part. For some of these recipes, I also suggest a good salsa or cabbage in place of the lettuce. At the end of this chapter, there are two great recipes for homemade salsas that are more robust than anything commercially prepared.

BASIC BEEF TACOS

Serves: 8 | Serving size: 1 taco (sauce yields 5 cups) | Prep time: 20 minutes | Cook time: 1 hour 20 minutes

For beef tacos, I use lean ground beef, as it's simple to cook and easy to eat. Feel free to use thin slices of lean beef, such as sirloin or top round instead. Partially freeze the meat, and then slice it very thin and sauté with the onions and peppers. When selecting Anaheim chilies, look for bright shiny skins with good color that feel heavy for their size.

SAUCE

- 3 pounds fresh tomatoes, cored and quartered
- 2 Anaheim chilies, stemmed and seeded
- 1 large onion, quartered
- 1 garlic clove
- 1 1/4 cups apple cider vinegar
- 2 tablespoons sugar
- 1/2 teaspoon kosher salt
- 1/4 teaspoon ground cinnamon
- 1/4 teaspoon ground cloves
- 1/4 teaspoon ground ginger

MEAT MIXTURE

- 1 pound lean ground beef
- 1 large onion, chopped
- 1 green or red bell pepper, cored, seeded, and diced
- 2 garlic cloves, finely minced

SEASONING MIX

- 1 1/2 teaspoons hot or mild chili powder
- 1/2 teaspoon dried oregano leaves
- 1/2 teaspoon sweet paprika
- 1/4 teaspoon ground cumin
- 1/4 teaspoon freshly ground black pepper

8 small corn tortillas

GARNISH

- 1 cup shredded romaine lettuce
- 1/2 cup shredded reduced-fat cheddar cheese
- 3 medium tomatoes, cored and diced
- 1/2 cup commercial salsa
- 1/2 cup plain nonfat yogurt or fat-free sour cream

1. Add the tomatoes, chiles, onion, and garlic to a blender and puree. Add the puree to a saucepan and add in the remaining sauce ingredients. Bring to a boil. Lower the heat and simmer for 1 hour until thick.
2. Prepare the beef mixture. In a large 12-inch skillet, cook the beef over medium heat for about 5–6 minutes until cooked through. Remove the beef from the skillet to a plate with a slotted spoon and set aside.
3. Add the onion, pepper, and garlic to the skillet and sauté for 5–6 minutes until the onions are soft.

CALORIES	CALORIES FROM FAT	TOTAL FAT	SATURATED FAT	TRANS FAT	CHOLESTEROL	SODIUM	POTASSIUM
210	50	6.0 g	2.4 g	0.2 g	40 mg	220 mg	630 mg

TOTAL CARBOHYDRATE	DIETARY FIBER	SUGARS	PROTEIN	PHOSPHORUS	EXCHANGES/CHOICES:
24 g	4 g	7 g	16 g	275 mg	1 Starch; 2 Nonstarchy Vegetable; 1 Protein, lean; 1 Fat

4. Add back the beef. Combine the ingredients for the seasoning mix and add to the beef and sauté for 1 minute. Add about 1 cup of the chile sauce to the meat (reserve the remaining sauce for another use) and simmer on low heat for 5 minutes.
5. While the sauce simmers, add a corn tortilla to an ungreased skillet and cook over medium-high heat for 30 seconds per side. Keep warm.
6. To serve, spoon the beef mixture into a warmed corn tortilla. Top with your choice of garnishes.

ZUCCHINI

Serves: 1 | Serving size: 1/2 cup

1/2 cup zucchini

1. Steam zucchini and serve alongside taco and apple.

EXCHANGES / CHOICES
Free food

Calories 15; Calories from Fat 5; Total Fat 0.5 g; Saturated Fat 0.1 g; Trans Fat 0.0 g; Cholesterol 0 mg; Sodium 0 mg; Potassium 240 mg; Total Carbohydrate 2 g; Dietary Fiber 1 g; Sugars 2 g; Protein 1 g; Phosphorus 35 mg

• • • • • • •

APPLE

Serves: 1 | Serving size: 1 apple

1 small apple

1. Slice apple and serve alongside tacos and zucchini.

EXCHANGES / CHOICES
1 Fruit

Calories 50; Calories from Fat 0; Total Fat 0.0 g; Saturated Fat 0.0 g; Trans Fat 0.0 g; Cholesterol 0 mg; Sodium 0 mg; Potassium 110 mg; Total Carbohydrate 14 g; Dietary Fiber 3 g; Sugars 11 g; Protein 0 g; Phosphorus 10 mg

CHICKEN TACOS

Serves: 8 | Serving size: 1 taco | Prep time: 20 minutes + marinate time | Cook time: 1 hour 30 minutes

I chose chicken thighs for this taco filling, as the spicy chile sauce pairs better with it than chicken breasts. Feel free to use chicken breasts if you prefer. The difference in the method between the Basic Beef Tacos and these Chicken Tacos is that the chicken will marinate in the spice mixture. Chicken is blander in taste than beef, and it benefits greatly from a nice soak in a lime juice–laced spice blend. You can also prepare just the chicken filling (leave out the tortillas) and serve it with a few vegetables on the side for a nice lean, but definitely tasty, meal.

CHILE SAUCE

3 pounds fresh tomatoes, cored and quartered
2 Anaheim chilies, stemmed and seeded
1 large onion, quartered
1 garlic clove
1 1/4 cups apple cider vinegar
2 tablespoons sugar
1/2 teaspoon kosher salt
1/4 teaspoon ground cinnamon
1/4 teaspoon ground cloves
1/4 teaspoon ground ginger

1 pound boneless skinless chicken thighs, cut into thin strips

SEASONING MIX

1 1/2 teaspoons hot or mild chili powder
1/2 teaspoon dried oregano leaves
1/2 teaspoon sweet paprika
1/4 teaspoon ground cumin
1/4 teaspoon freshly ground black pepper
Juice of 1 lime

1 tablespoon olive oil
1 large onion, thinly sliced
2 garlic cloves, minced

8 small corn tortillas

GARNISH

1 cup shredded romaine lettuce
1/2 cup shredded reduced-fat cheddar cheese
3 medium tomatoes, cored and diced
1/2 cup commercial salsa
1/2 cup plain nonfat yogurt or fat-free sour cream

1. Add the tomatoes, chilies, onion, and garlic to a blender and puree. Add the puree to a saucepan and add in the remaining chile sauce ingredients. Bring to a boil. Lower the heat and simmer for 1 hour until thick.
2. In a bowl, add the chicken. Combine the ingredients for the seasoning mix and add to the chicken. Mix well, cover, and refrigerate for 1 hour.
3. Heat the oil in a large skillet over medium-high heat. Add the chicken and sauté for about 6–8 minutes until the chicken is cooked through. Remove the chicken with a slotted spoon, plate, and set aside.

CALORIES	CALORIES FROM FAT	TOTAL FAT	SATURATED FAT	TRANS FAT	CHOLESTEROL	SODIUM	POTASSIUM
210	60	7.0 g	2.2 g	0.0 g	55 mg	220 mg	510 mg

TOTAL CARBOHYDRATE	DIETARY FIBER	SUGARS	PROTEIN	PHOSPHORUS	EXCHANGES/CHOICES:
23 g	4 g	6 g	15 g	265 mg	1 Starch; 2 Nonstarchy Vegetable; 1 Protein, lean; 1 Fat

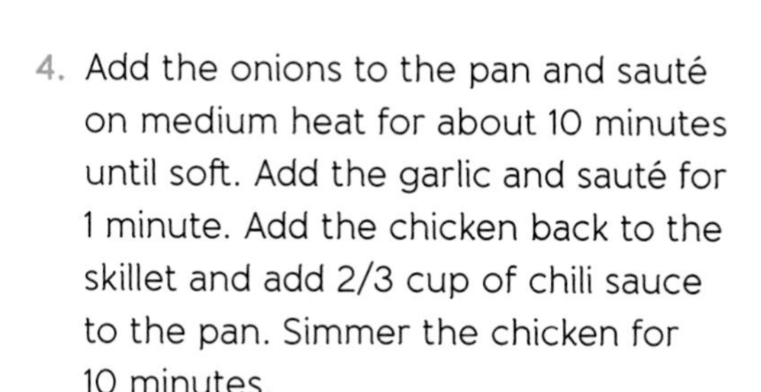

4. Add the onions to the pan and sauté on medium heat for about 10 minutes until soft. Add the garlic and sauté for 1 minute. Add the chicken back to the skillet and add 2/3 cup of chili sauce to the pan. Simmer the chicken for 10 minutes.
5. While the chicken simmers, add a corn tortilla to an ungreased skillet and cook over medium high heat for 30 seconds per side. Keep warm.
6. Spoon the chicken mixture into a warmed corn tortilla. Top with your choice of garnishes.

PINEAPPLE

Serves: 1 | Serving size: 1/2 cup

1/2 cup fresh pineapple

1. Serve pineapple alongside taco and green beans.

EXCHANGES / CHOICES
1 Fruit

Calories 40; Calories from Fat 0; Total Fat 0.0 g; Saturated Fat 0.0 g; Trans Fat 0.0 g; Cholesterol 0 mg; Sodium 0 mg; Potassium 90 mg; Total Carbohydrate 11 g; Dietary Fiber 1 g; Sugars 8 g; Protein 0 g; Phosphorus 5 mg

• • • • • • •

GREEN BEANS

Serves: 1 | Serving size: 1/2 cup

1/2 cup green beans

1. Steam green beans and serve alongside tacos and pineapple.

EXCHANGES / CHOICES
1 Nonstarchy Vegetable

Calories 20; Calories from Fat 0; Total Fat 0.0 g; Saturated Fat 0.0 g; Trans Fat 0.0 g; Cholesterol 0 mg; Sodium 0 mg; Potassium 90 mg; Total Carbohydrate 5 g; Dietary Fiber 2 g; Sugars 1 g; Protein 1 g; Phosphorus 20 mg

PORK TACOS

Serves: 8 | Serving size: 1 taco | Prep time: 20 minutes + marinate time | Cook time: 1 hour 30 minutes

Just like the Chicken Tacos, you can prepare just the pork portion of the recipe and serve with a crisp salad for a thoroughly satisfying meal.

CHILE SAUCE

3 pounds fresh tomatoes, cored and quartered
1 jalapeño chili, stemmed and seeded (if desired)
1 large onion, quartered
1 garlic clove
1 1/4 cups apple cider vinegar
2 tablespoons sugar
1/2 teaspoon kosher salt
1/4 teaspoon ground cinnamon
1/4 teaspoon ground cloves
1/4 teaspoon ground ginger

1 pound lean pork tenderloin, cut into 1/2-inch chunks

SEASONING MIX

2 teaspoons chipotle chili powder
1/2 teaspoon dried oregano leaves
1/2 teaspoon sweet paprika
1/4 teaspoon ground cumin
1/4 teaspoon freshly ground black pepper
Juice of 1 orange

1 tablespoon vegetable oil
1 large onion, thinly sliced
2 garlic cloves, minced
8 small corn tortillas

GARNISHES

1 cup shredded romaine lettuce
1/2 cup shredded reduced-fat cheddar cheese
3 medium tomatoes, cored and diced
1/2 cup commercial salsa
1/2 cup plain nonfat yogurt or fat-free sour cream

1. Add the tomatoes, chiles, onion, and garlic to a blender and puree. Add the puree to a saucepan and add in the remaining ingredients for the chile sauce. Bring to a boil. Lower the heat and simmer for 1 hour until thick.
2. Place the pork in a small bowl. Combine the ingredients for the seasoning mix and add to the pork. Mix well, cover, and refrigerate for 1 hour.
3. Heat the oil in a large skillet over medium-high heat. Add the pork and sauté for about 6–8 minutes until the pork is cooked through. Remove the pork to a plate with a slotted spoon, set aside.

CALORIES	CALORIES FROM FAT	TOTAL FAT	SATURATED FAT	TRANS FAT	CHOLESTEROL	SODIUM	POTASSIUM
200	50	6.0 g	1.7 g	0.0 g	35 mg	210 mg	580 mg
TOTAL CARBOHYDRATE	**DIETARY FIBER**	**SUGARS**	**PROTEIN**	**PHOSPHORUS**	**EXCHANGES/CHOICES:**		
23 g	4 g	6 g	16 g	285 mg	1 Starch; 2 Nonstarchy Vegetable; 1 Protein, lean; 1 Fat		

4. Add the onions to the pan and sauté on medium heat for about 10 minutes until soft. Add the garlic and sauté for 1 minute. Add back the pork to the skillet and add 2/3 cup of the chili sauce to the pan. Simmer the pork for 10 minutes.
5. While the pork simmers, add a corn tortilla to an ungreased skillet and cook over medium-high heat for 30 seconds per side. Keep warm.
6. To serve, spoon the pork mixture into a warmed corn tortilla. Top with your choice of garnishes.

STEAMED PEPPERS

Serves: 1 | Serving size: 1/2 cup

1/4 cup sliced red bell pepper
1/4 cup sliced green bell pepper
Pinch oregano

1. Steam peppers and top with a pinch of oregano.

EXCHANGES / CHOICES
1 Nonstarchy Vegetable

Calories 20; Calories from Fat 0; Total Fat 0.0 g; Saturated Fat 0.0 g; Trans Fat 0.0 g; Cholesterol 0 mg; Sodium 0 mg; Potassium 115 mg; Total Carbohydrate 5 g; Dietary Fiber 1 g; Sugars 3 g; Protein 1 g; Phosphorus 10 mg

• • • • • • •

ORANGE

Serves: 1 | Serving size: 1 orange

1 small orange

1. Slice orange and serve alongside tacos and steamed peppers.

EXCHANGES / CHOICES
1 Fruit

Calories 45; Calories from Fat 0; Total Fat 0.0 g; Saturated Fat 0.0 g; Trans Fat 0.0 g; Cholesterol 0 mg; Sodium 0 mg; Potassium 170 mg; Total Carbohydrate 11 g; Dietary Fiber 2 g; Sugars 9 g; Protein 1 g; Phosphorus 15 mg

BLACKENED FISH TACOS

Serves: 6 | Serving size: 1 taco | Prep time: 30 minutes | Cook time: 15 minutes

I suggest adding a cast iron skillet to your kitchen equipment collection, if you don't already own one, as this recipe really works best when one is used. The dark surface of the pan coupled with the spice mixture makes a true blackened fish. This method deepens the flavor and the blackening mixture is mostly spices and herbs with just a tiny touch of salt added. Other fish varieties that work well blackened are grouper and sea bass.

SEASONING MIX

- 2 teaspoons chipotle chili powder
- 1/2 teaspoon dried oregano leaves
- 1/2 teaspoon sweet paprika
- 1/4 teaspoon ground cumin
- 1/4 teaspoon freshly ground black pepper
- 1/4 teaspoon sea salt

- 1 pound fish filets such as mahi, red snapper, or tilapia
- 2 tablespoons vegetable oil, divided use
- 1 large onion, thinly sliced
- 2 garlic cloves, minced
- Juice of 1 lime
- 8 (6-inch) corn tortillas

GARNISHES

- 1 cup shredded romaine lettuce or green cabbage
- 3 fresh medium tomatoes, diced
- 1/2 cup plain nonfat yogurt or nonfat sour cream

1. Combine the seasoning mix. Coat the fish filets with the seasoning mix and let stand on a plate at room temperature for 10 minutes.
2. Meanwhile, heat 1 tablespoon of oil in a large skillet, preferably cast iron. Add the onion and sauté on medium heat for about 10 minutes until soft. Add the garlic and sauté for 1 minute. Remove the onions and garlic from the pan to a plate and set aside.
3. Add the remaining oil to the pan. Sauté the fish on both sides for about 4–5 minutes per side until cooked through. Remove the fish from the skillet and cut into chunks. Mix the fish with the lime juice.
4. Heat the tortillas, one at a time, in an ungreased skillet over medium-high heat for 30 seconds per side.
5. To serve, add the fish and onion to the tortillas and top with your choice of garnishes.

CALORIES	CALORIES FROM FAT	TOTAL FAT	SATURATED FAT	TRANS FAT	CHOLESTEROL	SODIUM	POTASSIUM
170	45	5.0 g	0.5 g	0.0 g	45 mg	140 mg	530 mg

TOTAL CARBOHYDRATE	DIETARY FIBER	SUGARS	PROTEIN	PHOSPHORUS	EXCHANGES/CHOICES:
19 g	3 g	4 g	14 g	215 mg	1 Starch; 1 Nonstarchy Vegetable; 1 Protein, lean; 1/2 Fat

ZUCCHINI

Serves: 1 | Serving size: 1/2 cup

1/2 cup zucchini

1. Steam zucchini and serve alongside tacos and grapes.

EXCHANGES / CHOICES
Free food

Calories 15; Calories from Fat 5; Total Fat 0.5 g; Saturated Fat 0.1 g; Trans Fat 0.0 g; Cholesterol 0 mg; Sodium 0 mg; Potassium 240 mg; Total Carbohydrate 2 g; Dietary Fiber 1 g; Sugars 2 g; Protein 1 g; Phosphorus 35 mg

• • • • • • •

RED GRAPES

Serves: 1 | Serving size: 12 grapes

12 grapes

1. Serve grapes alongside tacos and zucchini.

EXCHANGES / CHOICES
1 Fruit

Calories 40; Calories from Fat 0; Total Fat 0.0 g; Saturated Fat 0.0 g; Trans Fat 0.0 g; Cholesterol 0 mg; Sodium 0 mg; Potassium 115 mg; Total Carbohydrate 11 g; Dietary Fiber 1 g; Sugars 9 g; Protein 0 g; Phosphorus 10 mg

SHRIMP AND FRUIT TACOS

Serves: 4 | Serving size: 1 taco | Prep time: 10 minutes | Cook time: 5 minutes

Both mangoes and avocados have the same indicator of ripeness; press the skin on each and it should give just a little. Look for well-rounded mangoes that feel heavy for their size. While most mangoes have a beautiful red and yellow skin color, color isn't always an indicator of ripeness as some ripe mangoes retain quite a bit of green color on the outside. Better to choose large mangoes that yield a lot of fruit. In addition to pressing on the skin of an avocado, flick off the stem end. Underneath you should find the color green indicating your avocado is ready to eat.

SEASONING MIX

2 teaspoons chipotle chili powder
1/2 teaspoon dried oregano leaves
1/2 teaspoon sweet paprika
1/4 teaspoon ground cumin
1/4 teaspoon freshly ground black pepper
1/4 teaspoon sea salt

1 1/4 pounds large peeled and deveined shrimp
1 tablespoon olive oil
Juice of 1 lime
8 (6-inch) corn tortillas
1 large mango, peeled and cut into thin slices
1 small avocado, peeled and cut into thin slices

GARNISHES

1 cup shredded romaine lettuce
3 fresh medium tomatoes, cored and diced
1/2 cup nonfat plain yogurt or nonfat sour cream

1. Combine the ingredients in the seasoning mix and add the shrimp. Toss to coat.
2. Heat the olive oil in a large skillet. Add the shrimp and sauté for 4–5 minutes until shrimp are cooked through. Sprinkle with lime juice and remove from the heat.
3. Heat the corn tortillas one at a time in an ungreased skillet for 30 seconds per side.
4. To serve, add the shrimp to the tortilla and top with mango and avocado. Garnish with lettuce, tomatoes, and yogurt or sour cream.

CALORIES	CALORIES FROM FAT	TOTAL FAT	SATURATED FAT	TRANS FAT	CHOLESTEROL	SODIUM	POTASSIUM
210	45	5.0 g	0.7 g	0.0 g	140 mg	180 mg	550 mg

TOTAL CARBOHYDRATE	DIETARY FIBER	SUGARS	PROTEIN	PHOSPHORUS	EXCHANGES/CHOICES:
23 g	4 g	8 g	21 g	310 mg	1 Starch; 1/2 Fruit; 2 Protein, lean

FRESH SPINACH SALAD

Serves: 1 | Serving size: 1 1/2 cups

1 cup fresh spinach leaves
5 cherry tomatoes, halved
1/4 cup red onion, thinly sliced
1 teaspoon olive oil
1/2 teaspoon lemon juice

1. Combine spinach, tomatoes, and onion slices in a small bowl. Drizzle with olive oil and top with lemon juice.

EXCHANGES / CHOICES
1 Nonstarchy Vegetable; 1 Fat

Calories 70; Calories from Fat 45; Total Fat 5.0 g; Saturated Fat 0.7 g; Trans Fat 0.0 g; Cholesterol 0 mg; Sodium 25 mg; Potassium 360 mg; Total Carbohydrate 7 g; Dietary Fiber 2 g; Sugars 3 g; Protein 2 g; Phosphorus 40 mg

• • • • • • •

ZUCCHINI

Serves: 1 | Serving size: 1/2 cup

1/2 cup zucchini
Pinch oregano

1. Steam zucchini, top with a pinch of oregano, and serve alongside salad and tacos.

EXCHANGES / CHOICES
Free food

Calories 15; Calories from Fat 5; Total Fat 0.5 g; Saturated Fat 0.1 g; Trans Fat 0.0 g; Cholesterol 0 mg; Sodium 0 mg; Potassium 240 mg; Total Carbohydrate 2 g; Dietary Fiber 1 g; Sugars 2 g; Protein 1 g; Phosphorus 35 mg

TOFU TACOS

Serves: 8 | Serving size: 1 taco | Prep time: 40 minutes | Cook time: 10–12 minutes

Tofu is really a blank slate and a terrific vehicle for taking on bold flavor. I use extra-firm tofu, which is available in most grocery stores and markets. I also "press" the tofu to remove most of its liquid, prior to using it. If you cannot find tofu that has been pressed, it's easy enough to do yourself. Simply wrap the block of tofu in several wrappings of paper toweling. Place the block on a plate. Put another plate on top of the tofu and then weight it down with a heavy pot or pan. Set aside for a few hours at room temperature or in the refrigerator. Remove the weight, top plate, and paper toweling. Pat dry and discard all the liquid that has accumulated around the tofu. The tofu should look compressed, and have a texture similar to chicken breast.

SEASONING MIX

1 tablespoon chipotle chili powder
1 teaspoon dried oregano leaves
1 teaspoon sweet paprika
1/2 teaspoon ground cumin
1/4 teaspoon freshly ground black pepper
1/4 teaspoon sea salt

1 pound extra-firm pressed tofu, cut into 8 slabs
2 1/2 tablespoons vegetable oil, divided use
1 1/2 cups shredded green cabbage
2 large carrots, shredded
1 large shallot, minced
8 (6-inch) corn tortillas
1/4 cup nonfat mayonnaise
1 teaspoon hot sauce
1 teaspoon rice vinegar
1/4 cup minced fresh cilantro (garnish)

1. Combine all the ingredients for the seasoning mix. On a flat plate, dredge the tofu slabs in the seasoning mix. Set the tofu in the refrigerator for 20 minutes.
2. Heat 2 tablespoons of the oil in a large skillet over medium-high heat. Add the tofu and brown 3–4 minutes per side or until golden. Remove the tofu from the skillet. Add the remaining oil. Add in the cabbage, carrots, and shallot and sauté for 6–7 minutes until vegetables are soft, but still crisp.
3. Heat the tortillas one at a time in an ungreased skillet over medium-high heat for 30 seconds per side.
4. Combine the mayonnaise, hot sauce, and rice vinegar. To serve, add the tofu to the tortilla, top with the cabbage mixture, and a dollop of the mayonnaise sauce. Sprinkle with cilantro.

CALORIES	CALORIES FROM FAT	TOTAL FAT	SATURATED FAT	TRANS FAT	CHOLESTEROL	SODIUM	POTASSIUM
170	80	9.0 g	0.8 g	0.0 g	0 mg	170 mg	240 mg

TOTAL CARBOHYDRATE	DIETARY FIBER	SUGARS	PROTEIN	PHOSPHORUS	EXCHANGES/CHOICES:
18 g	3 g	3 g	8 g	180 mg	1 Starch; 1 Nonstarchy Vegetable; 1 Protein, medium fat

PINEAPPLE

Serves: 1 | Serving size: 1/2 cup

1/2 cup fresh pineapple

1. Serve pineapple alongside tacos and green beans.

EXCHANGES / CHOICES
1 Fruit

Calories 40; Calories from Fat 0; Total Fat 0.0 g; Saturated Fat 0.0 g; Trans Fat 0.0 g; Cholesterol 0 mg; Sodium 0 mg; Potassium 90 mg; Total Carbohydrate 11 g; Dietary Fiber 1 g; Sugars 8 g; Protein 0 g; Phosphorus 5 mg

. . . .

GREEN BEANS

Serves: 1 | Serving size: 1/2 cup

1/2 cup green beans

1. Steam green beans and serve alongside tacos and pineapple.

EXCHANGES / CHOICES
1 Nonstarchy Vegetable

Calories 20; Calories from Fat 0; Total Fat 0.0 g; Saturated Fat 0.0 g; Trans Fat 0.0 g; Cholesterol 0 mg; Sodium 0 mg; Potassium 90 mg; Total Carbohydrate 5 g; Dietary Fiber 2 g; Sugars 1 g; Protein 1 g; Phosphorus 20 mg

BLACK BEAN TACOS

Serves: 8 | Serving size: 1 taco | Prep time: 15 minutes | Cook time: 20 minutes

Black bean tacos are the fastest tacos to prepare. If you stock your pantry with the ingredients included here, you'll have dinner on the table in about a half hour! Mashed kidney beans are also great in these vegetarian tacos. Sometimes I like to serve a small portion of the filling only as a side dish to accompany a piece of grilled fish.

2 teaspoons olive oil
1 medium onion, chopped
2 garlic cloves, minced
1 teaspoon ground cumin
1 teaspoon chipotle chili powder
2 cups cooked black beans (canned, drained, and rinsed, or fresh)
1 cup commercially prepared hot or mild salsa

8 (6-inch) corn tortillas

GARNISHES
1/2 cup finely minced fresh cilantro
3 medium tomatoes, cored and diced
1 small avocado, peeled and diced

1. Heat the olive oil in a large skillet over medium-high heat. Add the onion and sauté for 6 minutes. Add in the garlic, cumin, and chipotle chili powder and sauté for 1 minute. Add the beans and salsa and simmer over medium-low heat for 10 minutes. Mash the mixture slightly.
2. Heat the corn tortillas, one at a time, over medium-high heat for 30 seconds per side.
3. Add the black bean mixture to the tortillas and top with the garnishes.

CALORIES	CALORIES FROM FAT	TOTAL FAT	SATURATED FAT	TRANS FAT	CHOLESTEROL	SODIUM	POTASSIUM
170	35	4.0 g	0.6 g	0.0 g	0 mg	250 mg	530 mg

TOTAL CARBOHYDRATE	DIETARY FIBER	SUGARS	PROTEIN	PHOSPHORUS	EXCHANGES/CHOICES:
30 g	8 g	5 g	7 g	180 mg	1 1/2 Starch; 1 Nonstarchy Vegetable; 1 Protein, lean

GARDEN SALAD WITH BALSAMIC VINAIGRETTE

Serves: 8 | Serving size: 1 cup | Prep time: 7 minutes | Cook time: 4 minutes

3/4 cup walnuts
2 tablespoons sugar

DRESSING
1/4 cup balsamic vinegar
1 garlic clove, minced
1 teaspoon coarse Dijon mustard
1 teaspoon honey or sugar
3 tablespoons olive oil
1/4 teaspoon sea salt
1/4 teaspoon freshly ground black pepper

SALAD
5 cups mixed greens
1 cup halved cherry tomatoes
2 large carrots, peeled and grated
1/2 medium red onion, thinly sliced

1. In a small sauté pan or skillet over medium-high heat, toss the walnuts with the sugar for 3 to 4 minutes or until the sugar melts and caramelizes. Watch that the nuts do not burn. Remove the nuts from the pan and let cool.
2. In a large bowl, combine dressing ingredients and whisk well.
3. Add the salad ingredients to the dressing and quickly toss together. Serve on individual plates, top with the nuts.

EXCHANGES / CHOICES
1/2 Carbohydrate; 1 Nonstarchy Vegetable; 2 1/2 Fat

Calories 160; Calories from Fat 120; Total Fat 13.0 g; Saturated Fat 1.4 g; Trans Fat 0.0 g; Cholesterol 0 mg; Sodium 105 mg; Potassium 250 mg; Total Carbohydrate 11 g; Dietary Fiber 2 g; Sugars 7 g; Protein 3 g; Phosphorus 65 mg

This recipe also in Salads page 150

PORTOBELLO MUSHROOM AND ONION TACOS

Serves: 8 | Serving size: 1 taco | Prep time: 15 minutes | Cook time: 20 minutes

When I first discovered Portobello mushrooms, I became totally hooked on adding them whenever I wanted to mimic meat in a recipe. Be sure to remove the mushroom stems and discard them; unlike a lot of other mushrooms, Portobello stems are often thick and woody with minimal flavor. Remember that mushrooms are highly perishable. The best way to store them is in a large brown paper bag set on a refrigerator shelf. The produce bin in your refrigerator is actually too cold and humid for mushrooms.

- 2 teaspoons olive oil
- 1/2 large red onion, thinly sliced
- 6 large Portobello mushrooms, stems removed, caps wiped clean, and thinly sliced
- 1 small jalapeño pepper, seeded and minced
- 1 tablespoon hot or mild chili powder
- 2 teaspoons ground cumin
- 1 teaspoon dried oregano
- 1/4 teaspoon sugar
- 1/8 teaspoon cayenne pepper
- 1/8 teaspoon sea salt
- 1/8 teaspoon freshly ground black pepper
- 2 tablespoons water
- 8 (6-inch) corn tortillas
- 2 cups finely shredded green cabbage
- 1/2 cup nonfat plain yogurt or nonfat sour cream
- 1/4 cup finely chopped cilantro

1. Heat the oil in a large skillet over medium-high heat. Add the onion and sauté for 3 minutes. Add the mushrooms and jalapeño pepper and sauté until mushrooms brown and are soft.
2. Combine the chili powder, cumin, oregano, sugar, cayenne pepper, salt, and black pepper in a small bowl. Add to the onion-mushroom mixture and sauté for 1 minute. Add the water and simmer on low heat for 1 minute.
3. Heat the tortillas, one at a time, in an ungreased skillet over medium-high heat for 30 seconds per side.
4. Fill each warmed tortilla with some of the onion and mushroom mixture. Garnish with shredded cabbage, sour cream, and cilantro.

CALORIES	CALORIES FROM FAT	TOTAL FAT	SATURATED FAT	TRANS FAT	CHOLESTEROL	SODIUM	POTASSIUM
100	20	2.0 g	0.3 g	0.0 g	0 mg	65 mg	360 mg
TOTAL CARBOHYDRATE	**DIETARY FIBER**	**SUGARS**	**PROTEIN**	**PHOSPHORUS**	**EXCHANGES/CHOICES:**		
19 g	3 g	4 g	4 g	170 mg	1 Starch; 1 Nonstarchy Vegetable		

PAN GRILLED PORK CHOPS

Serves: 4 | Serving size: 3 ounces

Cooking spray
1 pound boneless pork loin chops, trimmed of fat, brought to room temperature
1/2 teaspoon kosher salt
1/4 teaspoon freshly ground black pepper

1. Coat a nonstick ridged grill pan with cooking spray. Set the pan on high heat until hot, about 2 minutes. Sprinkle the chops with salt and pepper. Add the chops and cook on each side for about 2 minutes per side.
2. Lower the temperature to medium and cook for an additional 3–4 minutes per side or until an internal temperature of 135°F is reached. Remove from the pan and set aside. The internal temperature will reach 145°F as the pork rests.

EXCHANGES / CHOICES
3 Protein, lean

Calories 140; Calories from Fat 30; Total Fat 3.5 g; Saturated Fat 1.4 g; Trans Fat 0.0 g; Cholesterol 55 mg; Sodium 300 mg; Potassium 310 mg; Total Carbohydrate 0 g; Dietary Fiber 0 g; Sugars 0 g; Protein 24 g; Phosphorus 235 mg

This recipe also in Master Proteins page 9

MANGO

Serves: 1 | Serving size: 1/2 cup

1/2 cup mango

1. Slice mango and serve alongside pork and tacos.

EXCHANGES / CHOICES
1 Fruit

Calories 60; Calories from Fat 5; Total Fat 0.5 g; Saturated Fat 0.1 g; Trans Fat 0.0 g; Cholesterol 0 mg; Sodium 0 mg; Potassium 150 mg; Total Carbohydrate 14 g; Dietary Fiber 1 g; Sugars 13 g; Protein 1 g; Phosphorus 15 mg

ROASTED PEPPER AND CHERRY TOMATO SALSA

Serves: 16 | Serving size: 2 tablespoons | Prep time: 15 minutes | Cook time: 10 minutes

2 red peppers
1 yellow pepper
1/2 cup diced cherry tomatoes
1 jalapeño pepper, seeded and minced
1/2 red onion, minced
1 1/2 tablespoons fresh lime juice
1 1/2 tablespoons red wine vinegar
2 tablespoons minced cilantro
2 teaspoons olive oil
1 teaspoon chili powder
1/2 teaspoon smoked paprika

1. Place the whole red and yellow peppers directly on an open stove flame. With long-handled tongs, keep turning the peppers until most of the skin has blackened. Place the peppers in a bowl and cover with plastic wrap. Set aside to cool. (Alternatively, if you do not have a gas stove, cut the peppers in half and remove the seeds and white membrane. Place the peppers, skin side up, under an oven broiler, about 4–5 inches from the heat source. Broil the peppers until they are blackened. Remove the peppers to a bowl, cover with plastic wrap and set aside to cool.) You may also place whole peppers on an outdoor charcoal or gas grill. Place the peppers directly on the grill rack that has been coated with nonstick cooking spray. Set the heat to medium-high. Cover the grill. Using long-handled tongs, keep checking the peppers by turning them to make sure all sides have blackened. Follow the instructions above for cooling the peppers.
2. Once the peppers have cooled, remove them from the bowl. Peel off the charred skin with your fingertips, using a paper towel for assistance to remove most of the charred skin. (A little bit of charred skin is tasty, so there is no need to get every bit of charred skin removed.)
3. Discard the seeds and chop the peppers into a medium dice. Add them to a medium bowl. Add the remaining ingredients, cover, and let the flavors marinate for about 1 hour.
4. Use this salsa on top of any of the tacos.

CALORIES	CALORIES FROM FAT	TOTAL FAT	SATURATED FAT	TRANS FAT	CHOLESTEROL	SODIUM	POTASSIUM
20	5	0.5 g	0.1 g	0.0 g	0 mg	0 mg	95 mg
TOTAL CARBOHYDRATE	**DIETARY FIBER**	**SUGARS**	**PROTEIN**	**PHOSPHORUS**	**EXCHANGES/CHOICES:**		
3 g	1 g	2 g	0 g	10 mg	Free food		

MANGO PINEAPPLE SALSA

Serves: 20 | Serving size: 2 tablespoons
Prep time: 15 minutes

2 small ripe mangoes, peeled and diced
1 cup diced fresh pineapple
1/2 small red onion, diced
1/4 cup minced fresh cilantro
3 tablespoons fresh lime juice
1/16 teaspoon salt

1. Combine all the ingredients and let the flavors blend for 1 hour prior to serving.

EXCHANGES / CHOICES
1/2 Fruit

Calories 20; Calories from Fat 0; Total Fat 0.0 g; Saturated Fat 0.0 g; Trans Fat 0.0 g; Cholesterol 0 mg; Sodium 10 mg; Potassium 50 mg; Total Carbohydrate 5 g; Dietary Fiber 0 g; Sugars 4 g; Protein 0 g; Phosphorus 5 mg

Chicken Tacos page 210

INDEX

Note: Page numbers followed by *ph* refer to photographs.

T

V

W

Y

Z

ADVANCED PRAISE FOR
The Perfect Diabetes Comfort Food Collection

"Robyn clearly understands that having diabetes doesn't mean the end of good eating. As a diabetes educator, I love *The Perfect Diabetes Comfort Food Collection*. It's a system of meal planning chock full of easy recipes, paired with 1–3 suggested sides to make the perfect meal. If you're a novice in the kitchen, Robyn's taken care of that too. She gives tips for buying equipment, stocking your pantry, and teaches techniques to ensure each recipe is a culinary delight."

—CONSTANCE BROWN-RIGGS, MSEd, RD, CDE, CDN, author of *The African American Guide to Living Well with Diabetes*

. . . .

"Robyn is a gifted cook and teacher. She makes preparing healthy meals effortless, delicious, and attainable even for the busiest of families. This gorgeous book is filled with mouth-watering diabetes friendly recipes. It is a must have for anyone who wants to improve their health and look like a culinary rockstar."

—DAWN LERMAN is a top Manhattan nutritionist, contributor to the Well blog of the *New York Times*, and author of the best-selling book, *My Fat Dad: A Memoir of Food, Love and Family, With Recipes*

"Robyn Webb's latest cookbook, *The Perfect Diabetes Comfort Food Collection*, is a must have for anyone with diabetes. Each nutritious recipe is easy to prepare and absolutely delicious! As a registered dietitian, nutritionist, and certified diabetes educator, I am constantly searching for healthy and diabetes-friendly recipes for my patients. Robyn recipes are masterfully crafted to ensure a perfect outcome. Robyn guides us through the recipes while taking the guesswork out of meal preparation. Whether you are newly diagnosed with diabetes, or are experienced with diabetes meal planning, this book will provide you with delicious recipes for you and your entire family. THANK YOU Robyn for creating recipes that are delicious, nutritious, and easy to prepare for people with diabetes and their families."

—SUSAN WEINER, MS RDN, CDE, CDN, and 2015 AADE Diabetes Educator of the Year

"Author Robyn Webb really hits it out of the park with her latest book *The Perfect Diabetes Comfort Food Collection*. Her book approaches cooking in a simple, yet effective way by first concentrating on a few cooking techniques. She then describes a few core kitchen ingredients that she cross utilizes in many of her recipes. What I really adore about this book is how it focuses on popular food items, such as burgers, chicken breast, and meatloaf, and how to master the classic styles of each food. As a registered dietitian and someone that loves food, I would recommend this book to anyone because it takes comfort food to a new level with its variety and craftiness. Robyn dispels the myths behind diabetic diets and shows how simple eating a whole foods diet really is. Get ready to take your taste buds on a flavor packed roller coaster ride."

—MANUEL VILLACORTA, MS, RD, and author of *Whole Body Reboot*

"For those with diabetes, or health conscious people in general, Robyn Webb's *Perfect Diabetes Comfort Food Collection* offers myriad great tasting, yet simple, creative meals that reflect how real people cook. The collection is a godsend and sure to become a go-to classic in homes everywhere."

—NATHALIE DUPREE, cookbook author and television host